D1264592

TROUBADOURS
AND
ELOQUENCE

TROUBADOURS
AND
ELOQUENCE

—•••—

Linda M. Paterson

OXFORD
AT THE CLARENDON PRESS
1975

Oxford University Press, Ely House, London W. 1

GLASGOW   NEW YORK   TORONTO   MELBOURNE   WELLINGTON
CAPE TOWN   IBADAN   NAIROBI   DAR ES SALAAM   LUSAKA   ADDIS ABABA
DELHI   BOMBAY   CALCUTTA   MADRAS   KARACHI   LAHORE   DACCA
KUALA LUMPUR   SINGAPORE   HONG KONG   TOKYO

ISBN 0 19 815711 8

© *Oxford University Press 1975*

*Printed in Great Britain
at the University Press, Oxford
by Vivian Ridler
Printer to the University*

FOREWORD

WHEN Dante praised Arnaut Daniel as the greatest poet of love in the vernacular, he recognized the supreme reputation, in his day, of the Provençal love lyric. When he took Arnaut Daniel as his model, he also showed his preference for those troubadours who composed in a contemplative, allusive, and metaphysical style. Such poets were all dissatisfied in some measure with the courtly songs of praise, homage, and service to the lady, which were expected from the troubadour who sang, in the 'clear' style, of a joy and a love which were defined by courtly values and limited by social convention. Such profane certainty was suspect to these poets. They were all, in some degree, unsure of themselves, aware of the vanity of earthly existence, disturbed by the conflict between the flesh and the spirit, between folly and reason, personal happiness and social convention, between love for the lady and love of God. To express this sense of conflict they used dark and coloured words, and interwove and unfolded levels of meaning within their poetry. They could and did compose clear courtly songs 'such as knights sing'. But it was their serious songs with their rich texture of theme, style, and language which won fame and authority for the Provençal love song throughout Europe.

This book is about the ideas on style and the methods of composition of some of these remarkable troubadours, whose poetic intention and achievement have not been understood or even apprehended until recently. Dr. Paterson's work shows clearly, for the first time, the variety of their coloured styles and the inadequacy of the term *trobar clus* which has been applied to their poetry. It traces their methods of composition to twelfth-century principles of rhetoric which drew on the traditions of Cicero, Horace, and Quintilian, and from knowledge of their eloquence there comes a new insight into this poetry which Dante chose as his example, and a better understanding of the poetic skills of the courtly troubadours whose ideas and poetic techniques they enriched.

L. T. TOPSFIELD

St. Catharine's College, Cambridge

ACKNOWLEDGEMENTS

I wish to thank the following for their kind permission to reproduce editions of certain texts: Dr. J. H. Marshall, for Raimbaut d'Aurenga's poem 'Cars, douz'; Professor A. Roncaglia, for Marcabru's 'D'aisso lau Dieu'; G. C. Sansoni Editore for Professor G. Toja's edition of Arnaut Daniel's 'Lo ferm voler'; Loescher Editore, for Professor A. Del Monte's edition of Peire Alvernhe's 'Be m'es plazen'; and the University of Minnesota Press, for Raimbaut d'Aurenga's 'Ar vei', together with other quotations from Professor W. T. Pattison's edition.

I should also like to thank the staff of The Chilton Atlas Laboratory for the use of their computing facilities.

Above all I am deeply grateful to Dr. L. T. Topsfield for his unreserved help and encouragement during the past several years, and for the many personal kindnesses he has shown me. It would be impossible to acknowledge all my debts to him as regards this book. While he is in no way responsible for its shortcomings, it would not have been written without his constant advice.

CONTENTS

INTRODUCTION

DANTE praised the troubadours for their eloquence. He called them the first 'vulgares eloquentes', the 'antiquiores doctores' of the vernacular.[1] What was their *eloquentia*? Dante placed it within the tradition of medieval Rhetoric;[2] but the rhetoric of the troubadours was not necessarily the rhetoric of Dante, or of the medieval schools. It developed, perhaps independently of these, to suit a secular, courtly audience. The purpose of this book is to investigate the vernacular 'eloquence' of certain major twelfth-century troubadours: of these, some were specifically admired by Dante, while others contributed equally to this eloquence through the literary polemics of the classical and pre-classical period in the south.

My starting-point was a cluster of theories, put forward by several distinguished scholars, which seek to explain the so-called 'uniformity' of the courtly lyric in France.[3] These scholars see the northern French lyric in particular as a poetry of form: not so much because the trouvères set out to produce learned, rhetorical compositions,[4] as because they sought to express and renew typical, ideal emotions by means of ever varying combinations of traditional clichés.[5] According to these scholars the poet's task is not to express 'sincere' feelings, in other words emotions drawn from his personal life, but to create an emotional fiction which he then 'lives' symbolically. The beauty of a song would lie in the style, which would result from the art of combining clichés. Such a method of composition would almost necessarily exclude individuality or originality: although these would be theoretically possible within the framework of an 'imposed rhetoric',[6] the most effective works would avoid them,

---

[1] A. Marigo, *DVE* I. x. 2.

[2] I use 'Rhetoric' to denote the art of speaking and writing as it was taught in the schools of Antiquity and in the Middle Ages, and 'rhetoric' to mean this art in general.

[3] H. Binet, *Le Style de la lyrique courtoise en France aux XIIᵉ et XIIIᵉ siècles*, (Paris, 1891), p. 103; A. Jeanroy, *Poésie lyrique*, ii. 94, 116.

[4] D. Scheludko, 'Beiträge', *Arch. Rom.* xi (1927), 304–5.

[5] R. Dragonetti, especially pp. 137, 139, 191, 543, 545; R. Guiette; E. Vinaver; P. Zumthor, *Langue et techniques*, also 'Recherches'.

[6] Dragonetti, pp. 225, 545.

since they seek abstract, typical expression. The audience's attention would thus be concentrated not on the theme, which would be a mere pretext for the existence of the poem, but on the subtle interplay of stylistic figures, clichés, rhythm, and music. For the most part such theories have been concerned with the lyric of the northern French trouvères, but sometimes they have been extended to include the southern troubadours.[1]

The existence of different styles of composition in troubadour poetry: *trobar clus, leu, braus, plan, prim, naturau, car*, at once indicates its many-sidedness. A single theory, of a traditional poetry composed by means of inherited clichés and consciously avoiding individuality, is clearly inadequate to account for these different kinds of *trobar*; this alone invites a decidedly different approach to troubadour poetry from that taken with the northern poets. There exist a number of works which offer brief definitions of *trobar clus, trobar leu*, or *trobar plan*,[2] and a few which treat in more detail the distinction between *trobar clus* and *trobar leu*,[3] but no one has yet examined extensively the variety of styles mentioned above, both by fully investigating the troubadours' literary terminology and by relating this to their methods of composition.

The fundamental stylistic division in troubadour poetry has usually been thought of in terms of *trobar clus* and *trobar leu*; however, these terms were not formalized until the second generation of troubadours, most probably by two outstanding

---

[1] Dragonetti, pp. 59–61, notes the different lines taken in the south by poets of *trobar clus* and *trobar ric;* Guiette, p. 63, and Vinaver, p. 13, confine their remarks to the trouvères. Zumthor's book extends beyond the trouvères: 'Mon dessein est d'esquisser dans ce livre une définition de la langue poétique du moyen âge' (*Langue et techniques*, p. 7), and he includes in his discussions Jaufré Rudel (ibid., pp. 205–17) and Bernart de Ventadorn (ibid., pp. 180, 182 and 'Recherches', pp. 410–11).

[2] E. Wechssler, *Das Kulturproblem des Minnesangs* (Halle, 1909), i. 112; K. Vossler, 'Der Trobador Marcabru'; C. Appel, 'Zu Marcabru', pp. 462–3; H. Brinkmann, *Zu Wesen und Form mittelalterlicher Dichtung* (Halle, 1928), p. 99; J.-J. Salverda de Grave, *Observations*, p. 81; Scheludko, 'Beiträge', *Arch. Rom.* xv (1931), 142 ff.; Jeanroy, *Poésie lyrique*, ii. 36, 47 ff.; A. Viscardi, 'La tradizione aulica e scolastica e la poesia trobadorica', *SM* vii (1934), 151–64 (158–60); E. Auerbach, 'Sacrae Scripturae sermo humilis', *NMi* xlii (1941), 57–67; H. Briffault, *Les Troubadours et le sentiment romanesque* (Paris, 1945), p. 97; J. Wettstein, '*Mezura*', *l'idéal des troubadours* (Zürich, 1945), pp. 13–14; H. J. Chaytor, *From Script to Print*, pp. 67–73; M. de Riquer, *Lírica*, vol. i, pp. xviii–xix; A. Del Monte, *Studi*, *passim*, especially pp. 23 ff., 34–8, 48; Dragonetti, pp. 59–61; F. Quadlbauer, pp. 128–9; L. Arbusow, *Colores rhetorici* (Göttingen, 1963), p. 19.

[3] E. Köhler, pp. 133–52; L. Pollmann, '*Trobar clus*'; U. Mölk.

individuals: Giraut de Bornelh and Raimbaut d'Aurenga. Earlier poets, especially Marcabru, undoubtedly provided models for later *clus* poets, but did not term their own style *clus*. Marcabru called his own style of composition *trobar naturau*. Other early troubadours, Cercamon and Jaufré Rudel, praised their style as *plan*, although the expression *trobar plan*, as *trobar clus* or *leu*, does not appear until the middle of the twelfth century with the poetry of Giraut de Bornelh and Raimbaut d'Aurenga. Peire d'Alvernhe, their contemporary, composes *clus* and non-*clus* songs, but devotes more attention to his concept of *vers entiers*. In this interest he follows Marcabru's example (while diverging from it), and is in turn followed and challenged by Bernart Marti. Bernart de Ventadorn, thought to be an exponent of the *trobar leu*,[1] in fact never mentions this or indeed any particular style. Other styles besides *trobar clus* and *trobar leu* emerge in the middle of the twelfth century: the *trobar prim*, which appears in the songs of Giraut de Bornelh, Raimbaut d'Aurenga, and Arnaut Daniel; the *trobar car*, a term which appears with Raimbaut d'Aurenga and Peire Vidal; the *trobar braus*, a term first used by Raimon de Miraval but practised as a style by Marcabru and other major troubadours. *Clus* and *leu* are never explicitly used by Arnaut Daniel, but his practice is related to the *trobar clus*. So while the distinction between *trobar clus* and *trobar leu* is an important one in troubadour poetry, it by no means represents the only stylistic interest of the twelfth-century troubadours, and is only a part of their *eloquentia*.

It would be possible to take the different styles: *trobar clus*, *leu*, *prim*, and so on, as points of departure in considering this *eloquentia*. But I have rejected such an approach for two reasons. The first is the problem of defining and recognizing the styles in isolation from the context of the entire surviving works of a given poet. References to them are infrequent and vague; when they can be found, they may apply only to a particular context or situation. Giraut de Bornelh, for example, only mentions the *trobar clus* when he is abandoning it[2] and this tells us little of how it was conceived of and practised. Or theoretical remarks by the troubadours may appear only as retrospective comment on what has long been practised: because Marcabru does not mention the *trobar clus* explicitly, this does not mean that he never composed

---

[1] M. Lazar, p. 11.　　　[2] See p. 90.

in an essentially *clus* style. So any theoretical remarks made by the troubadours must be related to their practice. But how do we know which songs belong to which style? The troubadours do not usually tell us that one song is *clus*, another *leu*, and so on. Even when they mention a style it is not necessarily the one in which that particular song is composed: Giraut and Linhaure discuss the *trobar clus* in their *tenso*[1] but their style is not *clus*. In recognizing a particular style it is, of course, self-defeating to rely on some preconceived criterion such as 'obscurité systématique'.[2] The second reason, obviously related to this, concerns the limitations imposed by such an approach on the way in which we look at the *eloquentia* of each poet. Rather than to assume that in a given work troubadours set out to compose in a particular preconceived style—that Raimbaut d'Aurenga set out to write *clus* poetry, Giraut de Bornelh *leu*, for example—it seems preferable to look at the *trobar clus* and the other styles as the outcome, and not the force behind, certain ideas and practices: in other words, to see these styles as part of a wider background of *eloquentia*, which is best understood in terms of the contributions towards it of certain major poets.

The poets examined most closely here: Marcabru, Peire d'Alvernhe, Giraut de Bornelh, Raimbaut d'Aurenga, Arnaut Daniel, represent or contribute substantially to an understanding of the different styles I have mentioned: *trobar naturau* (Marcabru), *trobar clus* (all of these poets), *trobar leu* (Giraut and Raimbaut), *trobar plan* (Giraut, Raimbaut, Arnaut), *trobar car* (Raimbaut), or to important stylistic concepts such as *vers entiers* (Marcabru, Peire). Each of these troubadours takes a keen interest in *eloquentia* and makes his own individual contribution to it. A notable absence from this selection is, of course, Bernart de Ventadorn. This is by no means intended to minimize his considerable influence on the 'eloquence' of both southern and northern poets; but he makes no overt contribution to the literary polemics of his time. Although he is a contemporary of Peire d'Alvernhe, Giraut de Bornelh, and Raimbaut d'Aurenga, and moreover in contact with them,[3] he displays none of their enthusiasm for

---

[1] See pp. 110 ff.   [2] Jeanroy, *Poésie lyrique*, ii. 33.

[3] He appears in Peire's satire on the troubadours (Del Monte, XII). See also W. Pattison, pp. 24–5, who argues that Raimbaut and Bernart addressed each other as 'Tristan'; see also M. Delbouille, and A. Roncaglia, 'Carestia'. Lazar, however, disagrees with Pattison (p. 274 n. 11).

poetic theory; he never mentions *trobar clus* or *trobar leu*, or indeed any other particular *trobar*. He appears to have shown no interest in *eloquentia*, and Dante ignores him. A craft concealed behind a fresh and apparently spontaneous expression of a range of emotions and psychological subtleties, his eloquence is a 'true' *trobar leu* which springs not from theoretical controversies but from his natural lightness of touch and sense of harmony.[1] He marks a different point of departure from the other troubadours I have mentioned; in terms of influence on later poets, Bernart seems turned towards the north, as a model for trouvères, the others with their interest in *eloquentia* towards the south and the Italian poets.[2]

My approach has been first to examine in detail the literary observations and terminology of each of these five major poets, both within the context of their own work and in relation to what is known of other troubadours; and second to analyse their methods of composition chiefly through individual works. When considering literary terminology one has to bear in mind that terms do not necessarily remain static, nor do they necessarily have a very precise sense for any one composer. Texts are also a limiting factor here since manuscripts disagree and sometimes, especially in the case of difficult but interesting *clus* works, only one manuscript of a work has survived. Individual songs whose composition is discussed in detail have been chosen partly to illustrate the ideas gathered from the poet's own literary observations, to see how far and in what way he puts them into practice; and partly to illustrate the most characteristic techniques of each troubadour.

In considering the *eloquentia* of the troubadours, it is impossible to ignore the wider context of medieval *eloquentia* in general, especially since Dante places troubadour poetry squarely within this context. There was undoubtedly some influence, direct or indirect, on the troubadours from the Rhetoric of the medieval

---

[1] For a study of Bernart's poetic world, see P. Bec, 'La douleur et son univers poétique chez Bernard de Ventadour', *CCM* xi (1968), 545–71, xii (1969), 25–33.

[2] Possibly one major difference between Bernart and the trouvères on the one hand, and these five poets with their interest in *eloquentia* on the other, is the importance of their music. 18 of Bernart's melodies are preserved, as opposed to 4 of Marcabru's, 1 of Peire's, 1 of Raimbaut's, 4 of Giraut's, 2 of Arnaut's. (See C. Appel, *Bernart*, pp. c–ci.) Only 273 melodies of the troubadours' as opposed to 1,700 of the trouvères have survived; see F. Gennrich, *Troubadours, Trouvères, Minne- und Meistergesang* (Köln, 1951), p. 5.

schools.[1] I have made a limited attempt to link the troubadours' ideas with those of Rhetoric, in order to help explain the Provençal works concerned. But the troubadours themselves are the point of departure, and no servile imitation of scholastic ideas and methods can be assumed. No attempt is made to analyse in any comprehensive way the influence of Rhetoric on these poets, which is beyond the scope of the present study.

Neither has any attempt been made to give a complete stylistic analysis of these five troubadours. It may be argued that one can make no secure statements about style without the support of the full statistical apparatus provided only by complete computations of vocabulary, stylistic devices, and so forth.[2] Setting aside the whole question of stylistic methods and the merit of applying them to troubadour poetry, we are simply not in a position to make such an analysis yet because of the state of the texts. Many of these are still dubiously established, and the meaning of poems is still often obscure or at least debatable. A large and crucial part of style concerns transference of meaning, but it is impossible to pinpoint a rhetorical device if one is unaware of ambiguity, irony, word-play, and allusions, or if the syntax is not even clear.[3]

However, I have included one piece of statistical information which concerns the size of vocabulary and the use of rare words of some important troubadours.[4] The purpose of this is once again to refute the idea that troubadour poetry, despite minor variations, is basically uniform and restricts itself to a limited, traditional vocabulary. Bernart de Ventadorn, who has been taken as typical in this,[5] can be seen to have limited himself far more than the leading figures examined in this book; Marcabru's vocabulary is half as large again, and he apparently uses twice the number of unusual words.

In spite of traditional or conventional elements which may sometimes give a superficial air of uniformity to troubadour poetry, major poets did not only *not* seek to conform to tradition,

---

[1] See Scheludko, *Arch. Rom.* xv (1931), 137 ff.

[2] See especially P. Boyde, *Dante's Style in his Lyric Poetry* (Cambridge, 1971).

[3] Labels can be quite misleading. Scheludko (*Arch. Rom.* xv (1931), 157–8) compared 'Ar non sui jes mals et astrucs' (Pattison, XXXVI) with examples from Latin poetry to show that Raimbaut was using a stock Rhetorical device when he repeated *malastruc* in some form in every line of the song, and that *therefore* he was simply imitating traditional practice. Raimbaut's intention was almost certainly to make fun of this kind of device; see p. 178.

[4] See p. 229.   [5] Zumthor, 'Recherches', pp. 410–11.

but attempted to shape a developing literature to their own individual concepts of eloquence. To what extent the northern French lyric must then have evolved quite independently of southern influence to cultivate a traditional poetry of form which eschewed individuality, or to what extent the apparent uniformity of the trouvères is due to other causes, is an open question.[1]

[1] In northern France the more interesting ideas on love and courtliness were being expressed in non-musical genres. The lyric may have been principally *musical* entertainment (cf. p. 5 n. 2), where a harmonious, elegantly turned poem was little more than the vehicle for its musical setting. See, however, the recent work of P. Zumthor, *Essai de poétique médiévale* (Paris, 1972), which appeared too late for me to give it more detailed consideration.

I

MARCABRU: ELOQUENCE AND MEANING[1]

Two aspects of Marcabru's composition are essential to his concept of style: one is his view of eloquence, the other, of *trobar naturau*. The first is dualistic: he blames false eloquence, 'la falsa razos daurada' or 'false, gilded speech' (XXV. 24); but as a poet he practises his own form of eloquence, which he calls *trobar naturau*.[2]

1. *Eloquence*

Marcabru's view of eloquence is ostensibly negative. He condemns the false use of words: in empty boasting, in glib lies, in contortion of the truth through 'broken' thinking or *frait cuidar* (XIX. 11).

The churl is typically garrulous: empty, stagnating members of society are full of *nauzas e bauducs*, 'clamour and disputes',[3] while the lover of *cortezia* must reject *fol sobreparlar*, 'foolish loquacity' (XXXII. 60). The enemies of liberality 'make great clamour over small deeds' (XI. 43), and good intentions expressed boastfully are often sterile:

> Joves homes de bel semblan
> Vei per Malvestat deceubutz;
> Que van gaban:
> 'De so mil essais encogan
> Farem, qan lo temps er floritz',
> Mas lai reman lo gabs e.l brutz.[4]   (IV. 19–24)

---

[1] Marcabru's career can be dated approximately 1129–49; see Boissonnade. I quote from the Dejeanne edition except in the case of songs III, IX, XV, XVI, XXII, and XXIII, which have been re-edited by Roncaglia (see Bibliography).

[2] 'Lo vers comens', 7.   [3] 'Al departir', 31.

[4] Dejeanne: 'Dizo, mil essais encogan: "Farem . . . floritz"' (22–3); Pillet's emendation, p. 13. K. Lewent, 'Beiträge', p. 317: *encogan*, 'noch heuer' (*SWB* ii. 442).

Young men of fair appearance I see deceived by Evil; for they keep boasting: 'Of this we shall give a thousand proofs this very year, once the season is in flower'; but there ends the boast and the noise.

He attacks not only fruitless boasting but deceitful eloquence, 'la falsa razos daurada', by which false love corrupts its victims. It speaks with smooth, sweet words:

> Cujatz vos qu'ieu non conosca
> D'Amor s'es orba o losca?
> Sos digz aplan' et entosca;   (XVIII. 55–7)

Do you think I fail to realize that Love is blind or one-eyed? It smoothes out and polishes its words;[1]

> Putan' es de tan mal engenh
> C'ab dous parlar cueill et asenh
> Totz cels que pot metr' en congrenh,
> 　　　　　　　　　　　　　　　(XLIV. 57–9)

The whore is so evilly minded that with sweet speech she welcomes and reasons with all those she can put to work.[2]

Above all he blames people who twist the meaning of words. Such are the 'acropitz lengua-plana, / Torbadors d'amistat fina',[3] or the 'menut trobador bergau / entrebesquill',[4] who torment noble people by contorting the truth because of the confusion of their own minds:

> Trobador, ab sen d'enfanssa,
> Movon als pros atahina,
> E tornon en disciplina

---

[1] Dejeanne: 'Ses paroles sont tout miel, mais cette douceur cache le poison'; Lewent, p. 334: entosca is not derived from toxicum but is a compound of toscar, 'polir' (see E. Levy, ZRP xv. 545, SWB ii. 474).

[2] Dejeanne: '. . . elle enveloppe tous ceux qu'elle peut lier dans ses entraves.' For asenh see SWB, i. 89, congrenh, Rayn. ii. 458. Cf. XIV. 11–12, 'Qu'ab doussa sabor azesca / Sos digz de felho(n) azesc', 'for with sweet savour she baits her words with evil bait'; XXI. 19–22 'Volpils lengua traversana / Qu'a lairo cossilha, / Ab sa messorgua baussana / Dezers' ez essilha' (see Dejeanne's correction, p. 228), 'The cowardly, perverted tongue that gives evil counsel tricks with its lying, ruins and destroys.'

[3] 'vile smooth-tongues, disturbers of noble friendship' (XXXVI. 17–18). Dejeanne: lenguas planas; Lewent, p. 440: s must be omitted for the rhyme.

[4] 'buzzing, petty troubadours who confuse the truth' ('Lo vers comens', 9–10). Cf. XXXI. 37–40: 'Gent sembel fai que trahina / Ves son agach lo brico, / Del cim tro qu'en la racina, / Entrebescat hoc e no;' '(Amars) sets a gracious trap when it lures the simpleton into its snare; from the top to the root it weaves together yes and no.' Cf. II. 34–5. Köhler, p. 173, links 'oc e no' in Provençal with Abailard's sic et non method of dialectic; perhaps Marcabru has in mind here the misuse of dialectic.

> So que veritatz autreia,
> E fant los motz, per esmanssa,
> Entrebeschatz de fraichura.   (XXXVII. 7–12)

Simple-minded troubadours cause distress to good people and make torment[1] out of what is granted by truth, and cause words to be interlaced with brokenness in their own thoughts.[2]

Every effort, Marcabru says, is needed to prevent one's words from being falsified or misinterpreted:

> Ben dey tot mon chan esmerar,
> Qu'om re no mi puesca falsar,[3]
> Que per pauc es hom desmentitz,   (XL. 5–7)

I certainly ought to perfect my whole song so that no one can falsify anything in it for me, for on the slightest pretext one is accused of lying.

This theme of the imprecise and corrupting use of words is bound up with Marcabru's concept of 'dos cuidars', the 'entier' and the 'frait', the right and illusory ways of thinking:

> En dos cuidars ai conssirier
> A triar lo frait de l'entier,   (XIX. 10–11)

In two ways of thinking I am anxious to distinguish the broken from the whole.

Behind his negative view of eloquence as glib, deceitful, and corrupting, there lies, however, an implicit appreciation of true eloquence and a concern to apply this to his work. In fact, as we shall see Marcabru is expertly versed in the science of *eloquentia* derived directly or indirectly from medieval Rhetoric.

His very condemnation of eloquence may reflect this science. Blame of garrulousness and of the false use of words is a medieval moralizing commonplace,[4] but as false eloquence belongs to any

---

[1] Dejeanne: 'tournent en contrainte ce que vérité octroie'; Lewent, 'Beiträge', p. 441 : *tornon en d.*, 'zur Züchtigung wenden, geisseln, tadeln'. *Disciplina* is linked with *atahina*, 'distress' (v. 8): the troubadours who make words 'broken' give anxiety and torment to the *pros* who have to sift the truth from the *fraichura*. For *disciplina* as 'torment', see *SWB* ii. 250, and Marcabru, XXXVI. 11–12.

[2] *per esmanssa:* Dejeanne: 'par à peu près'; Lewent, p. 441: 'durch Nachdenken, absichtlich'; Rayn. iii. 219: 'opinion, pensée', *SWB* iii. 327: 'Schätzung, Meinung, Ueberlegung', *prendre e.* 'erwägen, überlegen; sein Ziel nehmen, zielen; sich eine Meinung bilden, der Meinung sein.' As Marcabru attacks the stupid troubadours for their folly ('sen d'enfanssa', v. 7, 'folla cuida', v. 59), he probably means their illusory opinions rather than wilful vice.   [3] Dejeanne: *mi*; Lewent: *m'i* (p. 445).

[4] Vulgate, ed. Marietti (Casali, 1959); Psa. 33: 14; 38: 2; 51: 4–6; 119: 2; 140: 1–5; Prov. 6: 17, and 6: 24; 'Ut custodiant te a muliere mala, et a blanda lingua

consideration of true eloquence it is discussed and condemned by teachers of Rhetoric. The blame of empty eloquence practised for its own sake, and its misuse by unscrupulous speakers, is a *topos* which goes back at least to Plato's attacks on Isocrates.[1] Saint Augustine reinforced it by his emphasis on Christian doctrine as the only basis for true eloquence: 'In ipso etiam sermone malit rebus placere quam verbis; nec aestimet dici melius, nisi quod dicitur verius; nec doctor verbis serviat, sed verba doctori.'[2]

Marcabru's specific knowledge of Rhetorical techniques can be seen in certain Rhetorical, especially dialectical vocabulary such as *razo, argumens, esprovaire, lassar, entensa*, through a striking use of Rhetorical method to define and argue his ideas in the song 'Per savi.l tenc' (XXXVII), and above all in the *gap* 'D'aisso lau Dieu'.

In his works *razo* can mean not only 'reason', 'what is right and reasonable',[3] but 'speech', 'argument':

> Ai! com es encabalada
> La falsa razos daurada,[4]   (XXV. 23–4)

Ah, how well perfected is the false, gilded speech!;

> Ges l'estornels non s'oblida,
> Quant ac la razon auzida ...   (XXVI. 2–3)

The starling did not delay; when it had heard the speech ...

> Gent ha la razon fenida,   (XXVI. 67).

Graciously it finished the speech;[5]

---

extraneae'; 12: 18, 19; 15: 2, 4; 17: 4; 21: 6, 23; 28: 23; Iac. 1: 26; 3: 5–8; I Pet. 3: 10. In his *Summa de arte praedicandi, PL* ccx. 111 ff., Alanus ab Insulis gives model sermons including 'Contra verbositatem et linguae evagationem' (162) and 'Contra mendacium' (164). Cf. *Indices* to PL ccxx, *Index de Decalogo*, 414–20. Matthew of Vendôme (*Ars versificatoria*, ed. E. Faral, p. 110) attacks Arnulf of Orléans for his 'sterilis et infructuosa . . . loquacitas' (v. 5). Cf. R. Tobler, *Die altprovenzalische Version der Disticha Catonis* (Berlin, 1897), pp. 58–9, III. 4. a.

[1] H. Clark, *Rhetoric in Graeco-Roman Education* (New York, 1957), pp. 6 ff.

[2] *De Doctrina Christiana, PL* xxxiv. 119, and the whole of book IV. For an account of the Augustinian tradition of Rhetoric, see Quadlbauer.

[3] 'Lavar de ser e de maiti / Nos deuriam, segon razo' (XXXV. 10–11); 'Que sentenssa follatina / Manten encontra razo' (XXXI. 75–6); cf. XXXVII. 50–1, IX. 23.

[4] C. Appel, 'Zu Marcabru', p. 435: 'La (or even 'Na') falsa Razos-daurada', by analogy with 'Na Cropa-fort' (XXXIV. 41).

[5] Dejeanne (XXVI. 3): 'l'objet de son message'; (XXVI. 67) 'sa mission'. In the *estornel* songs (XXV–XXVI) Marcabru describes three 'speeches': of the poet to the starling, the starling to the woman (a prostitute), and the woman to the poet

or else it can mean 'theme', 'line of thought':[1]

> Aujatz de chan, com enans' e meillura,
> e Marcabrus, segon s'entensa pura,
> sap la razon e.l vers lassar e faire
> si que autr'om no l'en pot un mot traire.[2]

Hear of my song how it progresses and improves, and how Marcabru, according to his pure intention, knows how to bind up the theme and compose the *vers* so that no one can remove from it a single word.

> Per savi.l tenc ses doptanssa
> Cel qui de mon chant devina
> So que chascus motz declina
> Si cum la *razos* despleia,   (XXXVII. 1–4)

I consider that man indubitably wise who can divine in my song what each word means as the theme unfolds . . .[3]

The meaning of *razo* as 'speech', 'theme', 'line of argument', appears to have its origins in Rhetorical debate. *Ratio* can mean argumentation or reasoning: 'Ratio est autem, cum omnis quaestio non in scriptione, sed in aliqua argumentatione consistit',[4] or it can be the core of a controversy, the cause for the debate to take place: 'Ratio est ea quae continet causam, quae si sublata sit, nihil in causa controversiae relinquatur.'[5] In Provençal legal terminology *razo* has the same meaning: 'D'aquesta question naissunt doas actios, so es doas razos':[6] 'From this issue arise

through his messenger. The first two satirically accuse the woman of infidelity and try to persuade her to grant the poet her love; the third is a speech in her defence. In Peire d'Alvernhe's song (Del Monte, I) 'Rossinhols', closely related to the *estornel* songs, the nightingale is *emparlatz* (119), 'eloquent', and the theme of eloquence is prominent: see pp. 55–8.

[1] Cf. Jaufré Rudel, ed. A. Jeanroy, VI. 1–6: 'No sap chantar qui so non di, / Ni vers trobar qui motz no fa, / Ni conois de rima co-s va / Si razo non enten en si. / Mas lo mieus chans comens' aissi / Com plus l'auziretz, mais valra, a a.' 'He who cannot execute the melody does not know how to sing, nor can he compose songs if he cannot turn phrases, nor does he know anything of rhyme if he does not understand his theme within himself. But my song begins in such a way that the more you listen to it, the more it is worth.' Jaufré says not that other people cannot understand his *razo* (Mölk, p. 51), but that the poet himself must understand what he is doing. The *topos* 'my song improves the more it is heard' is not confined to the *trobar clus*: Bernart de Ventadorn also says, 'Lo vers, aissi com om plus l'au, / vai melhuran tota via' (Appel, 21. 57–8). For *razo* as 'theme' cf. also Arnaut Daniel, ed. G. Toja, VI. 1; XVI. 4; and Rayn. v. 51.

[2] 'Aujatz de chan', 1–4.   [3] See p. 16.

[4] Cicero, *De Inv.* I. xiii. 18; cf. Quintilian, III. xi. 4; 'Ratio autem est, qua id, quod factum esse constat, defenditur': 'The *line of defence* is the method by which an admitted act is defended', and v. xiv. 1; VII. viii. 3. I follow the translations of the last editions, unless otherwise stated.

[5] *De Inv.* I. xiii. 18.   [6] *SWB* viii. 61.

two actions, that is, two lines of argument.' A *razonador* is an advocate: 'Mais e si alcus pecara, razonador avem ves lo paire Jhesu Crist'; 'Et es coustuma que nulh hom sia juge en neguna cort . . . en (l)aquela causa en que sera estat . . . conselhayre o razonayre de deguna de las partidas.'[1] The same terminology of legal Rhetoric appears in Provençal debate poems:

> De Berguedan, d'estas doas razos
> Al vostre sen chausetz en la meillor,
> Q'ieu mantenrai tant ben la sordejor
> Q'ie.us cuich vensser, qui dreich m'en col jutgar.[2]

De Berguedan, according to your wisdom choose the better of these two lines of argument, for I will maintain the worse one so well that I, who must judge correctly in this, believe I shall vanquish you.

> Guilhem de Mur, lo mielhs d'est partimen
> Puesc leu chauzir e mostrar mas razos.[3]

Guilhem de Mur, the best of this debate I can easily choose, and prove my argument.

The *Leys d'Amors* defines the *tenso* in the legal terms of arguing a case: 'Tensos es contrastz o debatz en lo qual cascus mante e razona alcun dig o alcun fag':[4] 'A *tenso* is a dispute or debate in which each man maintains and defends some saying or some action.' The continuity of usage from Rhetoric to the language of Provençal law and the troubadours' debate poetry shows how the term *razo* was absorbed into their literary terminology, and that before meaning 'speech' or 'theme' in general it means 'argument, line of argument'.

In the song 'Soudadier, per cui es Jovens' (XLIV) he attacks the *argumens* of prostitutes:

> Entendetz los mals argumens
> De las falsas putas ardens;   (XLIV. 3–4)

Listen to the evil arguments of the false, burning whores.[5]

---

[1] Rayn. v. 53; *SWB* viii. 65. 'But if any man sins, we have Jesus Christ as advocate with the father; 'And it is custom that no man should be judge in any court... in the same case in which he has been counsellor or advocate of either of the parties.'

[2] *Tenso* of Aimeric de Peguilhan and Guilhem de Berguedan, quoted in *SWB* viii. 62; v. 4 *col* = *cal*?

[3] *Tenso* of G. de Mur and Giraut Riquier, quoted by R. Zenker, *Tenzone*, p. 15 (C. A. F. Mahn, *Werke*, iv. 250).   [4] M. Gatien-Arnoult, p. 344.

[5] Appel, 'Zu Marcabru', p. 427: 'hört, was ich Uebles von den falschen geilen Huren sage.' Either translation is possible, but as Marcabru describes the 'dous parlar' of the *putana* (v. 58) used for deceit, he probably means the arguments spoken by the *putas*, rather than his own arguments about them.

Argumens is rare in Provençal lyric poetry[1] but it does occur in connection with dialectic in Peire de Corbiac's outline of the liberal arts in his *Tesaur* (thirteenth-century):[2]

> Per Dialectica sai arrazonablamens
> apauzar e respondre e falsar argumens;

Through Dialectic I know how to present a case and make replies by means of reasoning, and to falsify arguments.

Marcabru's use of this word at least suggests that he is here thinking of eloquence in terms of Rhetoric.

He certainly seems to have been conscious of arguing his ideas in a legal way. He sees himself as 'accuser, defender and inquisitor' in judicial inquiry into the truth about *Amors*:

> Qu'ieu sui assatz esprovaire,
> Deffendens et enquistaire,
> E vei cum Jovens se tuda,
> Per que Amors es perduda
> E de Joi deseretada
> E cum Amors es cujaire.
>
> L'amors don ieu sui mostraire
> Nasquet en un gentil aire . . .   . (V. 43-50)

For indeed I am investigator,[3] defender[4] and inquisitor,[5] and I see how Youth is being extinguished, so that Love is lost and disinherited from Joy, and how Love follows vain illusions. The love of which I testify[6] was born of noble lineage . . . .

The idea of being *mostraire* of Love may be derived from the *genus demonstrativum* of Rhetoric,[7] the genre of praise and blame.

---

[1] Rayn. and *SWB* give no examples of it in lyric poetry and it does not appear elsewhere in the troubadours considered in this book.

[2] Ed. Sachs, vv. 550-1; cf. p. 26.

[3] Rayn. iv. 652; *SWB* iii. 278.

[4] Rayn. iv. 361; *SWB* ii. 40.

[5] Rayn. v. 21 and 361; *SWB* iii. 24; L & S 961 B: in particular, an *inquisitor* is one who searches for proofs to support an accusation. Marcabru seems to be enumerating all participants in an enquiry (cf. Rayn. v. 21 OF, 'Il est juge, enquesteur e tesmoin tout ensemble').

[6] Or 'give proofs'? cf. Rayn. iv. 21 *monstranssa, mostramen, demonstranssa*, 'démonstration, preuve', and *SWB* v. 329. Peire d'Alvernhe, probably referring to Marcabru, speaks of one who in the eyes of the ignorant world 'fai avol demonstransa' because he attacked wordly pleasures (Del Monte, XIII. 22-8), and this suggests that Marcabru's way of 'demonstrating' his ideas on love became part of his reputation. (For the interpretation of Peire's lines I follow Appel, 'Zu Marcabru', p. 419, rather than A. Del Monte, *Peire*, p. 140.)

[7] See H. Lausberg, *Registerband*, p. 682.

Here Marcabru praises the love of which he is *mostraire*. Praise and blame are obviously essential to his moral didacticism. He himself complains that 'Lo plus d'aquest segle carnau' have over-turned *Joven*, 'e non prezon *blasme ni lau* / un gran de mill.'[1] Marcabru seems to have seen eloquence, including his own eloquence, in Rhetorical terms of the proper use of argument. When he wants to 'bind up' his theme 'according to his pure intention':

> e Marcabrus, segon s'entensa pura,
> sap la razon   e.l vers lassar e faire . . .[2]

he may again be using Rhetorical terms, although these may already have been so absorbed into the language that Marcabru was not aware of them as such. The 'binding up' of the song, a troubadour *topos*,[3] goes back to Rhetoric: 'argumenta in catenas ligare',[4] 'sententiam verbis illigare',[5] while *intentio* means some-times the intention behind a written document, as opposed to the facts in it,[6] or the 'intended meaning' of an allegorical work.[7] Giraut Riquier mentions the 'bon' entension' behind an argument he has made:

> Assatz ai dig breumen
> E mostrat per razon
> Ab bon' entension
> Per que devem amar,[8]

I have briefly and sufficiently stated and demonstrated by argument with noble intention why we ought to love.

Rhetorical influence on these terms may have been indirect; but other passages in Marcabru's work indicate that he had a detailed knowledge of Rhetorical ideas and techniques, especially those of argument and debate. The song 'Per savi.l tenc' is an outstanding example of this.

---

[1] 'Lo vers comens', 35–6.   [2] See p. 12.
[3] Cf. B. Marti, ed. E. Hoepffner, V. 75–6: 'E qui belhs motz lass' e lia / De belh' art s'es entremes'; Guilhem IX, ed. A. Jeanroy, VI. 6–7: 'E puesc ne traire. l vers auctor / Quant er lassatz.'
[4] Quintilian, v. xiv. 32 (L & S 1065).
[5] Cicero, *De Oratore*, III. xliv. 175 (L & S 1065).
[6] Lausberg, *Registerband*, p. 727, *intendere* II.
[7] *Intentio* is the technical term given to the (supposed) hidden intention of an author such as Ovid subjected to exegesis: see F. Ghisalberti, 'Biographies', pp. 10–59, especially pp. 11, 16.
[8] *SWB* vii. 64: 16) Guir. Riq. 71, 351 *per razon* 'in vernünftiger, angemessener, passender Weise'; but see p. 11.

He begins by stressing the need for clear thinking, on the part both of the poet and of his audience. :

> Per savi.l tenc ses doptanssa
> Cel qui de mon chant devina
> So que chascus motz declina,
> Si cum la razos despleia,
> Qu'ieu mezeis sui en erranssa
> D'esclarzir paraul' escura.   (XXXVII. 1–6)

I consider indubitably wise the man who divines in my song what each word indicates as the theme unfolds; for I myself am uncertain how to clarify obscure speech.[1]

This, he explains, is because foolish troubadours confuse the truth and in the vagueness of their thoughts make the words 'entrebeschatz de fraichura',[2] falsely equating true and false love:

> E meton en un' eganssa
> Falss' Amor encontra fina,   (13–14)

and place true and false love together on the same level.

As Lewent says,[3] Marcabru does not intend his words to be obscure, but they become cloudy in the minds of foolish troubadours; and it takes a wise man to concentrate on the meaning of each word in order not to misinterpret the whole. The mistake the foolish troubadours make is to think that true and false love are the same, and that when Marcabru attacks one, he is attacking love as a whole.[4]

When Marcabru introduces the problem of *paraul' escura*,[5] he may well be thinking of the Rhetorical *causa obscura*: the kind of

---

[1] *declina*(3) : cf. *SWB* ii. 30 : 'Que vench del cel en terra / Soffrent trebayl e guerra / E la vida mesquina, / Quel noms d'Eva declina . . .' 'For he came from heaven to earth, suffering travail and war and a wretched life, which the name of Eve signifies . . .'. This is Marcabru's meaning (but cf. P. Rajna, *R* xiv (1897), 410 : 'dice'), since the *savis* has to 'divine' what each word means. *en erranssa*: Dejeanne 'sujet à l'erreur'; Lewent, 'Beiträge', p. 441, *erranssa* = 'Not, Bedrängnis'.   [2] See p. 10.

[3] p. 441 ; cf. U. Mölk, p. 72. See, however, G. Errante, p. 189, and D. W. Robertson, 'Five Poems', p. 554.

[4] Cf. the *tenso* with Uc Catola, where Marcabru emphasizes that he is talking of '*fals*' amistat' (VI. 6), and points to the difference in possible kinds of love: 'Catola, l'amors dont parlaz', 'Catola, the love of which *you* speak . . .' (29).

[5] Lewent ('Beiträge', p. 441) and Mölk (p. 72; see n. 3) are probably right to refuse to see in *paraul' escura* a reference to the *trobar clus*. But the first stanza of this song reveals two features which reappear in future *clus* poems. The first is an awareness that the audience is divided into the wise and the foolish, which Raimbaut mentions when he says he will never seek the praise of the *fatz* (see p. 146). The second is the way in which the theme only unfolds gradually, and requires concentration to be understood. This is an essential ingredient of Giraut de Bornelh's *trobar clus* (see pp. 93 ff.).

case 'in quo aut tardi auditores sunt aut difficilioribus ad cogno-
scendum negotiis causa est implicata'.[1] His own 'case' could be
described as obscure both because the subject is difficult—it takes
a wise man to perceive the exact truth in it—and because the
foolish troubadours are *tardi*. The *De Inventione* says that in such
a case the speaker must make the audience receptive in the introduction: 'In obscuro causae genere per principium dociles
auditores efficere oportebit',[2] and this is done by explaining the
essence of the case in plain language: 'Dociles auditores faciemus
si aperte et breviter summam causae exponemus, hoc est, in quae
consistat controversia.'[3] This is what Marcabru does. He tries to
gain the good will of the audience by discreet flattery: 'Per savi.l
tenc . . .', and a 'modesty formula': 'Qu'ieu mezeis sui en erranssa
. . .';[4] he then states the nature of the subject: 'paraul' escura', and
after explaining the reason for his theme: that foolish troubadours
have been confusing the truth (stanza II), he states the subject as
simply and clearly as possible: 'E meton en un' eganssa / Falss'
Amor encontra fina' (13–14). False and true love are not to be
equated. This is followed by an attempt to define the difference
between the two as clearly and graphically as possible, and in
doing so Marcabru closely follows the basic pattern of *dispositio*
in Classical Rhetoric: introduction, exposition, definition or
division, defence of one's own case, refutation of the opponent's
case, and conclusion.[5] He defines the difference between two kinds
of love, *Amor* and *Amar* (15–30); he praises the virtues of
Amor (stanzas VI–VII),[6] and blames *Amar* (stanza VIII),[7]
praise and blame corresponding to *confirmatio* and *reprehensio*.

---

[1] *De Inv.* I. xvi. 20: 'in which either the audience is slow-witted or the subject
is bound up with matters which are fairly difficult to understand.' Cf. Brunetto
Latini, *Li Livres dou tresor*, ed. P. Chabaille, III. xvii. 4.   [2] *De Inv.* I. xvi. 21.

[3] Ibid. I. xvi. 23.   [4] For modesty formulae, see E. R. Curtius, p. 83.

[5] *De Inv.* I. xiv. 19: *exordium, narratio, partitio, confirmatio, reprehensio, conclusio*; a
digression is possible before the conclusion (I. li. 96). *Rhet. ad Her.* I. iii. 4 *exordium,
narratio, divisio, confirmatio, confutatio, conclusio*.

[6] 'C'Amors a signifianssa / De maracd' o de sardina, / E(s) de joi cim' e racina
. . .' (31 ff.).

[7] 'Sermonars ni predicanssa / Non val un ou de gallina / Vas cellui de qu'es
frairina / Follia de cor correia; / Qu'ieu sai s'Amars es amanssa, / Qu'a mains es
fals' e tafura . . .' 'It's not worth a hen's egg to sermonize and preach to someone
beset by foul, deceitful(?) folly (sin); / for I know that if *Amar* assumes a loving
appearance, to many it is false and treacherous.' *de cor*: 'of leather', or perhaps
'willingly' (*SWB* i. 358). *correia*: 'strap'; but *SWB* i. 379 indicates the *juec de
la correye* is often synonymous with a deceiving game, and a *jogaire de correia* is
a 'deceiver'.

The conclusion is divided into the summing up (*enumeratio*)[1] of his ideas:

> Fols pos tot cant au romanssa,
> Non sec razo, mas bozina,
> Car s'Amors viu de rapina
> Autrei c'Amors s'amoreia
> E que Costans es costanssa
> E fals usatges dreitura;   (stanza IX)

Since the fool spreads stories about everything that he hears, he does not follow reason but mumbles senselessly; for if *Amor* lives by rapine I grant that *Amor* is love-sick and Costans[2] is constancy and false conduct rectitude;[3]

and invective against 'un'avol gen canina' (*indignatio*):

> La defenida balanssa
> D'aquest vers e revolina
> Sobr' un'avol gen canina
> Cui malvatz astres ombreia,
> C'ab folla cuida bobanssa
> Ses faich de bon' aventura.
>
> La cuida per qu'el bobanssa
> Li sia malaventura.   (55–62)

The verdict[4] of this song hangs in the balance and comes down on a base, contemptible people, overshadowed by an evil star, for these people puff themselves up in foolish illusions without well-destined deeds. May the illusion with which they inflate themselves bring them ill fortune.

While other songs of Marcabru also show indications of Rhetorical *dispositio*,[5] this one is remarkable because the ideas in it are so

---

[1] *De Inv.* I. lii. 98: the conclusion has three divisions, *enumeratio, indignatio, conquestio*, 'summing up', 'exciting of indignation or ill will against the opponent', 'arousing of pity and sympathy'.

[2] *Costans* probably means a vacillating man; see A. Roncaglia, 'Al departir', pp. 18–20 n. 26.

[3] Dejeanne: 'Le fou raconte partout ce qu'il entend; il ne suit pas la raison, mais bousille, car son Amour vit de rapine. J'accorde alors qu'Amour . . .'. Pillet, p. 17, reads *s'amareja* (no MSS.): 'denn wenn Amor von Raub lebt, so gebe ich zu, dass Amor bitter wird (sich *amar* nähert) . . .'. Lewent, 'Beiträge', p. 443 is better: 'Fols, pos . . . romanssa, Non sec razo . . .': 'da der Tor alles, . . . weitererzählt, so folgt er . . .'. For *bozina*, see *SWB* i. 160.

[4] See p. 22, n. to v. 12.

[5] XVIII and VII are vituperative and belong to the *genus demonstrativum*, but show no defined *dispositio*: each stanza offers a new method of attack. V is made up of praise and blame used antithetically, but the song as a whole does not follow the clear pattern of 'Per savi'. 'Aujatz de chan' and 'Emperaire per vostre prez' both follow the arrangement of the epistolary style: introduction, *captatio benevolentiae*,

clearly arranged in this way, and because the Rhetorical structure coincides with an especially strong concern to clarify, define, and argue his ideas on love. It confirms that Marcabru knew how to use Rhetorical techniques for his own purposes.

This is especially plain in his *gap* 'D'aisso lau Dieu', which reveals his familiarity with Rhetorical debating procedures. This *gap* has been frequently discussed.[1] At first scholars tried to explain its apparently cynical and immoral tone, where Marcabru, contrary to all the moral principles expressed in the rest of his work, boasts of his ability to deceive and cuckold other men.[2] E. Köhler[3] suggested that he was composing on two levels of meaning: on one level, giving a profane public what it wanted by boasting of his sexual prowess; on the other, implicitly condemning the public's immoral taste. Köhler argues that Marcabru draws attention to the double meaning by mentioning his *gignos sens*, 'cunning meanings', and *cent colors*, 'hundred colours'. In this deliberate ambiguity Köhler, following an earlier suggestion of Jeanroy,[4] sees elements of the *trobar clus*. A. Roncaglia refused to see the *gap* as deliberately obscure[5] and interpreted it as a bitter polemical parody of those whom Marcabru attacks more openly in other songs.[6] L. Pollmann[7] reopened the question of whether the *gap* was composed in the *trobar clus*, and saw three levels of meaning in it, following the pattern of Christian exegesis which looked for literal, moral, and tropological levels of meaning in literary works; but U. Mölk[8] subsequently rejected this theory in favour of Roncaglia's.

The *gap* is reconsidered here because it contains a number of Rhetorical terms whose significance has not been recognized.

expositio, petitio, and a conclusion corresponding to the closing remarks of a letter (see Scheludko, *Arch. Rom.* xv (1931), 169). Marcabru does not always follow a Rhetorical pattern of *dispositio*, even in general outline: sometimes his theme unfolds through imagery (XXI, XXXIX, XLIV, XXXVIII, 'Al departir') or antitheses (XIV) or narrative (I, XXX, XXXI). The versatility of his approach makes the clear Rhetorical pattern in 'Per savi' all the more remarkable.

[1] See Roncaglia, 'Il *gap*', p. 46, for a bibliography of this song and an account of previous ideas of F. Diez, Vossler, Appel, H. Spanke, G. Errante, Dejeanne, Pillet, Lewent. See also Köhler, pp. 134 ff.; Pollmann, '*Trobar clus*', pp. 15 ff.; Mölk, pp. 66 ff.

[2] Vossler, 'Der Trobador Marcabru', p. 6, saw the song as a literary game in the *gap* genre. Appel, 'Zu Marcabru', p. 426, thought its apparently arrogant tone might be the result of the harshness of life which forced him to live by his wits.

[3] pp. 134 ff.   [4] *Poésie lyrique*, ii. 33.   [5] Op. cit., p. 46.
[6] Ibid., p. 47.   [7] '*Trobar clus*', pp. 15 ff.   [8] pp. 66 ff.

They point to a coherent *razo* which is distinct from the erotic
theme. This *razo* concerns the technique of verbal, Rhetorical
dispute; Marcabru claims to be its most astute exponent.

I   D'aisso lau Dieu
              e saint Andrieu
         c'om non es de major albir
            qu'ieu sui, so.m cuig,
            e no.n fatz bruig   5
         e volrai vos lo per que dir;

II   C'assatz es lait
             s'intratz en plait
         don non sabretz a lutz issir,   10
            e non es bo
            jutgetz razo
         si non la sabetz defenir.

III   De gignos sens
             sui si manens
         que mout sui greus ad escarnir;   15
            lo pan del fol
            caudet e mol
         manduc, e lais lo mieu frezir;

IV   Tant quant li dur
             li pliu e.il jur   20
         c'om no.m puosca de lui partir,
            e quan li faill
            mus e badaill
         e prenda del mieu lo dezir;

V   Qu'ieu jutg' a drei   25
             que fols follei
         e savis si gart al partir,
            qu'en dobl' es fatz
            e dessenatz
         qui.s laiss' a fol enfolletir.   30

VI   D'estoc breto
             ni de basto
         no sap om plus ni d'escrimir:
            qu'ieu fier autrui
            e.m gart de lui   35
         e no.is sap del mieu colp cobrir.

VII
        En l'autrui broill
        chatz cora.m voill
    e fatz mos dos canetz glatir,
        e.l tertz sahus   40
        eis de rahus
    bautz e ficatz senes mentir.

VIII
        Mos alos es
        en tal deves
    res mas ieu non s'en pot jauzir: 45
        aissi l'ai claus
        de pens venaus
    que nuills no lo.m pot envazir.

IX
        Dels plus tors sens[1]
        sui ples e prens,   50
    de cent colors per mieills chauzir;
        fog porti sai
        et aigua lai
    ab que sai la flam' escantir.

X
        Cascun si gart,   55
        c'ab aital art
    mi fatz a viure e morir;
        qu'ieu sui l'auzels
        c'als estornels
    fatz los mieus auzellos noirir.   60

I. For one thing I thank God and St. Andrew: that no one has better judgement than I, in my opinion, and I am not boasting in this, and I will tell you why;

II. for it is very disagreeable if you enter into a debate in which you will not be able to reach a conclusion, and it is bad to judge an argument if you do not know how to arrive at a true verdict.

III. I am so well endowed with cunning meanings that it is very hard to get the better of me; I eat the fool's bread while it is warm and soft, and leave my own to get cold:

IV. as long as his lasts I pledge and swear to him that I cannot be parted from him, and when he has none left let him muse and gape and start to desire mine;

V. for I rightly judge that the fool should fool and the wise man should take heed in the sharing, for one who lets himself be fooled by a fool is doubly foolish and senseless.

      [1] Roncaglia: 'Del plus torz fens'. See the notes.

vi. Of Breton staff or any stick no one knows more than I, nor of fencing: for I strike another and defend myself against him, and he does not know how to shield himself from my blow.

vii. In my neighbour's thicket I hunt where I will and make my two little dogs bark, and the third bloodhound rushes forward, bold and fixed on the prey: I'm not lying!

viii. My private property is in such a prohibited enclosure that no one but I can take pleasure in it: I have so closed it round with deceiving thoughts that no one can invade it.

ix. I am full and teeming with the most tortuous signs, with a hundred colours for the best choice; I bear fire here and water there with which I can extinguish the flame.

x. Let each beware, for with such an art I make myself live and die; for I am the bird that has its own fledgelings nurtured by the starlings.

NOTES

The text is Roncaglia's. See his notes in *SM* xvii (1951), 46–70.

3. *albir*: *SWB* i. 48: 'Ueberlegen, Besinnen', and *albirador* 'Beurteiler'.

8. *plait*: this can be a lawsuit, trial, or (legal) dispute, or an agreement or 'contract' between a poet and his lady: Rayn. iv. 547, *SWB* vi. 332 ('Prozess; Gegenstand eines Prozesses; Handel, Frage, Angelegenheit; Abmachung, Uebereinkommen, Vertrag . . .'). *Intrar en plait* can probably mean the same as *se metre en plait*, 'to begin': cf. Marcabru, XXXI. 15–16, 'Ieu.m met de trobar en plai / E dirai d'amor cum vai.'

11. *razo*: see pp. 12 ff.

12. *defenir*: 'define; finish' (*PD* 107), but also 'pronounce a verdict', as in the following passage quoted by Levy, *SWB* ii. 45: 'Ques aquil arbitrador . . . poguessan de las complanchas . . . de pla conoysser per sentencia o per mandament o per amicabla composition diffinir; en tal convenant agut entre las parta . . . ques aquela (sc. pena) forfacha o nesqualre tracha, le mandamentz o li sentencia o li diffinicions, qual que fossan, per aquo mens non aya(n) fermeza; e que aquil arbitre o arbitrador apres la deffenicion nesqualre poguessan de la pena connoyscer.' ('So that those judges . . . might judge the complaints with clear understanding, by sentence or decree or amicable arrangement, in such a skilful agreement between the parties . . . that the punishment, merited or treated in whatever way, the decree or the sentence or the verdict, whatever they might be, should not be any less firm on that account; and that those judges or arbitrators should be able to decide on the punishment after the verdict in any affair.') Cf. *Leys d'Amors*, Gatien-Arnoult, p. 344, which says that the *tenso* ends with 'doas tornadas en las quals devo jutge elegir, lo qual *definisca lor plag*'.

13. *sens*: Roncaglia: 'astuzie'; also 'meanings', cf. *SWB* vii. 560, 5.

31. *estoc breto*: Roncaglia, p. 65, n. 31, suggests this may have a special figurative meaning: cf. *Donatz provensals*, 28b, 45; *bretoneiar .i. loqui impetuose* (emended to *loqui impedite* by G. Paris, *R* i (1875), 235).

47. *pens venaus*: Roncaglia's note, p. 68, deals fully with attempts to explain this line. Dejeanne: 'pieux de vaisseaux' (following *C pes nauaus*), i.e. 'd'une palissade'; Lewent, 'Beiträge', p. 332: *d'empechs e vaus* (emendation), 'mit Brustwehren und Gräben(?)'. Roncaglia suggests the etymology *pinn-* for *pens*: cf. Isidore, *Etym.* xi. i 46 'pinnum . . . antiqui acutum dicebant'. *Navaus (C)* might, he

suggests, be derived from *nava*, 'a clearing': *pens navaus* could possibly be spikes surrounding a clearing (in a forest). *Venaus* (*ET*) might come from *venari*, Prov. *venar* (Rayn. v. 481, *SWB* viii. 624), *pens venaus* being perhaps sharpened hunting-spikes (as those used to make traps?). He prefers to derive *venaus* from *venna*, trellis-work used to catch fish, sometimes meaning hedge, enclosure, wattling (Jud, *R* xlvii (1921), 486 n. 1): *pens venaus* would be *pens* as of *venna* and might be an image of a chastity belt. He translates: 'sbarramenti'. However, *pens* does have the common meaning of 'thoughts' (*PD* 288). *Venals* can be applied to speech, not so much in the sense of 'venal', but 'perfidious', 'deceitful': cf. Raimbaut d'Aurenga, XII. 26: 'Istz lausengiers ab ditz venals'; and Aimeric de Peguilhan, quoted in *SWB* viii. 623:

> 'Ab proverbis dauratz de sen
> Et ab parauletas venals,
> Vol far creire del ben qu'es mals'.

'With proverbs gilded with reason and with deceitful little words I want to make people believe that good is evil.'

49. *AIK* Dels plus torsens, *CE* De pluzors sens, *T* De sens cortes. *Sens* here rhymes with *prens* (= *prenhs;* cf. Giraut de Bornelh: 'Mo trobar ab saber prenh', 'Ans que venia', v. 56, see p. 119), and therefore does not repeat the rhyme word of v. 13. Although *sens* is in all MSS., Roncaglia says that it does not make satisfactory sense and emends to *fens* (*fenhs*), 'infingimenti' (p. 56). For an explanation of *sens*, see the commentary below.

57. *mi fatz a*: Roncaglia, 'I play at living and dying', as in *se f. a un joc*, *SWB* iii. 388, 31. This is possible, but isn't the idea of 'play' in *joc* rather than *se f. a*?

Before we examine the Rhetorical elements of the *gap* we should recall its erotic theme, which is generally recognized.[1] Marcabru claims to be the universal cuckolder, whose 'fledgelings are nurtured by the starlings' (58–60). If the words in stanzas I–II are taken in a general sense, they mean: my way of thinking is the best, and this is no empty boast; for it is bad to begin something one cannot finish, or to express an opinion in ignorance. *Intrar en plait* has the general sense of 'to begin';[2] *a lutz issir* can mean 'to finish';[3] *razo* can be, in general, a 'matter' or 'affair'.[4] In the erotic context which becomes plainer subsequently, Marcabru implies here that some people may boast of sexual prowess, but only he carries out his boast successfully. He is so full of 'cunning ways'[5] that it is hard to fool him; he takes the fool's bread, or his wife,[6] and keeps his own to himself (stanzas III–V). The image of the *estoc breto*, of hunting with dogs (stanzas VI–VII) have erotic implications.[6] He has locked up his 'property' or his wife so that only he can enjoy her (VIII), and is full of a hundred

---

[1] See p. 19.   [2] See note to v. 8.
[3] *SWB* iv. 445: *gitar a lutz, traire a lutz* 'ausführen, vollenden'; also 'to succeed' (Roncaglia, p. 63).   [4] *PD* 315, 'matière, sujet'.
[5] See note to v. 13.   [6] See Roncaglia's notes.

deceiving appearances or *colors* (51).[1] 'Fire here' and 'water there'
(52–4) are the contrary appearances assumed by the cuckolder,
or perhaps they refer more specifically to sexual arousal and re-
lease, alluded to again in 'mi fatz a viure e morir' (57). On one
level the song is a sexual *gap* in the manner of Guilhem IX.[2]

But on another, it shows Marcabru's knowledge of the techniques of Rhetorical debate. The terminology of stanza II can have
a specific Rhetorical meaning. *Plait* can mean 'lawsuit' or 'debate'.[3]
Razo has the Rhetorical sense of 'theme, line of argument';[4] the
various readings for v. 11 concern the judging, stating, proposing,
or examination of an argument: *A* jutgetz razo, *IK* digatz razo,
CE qu'enquier razo, *T* ci mou razo. *Defenir* can have the specific
meaning of 'pronounce a verdict'.[5] *A lutz issir* can mean either 'to
complete, reach a conclusion' or 'to explain, make oneself clear'.[6]
Marcabru blames those who engage in a dispute without knowing
how to bring it to a successful conclusion, or perhaps without
knowing how to make themselves clear, and for expressing
opinions when they have no sense of judgement. He claims that
he has the best judgement (*albir*), and he challenges the accuracy
of thought of his competitors, and their ability to carry through
an argument.

The *gignos sens* of which he claims to be full (13–15) can mean
not merely 'astute ways' but 'cunning meanings'. Rhetorical
works mention the various *sensus* or figurative meanings of words,[7]
and an anonymous Provençal poet says that a *razo* can have
several *sens:*

Qui aquetz digs estriers enten,
Si mielhs hi dis, no lo.n repren,
Quar s'a trop sens una razos,
Mout m'es meiller quan quecx es bos.[8]

If someone understands these words in a different way, if he prefers to
explain them this way then I do not reproach him for it; for if a theme

---

[1] *SWB* i. 284; cf. Marcabru, XXIV. 4–5: 'Qui a drut reconogut d'una color /
Blanc lo teigna . . .'

[2] Köhler, p. 136, discusses the similarities between Marcabru's song and 'Ben
vuelh' of Guilhem (ed. Jeanroy, VI). Cf. Roncaglia's notes.

[3] See notes, p. 22.

[4] See pp. 12 ff.   [5] See notes, p. 22.

[6] See note 3, p. 22; also *SWB* iv. 445 *traire a lutz, venir a lutz* 'erklären, offenbar
werden'.

[7] Quintilian, VI. iii. 48 'non quia excludenda sint omnino verba duos sensus signi-
ficantia'; cf. Lausberg, *Registerband,* p. 803.   [8] *SWB* vii. 560.

has many senses, it's much the better for it, in my opinion, when each one is valid.

Gignos can mean either 'cunningly deceitful' or 'subtle'; subtlety or ingenuity is essential to the Rhetorical speaker[1] or poet: Dante says the poet must have *ingenium et scientia*,[2] and Peire d'Alvernhe that he should have *gienhs ginhos*.[3] If *gignos sens* is taken in the sense of 'cunning meanings', then Marcabru is explaining his superiority in arguing and judging a *razo:* he baffles his opponent by the cunning senses he puts into his words. The rest of the *gap* can be seen as a development of this theme: of the poet's superior skill in verbal combat.

In this context the imagery of the fool's bread, which Marcabru takes and eats while it is still warm, could mean that he is apparently friendly while he persuades his opponent to reveal his arguments; these he then demolishes, without allowing him to grasp any of his own arguments in turn (stanzas III–V). This is one sense of stanza VI, where their dispute is described in terms of fighting or fencing. Roncaglia suggested that the *estoc breto* might have a special figurative sense of 'Breton eloquence';[4] the imagery of fighting or fencing may be equivalent to the *arma eloquentiae*, the 'weapons of eloquence' which the Rhetorical disputant uses to confound his adversary.[5]

Marcabru 'hunts where he will' in his neighbour's estate (VII): he does what he likes with his opponent's arguments; but his own *alos* he keeps to himself to prevent all attacks (VIII). Whether or not *pens* (47) can mean 'spikes', as scholars have

---

[1] See Lausberg, *Registerband*, p. 723, *ingenium*, especially §1152, Quintilian, x. ii. 12, x. i. 130. Cf. Geoffrey of Vinsauf, *Poetria Nova*, vv. 213–17, ed. Faral, p. 203, where *ingenium* is 'native ability'.

[2] *DVE* II. iv. 11, 'genius and knowledge', i.e. innate ability and acquired skill.

[3] Del Monte, V. 11–13: 'Quar ses gaug grans sabers ni purs / ni gienhs ginhos / non er aut elegutz', 'For without joy, great and pure wisdom and subtle genius will not be highly esteemed'; cf. Peirol, ed. S. C. Aston, XXI. 6: 'Quar ylh m'a donat l'art e.l genh'.   [4] See notes, p. 22.

[5] L & S 162 *arma* II: 'tenere semper arma [*sc.* eloquentiae], quibus vel tectus ipse esse possis, vel ...' (Cic. *De Or.* I. viii. 32); 'arma ... eloquentiae', Quintilian, v. xii. 21. Cf. Quintilian, III. xi. 26; 'Nec tam hoc praecipiendum est, ut quaestionem, continens, iudicationem inveniamus (num id quidem facile est), quam ut intueamur semper, aut certe si digressi fuerimus saltem respiciamus, ne plausum adfectantibus arma excidant.' 'We should teach not so much that it is our duty to discover the question, the central argument, and the point for the decision of the judge (an easy task), as that we should continually keep our attention on the subject, or if we digress, at least keep looking back to it, lest in our desire to win applause we should let our weapons drop from our grasp.'

suggested with some reservation,[1] it can certainly mean 'thoughts'. By analogy with *parauletas venals*, 'deceitful little words',[2] *pens venaus* means 'deceitful, misleading thoughts'; the misleading, figurative meanings, the 'figures of thought' which Marcabru puts into his words, the *gignos sens* which defeat his tardy opponent. He is full of *cent colors per mieills chauzir:* not merely 'deceiving appearances' but also Rhetorical 'colours' or figurative meanings.[3] *Sens (senhs)* in v. 49 could have a similar sense: it means 'signs' or 'indications',[4] and *signa* in Rhetoric can be the signs, indications, and circumstantial evidence which a speaker uses to cast suspicion on the accused:

> Ab argumentis et signis et ceteris locis quibus augetur suspicio dicere hoc modo convenit: Cum multa concurrant argumenta et signa quae inter se consentiant, rem perspicuam, non suspiciosam videri oportere. Item plus oportere signis et argumentis credi quam testibus . . .[5].

Again Marcabru appears to be saying that he can draw the most tortuous conclusions from the facts, or produce the most cunning and devious arguments, to defeat his verbal opponent.

The techniques described by Marcabru in the *gap* were probably derived from standard ingredients of the quadrivium. In a thirteenth-century encyclopedia Peire de Corbiac[6] outlines the main items to be learned in the seven liberal arts, and his comments about Dialectic, Rhetoric, and Law have features in common with Marcabru's boast:

> *Per Dialectica* sai arrazonablemens
> a pauzar e respondre e falsar argumens,
> sofismar e conduire, e tot gignozamens
> menar mon aversaire ad inconveniens.

---

[1] See notes, pp. 22–3.   [2] See notes, p. 23.

[3] Either the deceiving 'gloss' or 'varnish' used to touch up a bad cause: Lausberg §329 and §538, Quintilian, IV. ii. 88; *SWB* i. 284: 'Te dic color? / Non ieu, ans mescle sen ab ver', 'Do I speak to you with (deceiving) colour? Not I, I rather mingle meaning with truth'; or stylistic ornaments, figures, and tropes. Cf. Köhler pp. 136–7.   [4] Rayn. v. 226; *SWB* vii. 568.

[5] *Rhet. ad Her.* II. vii. 11; 'In favour of presumptive proof, signs, and the other means of increasing suspicion it is advantageous to speak as follows: when there is a concurrence of many circumstantial indications and signs that agree with one another, the result ought to appear as clear fact, not surmise. Again, signs and presumptive proof deserve more credence than witnesses . . .'. For example, see IV. xl–xli. 53; II. ii. 3; II. iv. 6. Cf. Lausberg, *Registerband*, p. 811.

[6] Sachs, vv. 550–67.

Per Retorica sai per bels affaitamens
colorar mas paraulas e dir adautamens,
acaptar benvolensa en primas dels auzens,
acuzar e deffendre de manz encolpamens,
car puesc retener las proezas ni'l sens
e retenrai sivals can poirai bevolens.
De Ley ni de Decretz n'ai apres anc granmens,
mas en aitals cortz nostras sai de platz jutjamens,
e soi pron rasonables e parliers avinens
si qu'al partir s'en lauzon sil sui son captenens.

Through Dialectic I know how to present a case and reply and falsify arguments by reasoning, to use sophistries, to conduct and lead my adversary quite cunningly into discomfiture. Through Rhetoric I know how to colour my words with fine embellishments and to speak with charm, to capture the good will of the audience at the outset, to accuse and defend from many charges; for I can memorize proofs and reasons and will keep my sympathizers, at least as long as I am able. Of secular and canon law I never learned much, but in such courts as ours I know how to judge cases, and I am excellent at reasoning and a pleasing speaker, so that when a debate is proposed, those whom I champion are honoured.[1]

In the context of the Rhetorical theme of the *gap*, the last lines, where Marcabru says his 'fledgelings' are 'nurtured by the starlings', may have a figurative meaning distinct from the theme of cuckoldry. Why should Marcabru live at the expense of the starling in particular? In another song (XXV) he sends off a starling as a messenger. R. Lejeune[2] suggested that he chose this bird because its appearance made it a suitable parody of the nightingale, the usual messenger of love, but also because it had no song of its own but could be taught to speak parrot-fashion. This is a suitable image for a *joglar* who does not compose his own songs but imitates those of others, or sings songs for the troubadours; Raimbaut de Vaqueiras mocks at the *joglar* Perdigon by calling him 'N'estornels'.[3] Perhaps Marcabru means that he makes a living by the *joglars*: either because he is addressing his song to them, or because he can use his songs to damage the reputation of his enemies.

[1] *pauzar: SWB* vi. 155: 5) 'aufstellen, behaupten'; 6) 'den Fall setzen, annehmen'; 13) *se p. contra alc.*, 'sich entgegenstellen, entgegentreten'.
las proezas ni'l sens: corr. *ni.ls sens? Proezas* meaning 'noble deeds' (Rayn. iv. 659; *SWB* vi. 578) offers little sense. *Proezas* is perhaps *proazos, proansas*, 'proofs' (Rayn. iv. 651). Or perhaps the phrase is *las prezas ni.l cens*, 'rewards and payment'.
en aitals cortz nostras: Peire may be referring to courtly debates.
[2] R. Lejeune, 'Thèmes', p. 85.   [3] J. Linskill, IX. 51.

The terms in this *gap* which can have a specific meaning in the context of Rhetoric: *plait, jutgar razo, defenir, gignos sens, escrimir, pens venaus, sen(h)s, colors,* point to a coherent theme of Marcabru's skill in Rhetorical debate, distinct from the erotic boast. They show that while Marcabru usually only comments on the misuse of eloquence, he is well versed in Rhetorical techniques himself. The *gap* does contain a double meaning, conveyed through the use of words having more than one sense, or through *colors*. Possibly other layers of meaning are also intended: the element of irony or parody which Roncaglia emphasized[1] adds another dimension; the fool's 'bread' could perhaps be the soft and comfortable way of life of which Marcabru takes advantage temporarily, while maintaining his own inner integrity;[2] he may be describing not only his debating skill but his literary technique in the poem, where he confuses the listener with his *cent colors*.[3] But the basic ambiguity is between the erotic and the debating themes.[4]

2. 'Trobar naturau'

Except in the *gap*, Marcabru does not call attention to his Rhetorical skills. His inclination, as we have already remarked, is to be suspicious of eloquence. He prefers to compose according to *trobar naturau*:

> E segon trobar naturau
> port la peir' e l'esc' e.l fozill,
> mas menut trobador bergau
>   entrebesquill,
> mi tornon mon chant en badau
> e.n fant gratill.[5]

---

[1] See p. 19.

[2] This moral meaning was suggested by L. Pollmann, '*Trobar clus*', pp. 16–17.

[3] See Köhler, pp. 135 ff. Pollmann also sees a literary level of meaning.

[4] There was a tradition in medieval Latin poetry of word-play on terms of grammar, often erotic: see P. Lehmann, *Die Parodie im Mittelalter* (München, 1922; repr. 1963), pp. 49–54, 'Grammatische Spielereien' (also pp. 107–10), and pp. 223–4 'Erotische Grammatik'; authors played on such words as *declinare, coniunctio, copula, genetivus, interiectio.* Cf. P. Dronke, *Medieval Latin and the Rise of the European Love Lyric* (Oxford, 1965), i. 283: 'Tam dilecta lectio'. Guilhem IX played on literary terms in 'Ben vuelh': see L. Topsfield, *NMi*, vol. lxix, no. 2 (1968), pp. 281–4. The Rhetorical basis of ambiguity in the *gap* weakens Pollmann's theory that it contained three definite levels of meaning, literary, moral, and erotic ('*Trobar clus*', p. 18), corresponding to three levels of exegesis.

[5] 'Lo vers comens', vv. 7–12.

And according to the natural art of composing I bear the flint and tinder and steel, but buzzing, petty troubadours with confused thoughts turn my song into nothing and make a mockery of it for me.

This *trobar naturau* contributes to his reputation, for Peire d'Alvernhe later says that Marcabru used to sing according to an understanding of nature:

> Chantador, lo vers vos fenis:
> aprendetz la comensansa.
> Marcabrus per gran dreitura
> trobet d'altretal semblansa,
> e tengon lo tug per fol,
> *qui no conoissa natura*
> e no.ill membre per que.s nais!   (XIII. 36–42)

Singers, I complete the *vers* for you; learn of its beginning! Marcabru composed in a similar way, and he was right to do so; and let all consider him a fool who does not understand nature or recall why he was born!

Roncaglia rightly explains *trobar naturau* as the art of composing according to 'so que veritatz autreia',[1] as opposed to 'artificially' or 'falsely', in not only a formal but also a moral sense. The man who can distinguish between 'whole' and 'broken' thoughts Marcabru calls *naturau:*

> Be.l teing per deum naturau
> Qui de cuit conoisser es guitz[2]   (XIX. 12–13)

Someone who is a guide in discriminating about ways of thinking I certainly consider to be natural through God.

that is, God has given him true understanding according to 'nature'.

Roncaglia situates Marcabru's *trobar naturau* within the context of medieval theology and philosophy, which conceived of natural law as moral order and harmony;[3] 'ius naturale, quod natura docuit omnia animalia, ut est coniunctio maris et feminae, et similia'.[4] He argues that Marcabru thinks of his *trobar* as *naturau*, or in accordance with the moral order of things, because it opposes the new gallant eroticism of the courtly world.[5] Marcabru expresses his concern for what is in harmony with nature and

---

[1] Op. cit., p. 36; cf. XXXVII. 10.
[2] Dejeanne: *per devin n.*; all MSS., *AIK*, have *per deum.*
[3] *CN* xxix (1969), 5–55.
[4] William of Auxerre, see Roncaglia, op. cit., p. 49.
[5] Op. cit., pp. 50–1 and *passim.*

outside it, 'segon natura et estiers' (XLI. 5), either in terms of a contrast between the innocence of natural creatures and the corruption of man:

> Lur joys sec la via plana
> E.l nostre bruzilha,   (XXI. 15–16)

Their joy follows the smooth path, and ours stumbles,

or else in terms of nature as the world of base instinct as opposed to the rationality of man: summer, when nature is at its most teeming, is the season of renewed lusts,

> L'estiu plen de gandill
> Don nais puti' et enveia,   (XXXVIII. 6–7)

while Marcabru as a poet of *trobar naturau* composes according to the true nature of man, with rational control rather than outpouring of feeling and instinct:

> Bel m'es can s'esclarzis l'onda
> E qecs auzels pel jardin
> S'esjauzis segon son latin;
> Lo chanz per lo(s) becs toronda,
> Mais eu trop miels qe negus.
>
> Qe scienza jauzionda
> M'apres c'al soleilh declin
> Laus lo jorn, e l'ost' al matin,
> Et a qec fol non responda
> Ni contra musar(t) no mus.   (XII *bis*. 1–10)

It pleases me when the wave grows bright and each bird in the garden rejoices according to its own language; the singing gushes from their beaks, but I compose better than any. For joyful understanding taught me to praise the day at sunset and my host at sunrise (to count my blessings),[1] and not to answer back to every fool, nor to gape at the gaper.

In scholastic philosophical and moralizing tradition in the Middle Ages the natural world was seen as a reflection of divine truth, and a knowledge of the 'hidden meanings' of objects in the physical world was considered essential for a full understanding of Scripture. St. Augustine taught that 'Rerum autem ignorantia facit obscuras figuratas locutiones, cum ignoramus vel animan-

---

[1] Walther, 13562: 'Laudes nocte die pietati concine die! / Si sine laude manes, tibi noxia en ferunt manes.' 13555a; 'Laudem sero dies et mane minabitur hospes.' A. Tobler, *Proverbe*, no. 112: 'Nus ne puet deservir / Gre en felon servir, / Souvent l'avons vëu. / Servirs trop pou i vaut; / Qui une foiz li faut, / Si a trestout perdu. / *Au vespre loe on le jour, au matin son oste*.'

tium, vel lapidum, vel herbarum naturas, aliarumve rerum, quae plerumque in Scripturis similitudinis alicuius gratia ponuntur.'[1] Not only the Bible but the literature of Latin Antiquity was interpreted in the light of supposed symbolic meanings of natural objects, and handbooks were compiled as guides to the interpretation of texts in the form of herbaries, bestiaries, and lapidaries.[2] Isidore of Seville's method of discovering the supposed intrinsic meaning of an object through often hypothetical etymology was one manifestation of the medieval symbolic approach to worldly phenomena; Isidore believed that his method could discover the hidden force of words: 'Etymologia est origo vocabulorum, cum vis verbi vel nominis per interpretationem colligitur . . . . Nam cum videris unde ortum est nomen, citius vim eius intelligis.'[3] The twelfth century in particular saw the production of encyclopedias creating symbols to illustrate moral ideas and dogma.[4]

Roncaglia stresses the importance of examining Marcabru's poetic language in the tradition of moralistic–religious symbolism elaborated in the Middle Ages, especially through biblical exegesis.[5]

In general terms, Marcabru's view of nature corresponds to the Christian, scholastic one: nature is a reflection of hidden truth and moral order, requiring wisdom and effort to penetrate its outward form and discover its true significance. This attitude governs his use of nature imagery: imagery which not only illustrates moral truths, but in some cases, through the use of symbols, reflects the need to probe behind the outward appearance of natural objects to appreciate their true significance.

His plant imagery derives from the Christian tradition of spiritual fruitfulness: 'Arbor autem humanum genus significat . . . et fructum bonum, bona opera: malum vero mala opera.'[6] This imagery consists of two main groups: the first contains metaphors of flowering, bearing fruit, ripening, expressed in

[1] *De Doctrina Christiana*, ii. 24; PL xxxiv. 47. Quoted by D. W. Robertson, 'Gardens', p. 24.

[2] On the moral exegesis of Ovid, see S. Battaglia, 'La tradizione di Ovidio nel Medioevo', *FR* vi (1959), 185–224; F. Munari, *Ovid im Mittelalter* (Zürich, 1960); and especially F. Ghisalberti, 'Arnolfo d'Orléans', and 'Biographies', pp. 10–59. For an account of vernacular bestiaries see A. Kressner.

[3] *PL* lxxxii, 105.   [4] F. Saxl, pp. 118 ff.

[5] A. Roncaglia, 'Per un'edizione', p. 48.

[6] Rabanus Maurus, *De Universo*, xix, PL cxi. 509. Cf. PL ccxix. 123–242, *Index de allegoris, arbor* 197, *fructus* 202, *rama* 209.

general terms which are commonplace by Marcabru's time; the second includes trees mentioned by their individual names, usually having a specific, symbolic meaning.

The Bible provides many images of flowering and fruitfulness,[1] and Guilhem IX described his joy in these terms:

> Mas si anc nulhs joys poc florir,
> Aquest deu sobre totz granar.[2]

Marcabru depicts *fin' amors* as

> Blanch' e floria
> E presta de granar,   (XXXII. 66–7)

white and blossoming and ready to bear fruit; vices too flourish and bear their own evil fruit:

> D'una ren suy meravilhans
> Qu'ades vey granar e florir
> Escassetatz, oc! et Enjans,   (XXXIV. 8–10)

At one thing I am amazed: that I continually see Avarice blossoming, yes! and Deceit;

> Mas lor semensa frairina
> Geta malvatz fruit quan grana,
>
>   (XXXVI. 23–4)

But their despicable seed produces evil fruit when it ripens.

Such images, already commonplace in Marcabru's own works,[3] appear in the poetry of later troubadours as proverbs.[4]

In the song 'Al departir' Marcabru mentions several plants by name: *genest' e.l brucs* (broom and heather), *presseguier* (peach-tree), *sauzes e.l saucs* (willow and elder), *pomier* (apple-tree), *laur* (laurel), and *oliver* (olive), together with details associated with trees: *sucs* (sap), *branca* (branch), *l'empeut* (grafts), *frugs* (fruits), *ramils e festucs* (loppings and wisps of straw). D. W. Robertson[5] and A. Roncaglia[6] showed that these images express the poet's theme of the moral sterility of society through their symbolic meanings. In the *gran vergier* of society, willows and elders represent people who are sterile in good works,[7] but who have the initial appear-

---

[1] Matt. 7: 16–20; 12: 33; Marc. 4: 7–8; Luc. 3: 8–9; 6: 43–4; Joh. 15: 2–16; Psa. 103: 13; Prov. 11: 28, 30. Cf. Walther, 42, 82, 1241 ff, 8257–8.

[2] Ed. Jeanroy, IX. 9–10.   [3] II. 33; XI. 4, 32; XXVI. 77; XIX. 60; XLI. 30.

[4] E. Cnyrim, nos. 154 ff.   [5] 'Five poems', p. 539.

[6] 'Al departir', pp. 5 ff. Cf. also Scheludko, *Arch. Rom.* xv (1931), 180.

[7] Rabanus Maurus, *PL* cxi. 519: 'Item salices homines infructuosi sunt'; cf. Roncaglia, 'Al departir', p. 15 for numerous references in exegetical works and troubadour poetry.

ance of fruitfulness: their flowers and fruit 'paron de pomier',[1]
'appear to be those of the apple-tree'. Laurel and olive, absent
from the orchard, probably represent constancy and fecundity or
wisdom.[2] Broom and heather may have been included to make the
poem more colourful; but they bear no edible fruit and therefore
reinforce the idea of sterility; perhaps Marcabru wanted their
harsh sounds to produce an arid impression.[3] The trees in the
orchard appear to be fertile; the sap rises through the branch,
there are many groves of fine-looking plants, but their fruits are
empty, the fine old trees are dead, and the new ones merely
loppings and wisps of straw.[4]

Marcabru gradually unfolds his meaning through the images.
The first stanza only hints at the theme as he describes the new
season; the second introduces the poet's concern over the orchard
'Cossiros suy d'un gran vergier' (9), with its fine plants and 'frugs
bacucs' (11); and the theme is gradually linked more openly with
moral condemnation: 'dels fortz assays los vey damnucs' (19),
and with members of society:

> Quan son la nueg josta.l foguier
> n'Esteves, en Costans, en Ucs.[5]   (25–6)

Description of the activities of these people and imagery of the
plants in the orchard interweave and only in the last stanza does
Marcabru finally bind up the two:

> que.l ric malvatz paron saucs;
> per que.l segles es badalucs,   (50–1)

For the evil barons seem elder trees, so that life in this world is vain.

---

[1] The apple is an obvious image of fruitfulness. Marcabru may have had traditional imagery in mind: cf. Rabanus Maurus, *PL* cxi. 509: 'Poma significant fructus
sanctorum in virtutibus, ut est in Cantico Canticorum (5. 1): "Et manducet fructum
pomorum suorum".'

[2] The laurel is evergreen, the olive traditionally fruitful (Psa. 127: 3). Roncaglia
(p. 27) suggests *gloria* and *saggezza*; Robertson ('Gardens', p. 26) a more specifically
Christian meaning, the Tree of Life and Christ, though nothing in the text points
to this.

[3] Robertson, 'Five poems', p. 541, says Bersuire links *genesta* with sin. Roncaglia
(p. 11) thinks Marcabru may be mixing literary symbols with images drawn from
observation of his native Gascony.

[4] Bad branches are lopped off: Isaias 10: 33, Joh. 15: 2–6.

[5] See Roncaglia, op. cit., pp. 18–20: *Esteves* is probably associated with *estar* and
means 'idler'; *Costans* ironically means 'inconstancy'; *Ucs* means 'clamour'.

The structure, the gradual revelation of the theme, suggests poetically the way in which moral truth can be revealed through nature.

Although this song has seemed very difficult[1] it was probably not as difficult for Marcabru's listeners to understand as it has been in this century. His listeners would not need to know of learned symbolism to realize that some plants represented fruitfulness and others sterility, since Marcabru implies this in the text (11–15, 19, 21–2, 50–2), and reveals his theme if not by the first stanza than by the second and third. So it is certainly not obscure, even if many of the details might pass unnoticed by his less educated listeners.

In the moralizing and philosophizing tradition of medieval bestiaries animals and birds have diverse supposed meanings according to the whim of the author.[2] They are sometimes linked with Christian philosophy concerning man's rational and animal souls,[3] but in general the only unifying principle governing the allegorical interpretation of these creatures is 'ut in omnibus creaturis sola praedicatur virtus ac potentia creatoris'.[4] Some of Marcabru's images can be linked with this tradition, but although they have a moral function, they are used to create a strong visual impression rather than to draw a pedantic moral lesson.

Animals often represent sensual desires: adulterous husbands are 'moillerat ab sen cabri' (XVII. 31), 'husbands with goatish sensuality'; a woman who loves a wastrel is no better than a dog:

> Sa voluntatz la mastina[5]
> Cum fai lebrieir' ab gosso,   (XXXI. 48–9)

her lust covers her as the cur the hound;

---

[1] See Vossler, 'Der Trobador Marcabru', pp. 29–30, and W. Küchler, *Die neueren Sprachen*, xxvi. 79–80.

[2] The lion, for example, can mean kingship (Prov. 30: 30), the Devil (I Pet. 5: 8), God's faithful (Prov. 28: 1), arrogance (Marcabru, XLIV. 25–6), spiritual vigilance (Peter Damian, PL cxli. 768), the resurrection (Alcuin, PL c. 1118), God the judge (Rabanus Maurus PL cxii. 983).

[3] See Arnulf of Orléans, commentary on Ovid's *Metamorphoses* (Ghisalberti, 'Arnolfo d'Orléans', p. 181): 'Intencio est de mutacione dicere, ut non intelligamus de mutacione que fit extrinsecus tantum in rebus corporeis bonis vel malis sed etiam de mutacione que fit intrinsecus ut in anima, ut reducat nos ab errore ad cognitionem veri creatoris . . . Duo sunt motus in anima unus rationalis alter irrationalis. . . . Dedit enim deus anime rationem per quam reprimeret sensualitatem . . .'.

[4] Peter Damian, *De bono religiosi status, et varium animantium tropologia*, PL cxlv. 792.   [5] Lewent, 'Beiträge', p. 435: *l'amastina*.

Love is an insatiable mare (XVIII. 49–54), and unbridled passion could make the poet himself stronger than an Arab horse' (VIII. 36–40); the bastard is a mule, conceived by the bestial appetites of mixed parents:

> Eras naisson dui poilli,
> Beill burden ab saura cri
> Que.is van volven de blanc vaire
> E fan semblan aseni;
> Jois e Jovens n'es trichaire
> E malvestat eis d'aqui.   (XVII. 25–30)

Now two foals are born, fine mules with golden coats, who change from white to piebald and look like asses; Joy and Youth are cheating in this matter, and from this evil is born.[1]

These images appear as the poet's spontaneous visual expression of his ideas; even if these animals are traditionally images of *luxuria*[2] Marcabru make no attempt to link them with a tradition. The audience would need no education to understand them.

But some animals and birds, as the trees in 'Al departir', have a symbolic function. In the first stanza of 'Pois la fuoilla revirola' (XXXVIII), the symbolic significance of nature appears: the wind tears at the leaf as winter begins, the season which the poet defiantly values more highly than summer, the time of whoring and lust:[3]

> Mais pretz lo freich temporau

---

[1] v. 26 Dejeanne: *Beill, burden,* 'beaux, piaffant'. Marcabru is punning on the two meanings of *burden,* 'playful' and 'mules': see Rayn. i. 271: 'bardot, bardeau' and L & S 255, *burdo.*

[2] Ovid, *Ars,* i. 280 'Femina cornipedi semper adhinnit equo'; *Remedia Amoris* 514, 634; Peter Damian, *De decem Aegypti plagis,* PL cxlv. 691: men are given to *luxuria* 'sicut equus et mulus quibus non est intellectus'; Brunetto Latini, p. 240; cf. Guilhem IX, II. 18, I.

[3] 'Pois la fuoilla' may be a reply to an anonymous song 'Poc ve gent' (C. Appel, *Prov. Inedita,* p. 329), in which a poet complains of his lady's ill treatment of him, in intentionally rough, uncourtly, and provocative terms. He declares that now it is the rough season: implying, now that their relationship is turbulent, he will re-nounce love and speak out his true opinions, anticipating with delight any harm she might suffer. The rhyme schemes of this song and Marcabru's are similar:

> Poc ve gent: a b a b c d e   8 8 8 8 8 8 8
> Pois la f.:   a b a b c d e   7′ 7 7′ 7 7 7 7′   Frank 430.

This scheme is also used twice by Bernart Marti, and twice by later poets (A. Daniel, B. Rascas). The opening lines of both songs are similar, describing winter, violent weather, silent birds. The anonymous poet renounces love 'per lou freit del brun temporau' (v. 5); Marcabru says: 'Mais pretz lo freich temporau', because it is the time when pride comes before a fall, and when false love is shown up. He

> Que l'estiu plen de gandill
> Don nais puti' et enveia;[1]   (XXXVIII. 5–7)

I esteem the cold season more highly than the summer, full of discord, from which whoring and lust are born.

This is followed by a description of how arrogance is overthrown in winter, when the birds fall silent:

> Lo pics e la rossignola
> Tornon lor chant en tazer,
> Si.s fa.l gais e l'auriola,
> Don l'inverns fai son plazer;
> E l'orgoills torn' en canau
> Per garssos plens de grondill,
> Qu'en estiu contradenteia.   (8–14)

The woodpecker and the nightingale silence their singing, and so do the jay and the oriole, with which the winter does its pleasure; and pride, which bares its teeth in the summer, falls in the gutter because of surly ruffians.[2]

D. Scheludko[3] suggested that Marcabru wrote this stanza with a poem of Marbod in mind:

> Aurioli, merulae, graculi, pici, philomelae
> Certant laude pari varios cantus modulari,

but even if this were true, and catalogues of birds must have been a standard device used in Rhetorical descriptions of spring,[4] Marbod's poem is purely descriptive, whereas Marcabru specifically rejects the season of these birds because of its moral implications. The birds themselves have a symbolic meaning. The jay appears in another of Marcabru's poems as an image of pride and discord:

> Quan l'aura doussana bufa,
> E.l gais, desotz lo brondel,
> Fai d'orguoil cogot e bufa
> E son ombriu li ramel,
> Ladoncs deuri' hom chausir

may be directly attacking the attitude of the poet in 'Poc ve gent' who gives up loving in a courtly way when times are hard.

J. Mouzat (see Bibliography) suggests that 'Poc ve gent' was composed by Ebles, although there is no proof of this. If Marcabru replied to it, it would be early.

---

[1] *gandill* occurs only in *R*: see Dejeanne's note, p. 188.

[2] *Pics* occurs only in one MS., *A*; *I* Lauzel, *K* Lauzeill, *E* Lauzels, *a* Lauselz, *C* L'auzelh, *R* Neys ab sa par l'auriola.

[3] 'Natureingang', p. 269; Marbod, *Descriptio vernae pulchritudinis*.

[4] See Matthew of Vendôme's *descriptio loci* in Faral, pp. 148–9.

Verai' amor ses mentir
C'ab son amic non barailla.   (XLII. 1–7)

When the gentle wind blows, and the jay beneath the twig puffs itself
up with pride and disdain, and the branches are shady, then one ought
to choose true, undeceiving love, which causes no strife with its lover.[1]

Perhaps the vivid colours of the jay suggested this image to
Marcabru; but in vernacular tradition it is known for its ugly
cries, gossiping, and imitation of other birds' songs,[2] and possibly Marcabru links in his mind the sin of pride with the noise
of vainglorious boasting which he condemns elsewhere in the *menut trobador*.[3] The oriole was also reputed for its harsh and quarrelsome voice, and Marcabru means it to suggest the sort of people
who are full of 'nauzas e bauducs'.[4] The nightingale is the bird
of spring and love,[5] representing here superficial love which is
brought on by the arrival of fine weather or favourable circumstances, but soon disappears with the onset of winter. The woodpecker suggests harsh noise by both its name and habits. Rabanus
Maurus identifies it with 'futile loquacity'.[6]

After birds come reptiles and insects:

Graissans ni serps que s'amola
No.m fant espaven ni mau,
Mosca ni tavans que vola,
Escaravait ni bertau,
Aquist malvatz volatill
Non sent bruir ni oler,
Dont francs inverns nos neteia.   (15–21)

Neither swollen toad nor serpent brings me fear or harm; flying
insects and gadflies, beetles and gnats I no longer perceive buzzing and
smelling: those evil flying creatures from which noble winter puri-
fies us.[7]

---

[1] v. 4: Dejeanne has a semicolon after *ramel*. Cf. Peire d'Alvernhe, IX, stanza 1:
'En estiu quan crida.l jais . . . / adoncs es razo qu'on lais / fals' amor enganairitz /
als volpilhos acropitz.'   [2] W. Hensel, 'Vögel', p. 620 , no. 14.

[3] See p. 9.   [4] Hensel, op. cit., p. 616, no. 7. See p. 8.

[5] Hensel, op. cit., p. 596 n. 5.

[6] *PL* cxi. 247: 'Nam sonus vocis ejus loquacitatem haereticorum potest significare, vel philosophorum: sicut superius de graculo diximus.' ('Graculus a garruli-
tate nuncupatus . . . . Est enim loquacissimum genus, et vocibus importunum.
Quod vel philosophorum vanam loquacitatem, vel haereticorum verbositatem
noxiam significare potest.')

[7] v. 15 *que s'amola:* Lewent, 'Beiträge', p. 443: perhaps from *mola*, 'Mühlstein',
followed by L. Spitzer, p. 223, suggesting an image of roundness; cf. *PD* 19:
'*amolonat*, ramassé sur soi-même, ratatiné'. The sense could be 'crouching' or

D. Scheludko again points to a possible Latin source:[1]

> Bufo nunc turget et amica silvis
> Vipera laedit gelidusque serpens,
> Scorpius ictu vigilat paratque
>   Stellio pestem.
> Musca nunc saevit piceaque blatta
> Et culex mordax olidusque cimex,
> Suetus in nocte vigilare pulex
>   Corpora pungit.
> Tolle tot monstra, Deus, imprecanti,
> Pelle languorem, tribue quietem,
> Ut queam gratas placido sopore
>   Carpere noctes.

The toad now puffs itself out and the viper, friend of the woodlands, strikes, and the icy serpent; the scorpion lies in wait with its sting, and the newt prepares its poison. The fly now rages and the pitch-black moth, the biting gnat and smelling bug: the flea that is wont to wake at night stings our bodies. Take away all these monsters, God, from this suppliant, drive away sluggishness, grant me quiet, so that I may pass pleasant nights in peaceful sleep.

A moral meaning is implied in the Latin poem, if obliquely.

Marcabru adopts the images from this poem or a similar one for his commentary on courtly society. Individually some of these images have a traditional symbolism which Marcabru knew. In Latin moralizing tradition the fly represents sin: as flies sting imperceptibly but poison the whole body, so sin steals unnoticed into the soul and corrupts it.[2] Marcabru knew of this symbolism because in the song 'Dirai vos senes duptansa' (XVIII) he says of carnal love:

> Plus suau poing qu'una mosca
> Mas plus greu n'es hom sanatz.   (59–60)

perhaps 'swollen to the size of a millstone', where the image is closer to that of the Latin poem.

---

[1] 'Natureingang', p. 282; G. M. Drèves, *Analecta Hymnica* (Leipzig, 1891), xi. 24, 'Tempore estivali', 9th-century MS.

[2] Peter Damian, *De decem Aegypti plagis*, PL cxlv. 689–90; 'Sed quoniam ciniphes istae perexiguae sunt et noxiae, ut non tam pondus videantur habere quam morsus, qui vitio vagationis inserviunt, quod per ciniphes designatur, leve quidem arbitrantur esse peccatum, sed non levi reatus perfodiuntur aculeo. Non aggravat pondus, sed penetrat morsus . . .'; cf. Alanus ab Insulis, *PL* ccx. 121 ('*Contra luxuriam:* Haec est musca . . .'); Rabanus Maurus, *PL* cxi. 258.

It stings more gently than a fly, but with greater difficulty is one cured of it.[1]

The beetle was supposed to be produced from dung, and therefore vile;[2] Marcabru abuses the Angevins[3] with the comment:

> Per so, son Angevin aunit,
> E qui d'escarabot fai guit
> En avol loc perpren ostau;   (VIII. 60-1)

For this the Angevins are dishonoured; and whoever takes the beetle as his guide makes his dwelling in a vile place.

In 'Pois la fuoilla' Marcabru uses these symbols to reinforce his explicitly stated moral theme both by their immediate visual impact and their traditional associations.

The *rana*, one of Marcabru's favourite images although rare in Provençal,[4] represents false loquacity in Christian moralizing literature: garrulousness, or the speech of the Devil, or the fallacious arguments of heretics and false philosophers, and is associated with a squalid way of life.[5] Marcabru's *rana* is also, at times, an image of sterile verbosity: in 'Al departir' it is the frog that sings in the pond during a spring which gives promise of fruitfulness but ends in sterility, and the noise of the frog anticipates the 'nauzas e bauducs' of the dice-players.[6] In 'Lo vers comens' the frog falls silent, as the birds do in 'Pois la fuoilla' (XXXVIII), at the onset of winter:

> Lo vers comens quan vei del fau
> ses foilla lo cim e.l branquill,

---

[1] Dejeanne: 'abeille'.   [2] Rabanus Maurus, *PL* cxi. 256.

[3] See Dejeanne's notes, pp. 221-2.

[4] It is found also in Bernart Marti, ed. Hoepffner, III. 1-2, VII. 6, and Guilhem de Berguedan (see Rayn. v. 39).

[5] In the Apocalypse, 16: 13, 'unclean spirits like frogs' come from the Dragon's mouth; cf. Rabanus Marus, *PL* cxi. 228: 'ranae daemones'. The plague of frogs in Egypt is interpreted by Peter Damian as a plague of noisy heretics: 'Rana clamosum est animal, et in limosis vociferatur ex more paludibus. Cui similes judicantur haeretici, ac Philosophi, qui velut super paludes limosas, hoc est, inter turbas squalore perfidiae sordidas, vanis adversus Christum vociferantur obloquiis: et dum per argumenta fallaciae non definiunt importunis garrire clamoribus, inane quidem in auribus taedium, sed nullum mentibus vivendi afferunt cibum . . .' (*De decem Aegypti plagis*, *PL* cxlv. 689). Cf. Walther 26241a: 'Rana loquax heresis nomen reprobans Deitatis'. In Ovid's *Metamorphoses*, vi. 339 ff., boorish peasants are turned into frogs and curse from their pool; cf. the commentary of Arnulf of Orléans (F. Ghisalberti, 'Arnolfo d'Orléans', p. 217). See also Walther, 26241, 26241a, 26242-6.

[6] 'Al departir del brau tempier, / quan per la branca pueja.l sucs / don reviu la genest' e.l brucs / . . . e la rana chant' el vivier'; cf. stanza III.

> c'om d'auzel ni raina non au
> chan ni grazill,
> ni o fara jusqu'al temps soau
> que.l vais brondill.   (1–6)

I begin the song when I see the top and branches of the beech leafless,
when neither song nor croak of bird or frog is to be heard, nor will
be until the mild season when the hazel puts forth shoots.

In a song where Marcabru attacks the *joglar* Alegret for insincere
flattery of an undeserving patron,[1] he begins:

> Bel m'es quan la rana chanta
> E.l sucs pueja per la rusca,
> Per que.l flors e.l fueilhs e.l busca
> E.l frugz reviu en la planta,
> E.l rossinhols crid' e brama
> Sa par qu'a per joi conquisa,
> Ples d'orgueilh car el no sen
> Freg ni gel ni glaz ni bisa.   (XI. 1–8)

It pleases me when the frog sings and the sap rises through the bark
so that the flower and the leaf and the twig and the fruit revive in the
plant, and the nightingale cries and shrieks to its mate which it has
conquered through joy, filled with pride because it feels no cold or
frost or ice or north wind.

Although he says he is pleased at the season, these lines recall the
opening of 'Al departir' where the frog sings as the sap rises;[2] as
in 'Pois la fuoilla' the song of the nightingale is associated with
orgueilh,[3] which lasts only as long as wintry harshness is absent.
Marcabru's 'pleasure' in 'Bel m'es' is ironic: he mocks at the
brash confidence of the noisy frog and nightingale. Since his
song is an attack on Alegret, the *rana* may be an image of Alegret
himself: noisy with empty flattery, and perhaps raucous with poor
singing.[4] The image of the frog may have been suggested to
Marcabru from his own observation in the Midi; but its appearance in Christian moralizing works and in proverbs suggests that
he used it as a learned symbol.[5]

In conclusion, *trobar naturau* means to Marcabru the art of

---

[1] XI. 57–69; cf. Dejeanne, *AdM* xix (1907), 221–31 (p. 226).
[2] See p. 39 n. 6.   [3] XXXVIII. 15–21; see pp. 36 ff.
[4] The last lines of Peire d'Alvernhe's satire on the troubadours (Del Monte, XII),
where Peire praises his own singing, were altered to read: 'Peire d'Alvernhe a tal
voz / que canta cum granolh' em potz' (vv. 79–80, reading of *CRa*).
[5] Only in XXI. 7–16 the *rana* does not signify garrulousness: the frog and owl
are simple creatures of nature, contrasted with the corrupt ways of man.

composing according to an understanding of what is natural and unnatural, and of the moral truths which nature reveals. Through nature imagery he describes moral qualities in terms of fruitfulness and sterility, animal passions, vices and virtues. Sometimes this imagery illustrates a theme through immediate, visual impression; at other times it is the means of unfolding the *razo* gradually, through allusive metaphors or learned symbols.

U. Mölk[1] rejected L. Pollmann's theory[2] of the exegetical origins of the *trobar clus*. However, Marcabru's *trobar naturau* belongs to the scholastic view of nature as a pattern of symbols, which is the basis of Christian exegesis. He may not have developed his poetic method from exegetical method: the exegete draws a sententious and often far-fetched moral lesson from an object, whereas Marcabru uses an image creatively to present a picture or suggest an allusive meaning. But he shares with the tradition of exegesis common attitudes to nature, and follows it in the interpretation of individual images. This now leads us to consider Marcabru's contribution to the *trobar clus*.

3. Marcabru and the 'trobar clus'

Early in this century it was assumed that Marcabru composed in the *trobar clus* because his songs were so difficult. It was only undecided whether he intended to be obscure or not.[3] Gradually obscurities were resolved, and it became less certain that his songs would have been as difficult for a twelfth-century audience as they are for us.[4] With obscurity still the criterion for recognizing *trobar clus* it was not always easy to decide which songs belonged to this style, and recently U. Mölk[5] has claimed that Marcabru never composed in the *trobar clus*, as he was neither aware of a stylistic division between *clus* and *leu* nor intentionally obscure.

If Marcabru did not think of himself as a poet of the *trobar clus*

---

[1] pp. 140 ff.　　　　　　　　　　　　　　　[2] 'Trobar clus', pp. 47 ff.

[3] Vossler, 'Der Trobador Marcabru', pp. 1–65, saw Marcabru's style as the result of a conflict between confused thought and formal complexity. Jeanroy, *Poésie lyrique*, ii. 36, thought Marcabru wanted to be enigmatic.

[4] Appel, 'Zu Marcabru', pp. 462–3, thought that Marcabru was difficult because of his search for powerful visual expressions, and that these would have been familiar to his listeners. Roncaglia, 'Al departir', p. 6, also thought that many obscurities would eventually be resolved, but that three-quarters of his work was still not understood.

[5] pp. 55–90.

since this term did not, as far as we know, emerge until the generation after him,[1] he is still a model for poets who did: Peire d'Alvernhe, Giraut de Bornelh, Raimbaut d'Aurenga. Mölk claims
that they only borrowed from Marcabru techniques of language,
metre, and rhyme;[2] but there are other reasons why his poetry is
difficult, and other ways in which he could have been a model for
poets of the *trobar clus*.

In works which have been already discussed, we can see three
elements which anticipate this style. The first is Marcabru's
awareness that only the wise man can understand the truth
behind his words: the foolish man makes them 'broken'. His
awareness of a division in his audience between wise and foolish
does not, certainly, indicate his intention to address an exclusive
élite; he wants his truths to be understood by everyone, though
he realizes that this is a vain hope.[3] But it is not hard to see how
his recognition of such a division in his listeners might develop
into the more aristocratic attitude of Raimbaut d'Aurenga: that
the *clus* poet does not seek the applause of the masses.

Secondly, Marcabru unfolds his theme in some poems by
gradually revealing it through images or symbols. 'Al departir'
and 'Pois la fuoilla'[4] exemplify this method and Marcabru refers
to it in 'Per savi.l tenc',[5] when he says the wise man divines the
meaning of each word as the *razo* unfolds. As we shall see, Giraut
de Bornelh says that the *trobar clus* is valuable because of its fine
razo which gradually appears and 'yields itself up'.[6] U. Mölk
denied that Marcabru composed in the *trobar clus* partly on the
grounds that he did not seek systematically obscure compositions.[7]
But if the *trobar clus* sought, not deliberate obscurity, but the
gradual revelation of meaning, Marcabru is a model for such
a style.

Thirdly, the analysis of the *gap* showed one example of obscurity in Marcabru: not a completely esoteric style, but an
intention to mislead by 'cunning meanings' and to close the
thought round with 'misleading thoughts' and 'colours'.[8] This
use of 'colours' is also imitated by *clus* poets.[9]

I now intend to look at other sources of 'obscurity' or of the
trobar clus: firstly in the difficult song 'Ans que l'ivern' (XIV),

---

[1] Mölk, p. 55.   [2] Ibid., p. 89.   [3] See pp. 16–17.
[4] See pp. 32–4, 35–9.   [5] See p. 16.   [6] See p. 94.
[7] Mölk, p. 73.   [8] See pp. 19–28.   [9] See pp. 66, 117 ff., 147 ff.

secondly in poems where L. Pollmann thought he discovered the
influence on the *trobar clus* of Arabic poetry.

'Contra l'ivern que s'enansa'[1] is one of Marcabru's most difficult poems, 'évidemment du *trobar clus*' according to Dejeanne.[2]
It is found only in one manuscript, which suggests his contemporaries may also have found it difficult.

I   (Co)ntra (l'i)vern que s'e(n)ansa,
              ab cossi(ri)er que m'as(sa)lh
              m'es belh (q)ue del chant (m)'enans,
              ans (qu)'autre cossirs m'assalha;
              pus per un cosselh des(c)resc,   5
              no m'es ops qu'autre m'encresca.

II   Qu'ieu suy assis en trebalh
              e levatz en la balansa
              d'aquesta say que.m trebalha
              e.m ten en aquest balans,   10
              qu'ab doussa sabor azesca
              sos digz de felho(n) azesc.

III   Moś talans e sa semblansa
              so e no so d'un entalh,
              pueys del talent nays semblans   15
              e pueys ab son dig l'entalha,
              quar si l'us tray ab mal vesc
              lo brico, l'autre l'envesca.

IV   L'amar(s) d'aquesta no.m falh
              pels tricx enojos d'amansa,   20
              ab sol qu'en amar no.m falha
              e.m sia d'amar amans,
              ab guizardon que.m paresca
              plus tozetz que non paresc.

V   Per cujatz n'ay esperansa   25
              qu'enquer ab mi s'enguaṣalh,
              mas tan n'ay bons esperans
              estranhs de corta guaṣalha
              qu'en mieg mon afar folesc
              non dic paraula follesca.   30

[1] Dejeanne, XIV. I have re-edited it from the MS. (*C*); Dejeanne's version differs
only in a few minor details.
[2] p. 225.

VI   La musa port' e.l badalh
            selh qu'en amar a fizansa
            qu'estra grat mus' e badalh(a)
            soven, so vos afizans;
            qu'amors adoncx entrebresca,   35
            enginhos desentrebresc.

VII   Ab felhona deziransa
            e d'estranhatge baralh
            pays amors los dezirans
            cuy vir e vol(v) em baral*h*a,   40
            q'una.m n'a en ufanesc
            pagut d'aital ufanesca.

            (VIII missing; IX has the form of the odd stanzas.)

IX   D'*aqu*esta qu'ieu chant *sobransa*
            sos pretz senes devinalh,
            et en valor es *sobrans*   45
            neychas segon devinalha,
            quar si per lieys no m'espresc
            non aten qu'autra m'espresca.

X   Selh qui fes lo vers e.l tresc
            no sap don si mou la tresca.   50

XI   Marcabrus a fag lo tresc
            e no sap don si mou la tresca.

MS.: The first stanza is mutilated where a vignette has been removed. Letters in brackets have been added to fill gaps or to correct rhyme or grammar. Letters in italics are commented on in the notes. 26. *senguafalh*. 28. *guafalh*. 40. *baralla*. 49. *D'esta*; *es sobrans*. 51. *prezans*.

I. In the face of advancing winter, with the anxious thought which assails me, I wish to improve myself in song before another thought should assail me. Since I am brought low by one piece of advice, I do not need another to fill me with repugnance.

II. For I am fixed in torment and raised in the balance by this lady here who torments me and holds me in this uncertainty, for with sweet savour she baits her words with evil bait.

III. My desire and her appearance are and are not of the same sculpture, since the desire produces the appearance and then she sculpts it with what she says; for if the one (desire) leads the simpleton into the trap, the other (appearance) holds him fast in it.

IV. I do not cease to love this lady (I escape no bitterness from this lady) through the vexatious tricks of loving, provided that she does not fail me in love (bitterness) and is loving towards love (bitterness) for my sake, with a reward which might seem to me more childish than it appears.

V. In foolish fancy I have hope in this matter: that she may yet join company with me; but in this I have so many fine hopes which are alien to short-term reward that in the midst of my foolish condition I speak no foolish words.

VI. The man who puts his trust in (bitter) love possesses futile and illusory hopes, for he often hopes vainly and foolishly against his will, I assure you of this; therefore, what love entangles, let the cunning man disentangle.

VII. With evil desire and cruel conflict love nourishes those who desire it; I turn and twist in dispute against it, for one lady, acting with arrogant hypocrisy, has nourished me with similar arrogance.

IX. Of this lady of whom I sing the reputation is unsurpassed, without exercise of the imagination; and in worth she is supreme even in the light of investigation: for if I am not aroused through her, I expect no other lady to arouse me.

X. The one who composed the *vers* and the song (braid?) does not know where the dance began.

XI. Marcabru composed the song and does not know where the dance began.

NOTES

5–6. *encresca: SWB* ii. 457: 1) 'vermehren', 2) 'zuwider sein'. The double meaning was noticed by Spitzer, 'Lewent', p. 222. Lewent, 'Beiträge', p. 329 places a question mark after v. 6.

8–10. *balansa:* Rayn. ii. 171: 'balance; fig. agitation, doute, perplexité'. *Balans* can have the same meaning (ibid.), but also: *SWB* i. 121; 'Antrieb, Drang' (*balansar* 'stossen, werfen').

13–18. This stanza is the most obscure, partly because of the interplay of *semblans, semblansa, entalh, entalha,* all suggesting misleading appearances, partly because it is not clear to whom or what the possessive adjectives (*sa semblansa, son dig*) and *l'us* and *l'autre* (17–18) refer. Lewent, 'Beiträge' p. 330, translates as follows: 'Mein Wille und dessen Betätigung sind und sind auch wieder nicht von gleicher Form, da ja diese Betätigung aus dem Willen erwächst, anderseits aber die Geliebte sie mit ihren Worten formt. Denn wenn irgend jemand den Toren mit böser Lockspeise verführt, so verführt ihn auch ein anderer.' He sees Marcabru vacillating between his own desires and the lady's will which she imposes on him, as if these are two temptations. I take *sa semblansa* as the lady's appearance: her facial expression, or her outward appearance. This corresponds with the poet's desire in so far as it is the consequence of his desire; but it does not correspond with his desire in so far as she 'sculpts' her appearance by what she says, thus producing a deceiving impression through false speech (cf. 11–12). *L'us* and *l'autre* I take to mean 'talans' and 'semblansa': desire leads the fool into the trap initially, and deceiving appearances keep him there.

24. *tozetz:* 'youthful' in the sense of 'childish', 'foolish', cf. *SWB* viii. 328: *tos* 3):

'törichtes Kind, dummer Junge'. Marcabru equates childishness with folly in
VIII. 41–3, XIX. 53–4, XXXVII. 7.

26. *enguasalh,* MS. *enguafalh:* the latter is unattested and was emended by Dejeanne
(cf. *AdM* xvii. 482 n.), who thought *enguasalh* came from *gazalha,* 'company'
(*SWB* iv. 91). *Gazalha* can also mean 'profit' (Rayn. iii. 449), while *gazal* can
mean 'prostitute' (*SWB* viii. 91; cf. 92 *se gazalhar* 'Gemeinschaft haben mit, sich
zugesellen, sich vereinigen').

27. *esperans:* Lewent takes this as a participle (p. 330): 'aber es gibt so viele treulich
Harrende, die doch auch von der kürzesten Gemeinschaft mit ihrer Geliebten
entfernt sind.' But *tan n'ay* is first person. Marcabru is probably being intentionally ambiguous. *esperans* is probably a gerund meaning 'hopings (hopes)' or
'delayings (delays)' (*PD* 171: *esperar* 'espérer; attendre; accorder un délai');
corta can mean both 'brief' and 'cheap, worthless' (*SWB* i. 383, Rayn. ii. 495);
the meaning is either: 'I have so many fine hopes alien to cheap reward' (for
gazalha, see previous note) or: 'I have so many noble (ironic) delays alien to
short attachment', meaning that the lady, outwardly at least, delays rewarding
the poet with her company to test whether their relationship will be durable
(although the poet suspects this to be a trick).

34. Dejeanne, p. 225 n.: corr. *sui fizans?* But Pillet, p. 14, confirms *afizans.*

38. Dejeanne: *Ed estranhatge.*

39. Pillet, p. 14, Lewent, p. 330, take *Amors* as the subject of the verbs in v. 40;
Lewent: *em = en,* '. . . die Sehnsüchtigen, welche die Liebe in Wirrsal dreht
und wälzt'. vv. 41–2 however indicate that Marcabru is the subject: his lady's
arrogance has instilled a similar arrogance in him.

40. MS.: *baralla.*

49. MS.: *D'esta.* The line is one syllable short. For the emendations of v. 43 *es
sobrans* and v. 45 *prezans,* see Dejeanne.

50. *devinalh:* Rayn. iii. 35; 'énigme, sorte de poésie'; *SWB* ii. 200: 'Nachspüren'.
devinalha, in v. 46: *SWB* ii. 201: 'Nachspüren' or 'Gerede, Geschwätz' (rejects
Rayn. 'médisance, calomnie').

55–9. *tresc, tresca.* Two possible derivations exist for these words: the Gothic
þriskan, 'thresh' (Meyer-Lübke, 8715: Italian *trescare,* 'tanzen, herumhüpfen,
liebeln, klatschen': Spanish *triscar,* 'mit den Füssen trampeln, Mutwillen
treiben, scherzen': Italian *intrescare,* 'verwickeln, verwirren', *tresca* 'Liebelei');
and medieval Latin *trescia,* 'tress, braid' (Du Cange, vi. 655: 'Crines intexti,
implicati').

The earliest Provençal occurrence of *tresca* I know is in the *Chanson de Sainte
Foi d'Agen* (ed. A. Thomas (Paris, 1925), p. 3 st. 11):

'Canczon audi q'es bella 'n tresca,
Que fo de razo Espanesca;
Non fo de paraulla Grezesca
Ni de lengua Serrazinesca . . .'

'Bella 'n tresca' is translated as 'belle en danse' (see Thomas's note, p. 50 and
comment on p. xxxv, and C. Chabaneau, *RLR* xxxii (1888), 212). The examples
in Rayn. and *SWB* can be translated as 'dancing, whirling, leaping'; Giraut de
Bornelh uses *tresc (tresca?)* as a genre of song: 'Eu vi c'om prezava chansos / E
que plazian tresc e lais' (LXXIII, 80; *tresc' e lais?*), without specifying what kind.
SWB viii. 450 quotes the *Donatz Proensals: 'Trescar* .i. coream intricatam
facere' and suggests that *tresca* is 'eine Art Reihentanz'. Perhaps *tresca* and *tressa*
(Rayn. v. 419), 'tress' were not sharply distinguished. *Entrezar* which Rayn.
lists with *tressa* (loc. cit.) appears to be the same as Italian *intrescare* (see above)
which Meyer-Lübke lists under *þriskan.*

If the ideas of dancing and interweaving are both present in *tresca,* Marcabru may be taking advantage of this to suggest various meanings in his *tornadas*. *Tresc* may mean 'song' but also 'braiding': he has braided his song together, or bound it up, by its derivative rhymes and interweaving thoughts. *Tresca* might possibly be an allusion to the 'dance' or 'intricate complexities' brought about by love: Marcabru cannot imagine how this 'complicated dance' began, or how this lady has 'led him such a dance'.

The theme is the conflict in the poet's mind between desire and an awareness of the deceptions to which it leads. He is confused by the lady's sweet words and their evil bait (11–12), and the way words 'sculpt' false appearances (stanza III). Love is intermingled with bitterness (stanza IV) and anyone who trusts it is a fool (stanza VI); love is the cause of confusion and the cunning man disentangles himself from it (35–6).

There are two main causes of obscurity: the first is the use of derivative rhymes, which enables Marcabru to express the antithetical nature of his theme, to play on words to suggest paradoxes, and to suggest the entangled mind toiling to free itself. The second is his unwillingness to express his true theme directly until stanzas VI–VIII, because he wants to convey through the poem's structure the conflicts which have to be worked out before the mind can see clearly.

In the first stanza he makes no attempt to explain the nature of his 'anxious thoughts', or the 'advice' he has received. One piece of advice, linked with the 'anxious thought' which is already present in his mind, has 'brought him low', and he wants to sing before another one makes itself known. He plays on *enansar*, meaning 'advance' in the sense of both 'begin' and 'make progress',[1] suggesting that his song is a way of improving himself morally before winter, or adversity,[2] arrives, and of forestalling the new *cossirs*. He also plays on the meanings of *encresca*, 'increase' and 'be repulsive', implying a paradox: the new piece of advice would be both pleasant and unpleasant: it might perhaps seem advantageous, but be in fact harmful. From the subsequent development of the song it may perhaps be inferred that the first 'anxious thought' is the poet's desire for the lady, and the first 'advice', advice to give in to that desire, and that the new 'thought' and 'advice' concern the lady's appearance and his inclination to accept it as a true picture of reality. But these are initially left enigmatic.

[1] *SWB* ii. 416.   [2] Cf. XXXVIII, see p. 36.

The theme becomes clearer in stanza II: he is in a state of uncertainty because of the lady whose words are sweet but evil. Perhaps he plays on the meanings of *balansa* and *balans*: both can mean 'uncertainty', but *balans* can also mean 'impulse, urgency',[1] perhaps indicating the urgent desire with which she fills him.

Stanza III is the most difficult. With *semblansa, semblans, entalh, entalha,* he plays on the idea of appearances and false appearances. His desire and the lady's outward appearance, or her expression, correspond in one way and not another: they correspond because his desire gave rise to her expression in the first place, but then she 'sculpts' this expression, or the outward appearance of things, with her words, to suit her own ends. If desire traps him with 'lime'[2] on the one hand, deceiving appearances on the other hold him fast in the trap.

In stanza IV he carries through the pun on *amar*, 'love/bitterness', for four lines. On the surface he means: if she would love him, he would not give up loving her even in spite of the vexations attached to love; underneath he means that love with its tricks brings nothing but bitterness. *Paresc, paresca,* emphasize the theme of deceiving appearances. The play of the indicative *paresc* and the subjunctive *paresca* indicates that the poet may judge the 'reward' from this love as more foolish than it appears outwardly.

'Per cujatz' (25) means 'in vain illusion'.[3] If *enguasalh* is the correct reading in v. 26,[4] Marcabru says he still dreams of a relationship with the lady, but he is held back by hopes of something other than 'corta guasalha' (28): either 'temporary companionship', or 'worthless reward', or even 'cheap relationship'.[4] Again he seems to play on words to suggest various meanings and to reinforce the theme of illusory appearances.

In stanza VI he untangles the knot: openly he rejects the folly of love which controls a man against his will. 'What love entangles, let the cunning man disentangle.' The structure of the song reflects the confusion created by the double effect of desire and appearances, a confusion which the wise man eventually resolves for himself.

Marcabru openly attacks love in stanza VII, and explains that

---

[1] See notes.   [2] *envesca*, literally 'traps with bird-lime'.
[3] Cf. XIX. 32–4: 'Que per cuidar / Cuich esser bar / La cuid' es long' e.l faitz blasitz'; 'for he thinks he is noble by simply imagining it; the imagination is far-fetched and the fact withered.'   [4] See notes.

the lady's *ufanesca*, her arrogance coupled with false appearance,[1] has instilled the same quality in him. The idea of 'appearance' is alluded to again and indicates the way he has used the technique of entangling his theme to lead up to an attack on love. Stanza IX represents an apparent volte-face, for the poet praises the lady with conventional hyperbole. As there is a stanza missing before this one we do not know how the theme developed; perhaps this stanza was added later. Possibly *devinalh*, *devinalha*, imply some ambiguity: his lady's worth is supreme according to 'enigma'. Even if Marcabru praises this lady above all others, it is not necessarily a compliment, for elsewhere he says:

> Quez anc non amet neguna
> Ni d'autra non fo amatz. (XVIII. 71–2)

For never did he love any woman, nor was he loved by one.

In the *tornadas* he may be playing on the meanings of *tresc* and *tresca*. *Tresca* means 'dance' but is also a plaited strap or belt,[2] and may be derived from the Latin *trescia* meaning 'braid, plait'.[2] Perhaps Marcabru is referring to the way he has braided together the different strands of his theme.

The two main aspects of Marcabru's technique in this song: the gradual unfolding of the theme, as the poet clarifies his true ideas, and the playing on words or use of 'colours' to suggest meanings, are both found elsewhere in his poetry. The unfolding of the *razo* he referred to in 'Per savi.l tenc'[3] and practised in 'Al departir';[4] in the *gap* layers of meaning or *colors* were interwoven.[5] Both are to be important in future songs of the *trobar clus*.

L. Pollmann[6] claimed to find in Marcabru's poetry an equivalent of the *qufl* in the Zaǧal of Ibn Quzmān: that is, a method of rounding off a section of the poem, or a stanza, with a bizarre, obscure remark. I cannot compare Marcabru with Ibn Quzmān, but the examples Pollmann gives can be otherwise explained. He finds illogicalities and bizarre elements in the song 'Estornel, cueill ta volada' (XXV), which is admittedly difficult; but the

---

[1] *SWB* viii. 529 *ufanier*, 'prachtliebend . . . grosssprecherisch viel redend, aber nicht entsprechend handelnd; wortreich, lügnerisch'.
[2] See notes.
[3] See p. 16. [4] See pp. 32 ff. [5] See pp. 19 ff.
[6] '*Trobar clus*', p. 84.

commentary of A. Roncaglia[1] on this poem indicates that difficulties arise from Marcabru's far-ranging imagery, which may
have been much clearer to his audience than it is to us.

The other example of the *qufl* element Pollmann takes from 'Al
son desviat' (V), where he finds the last lines of stanzas III, IV, V,
VI, VIII, and the *tornada*, obscure.[2] Only stanza III is discussed
in detail:

> Non puosc dompnas trobar gaire
> Que blanch' amistatz no.i vaire,
> A presen o a saubuda
> N'aja vergoigna perduda,
> Si que la meins afrontada
> N'a laissat cazer un caire.   (V. 13–18)

I can hardly find any ladies in whom white friendship has not turned
piebald, or lost a sense of modesty secretly or openly, so that the least
barefaced among them has let fall a corner of it.[3]

Lewent[4] suggested that *caire* might be a piece of the clothing of
Vergoigna; but Pollmann thinks that the idea of 'letting fall' does
not fit in, and concludes that the image is incomplete, certainly
obscure, and notes that it falls more or less in the position of the
qufl.[5] The difficulty here seems in fact to be the result of Marcabru's fondness for puns, for playing on the meanings of words.
Afrontada means 'bold', but also literally 'barefaced' in the sense
of having the forehead, or *fron*, uncovered. *Cazer un caire* is a pun
in itself, for *caire* can be another form of *cazer*,[6] so the phrase
means 'to let fall a fall', probably 'to sin'. *Caire* also means a square
or corner. In v. 18 *n'* refers to *vergoigna*, so the ladies are letting
fall a corner or square of *vergoigna* (not of its 'clothing'). This can
be linked with *afrontada*: *vergoigna* is the veil which covers the
forehead of a modest lady, and even the least 'barefaced' of these
fickle ladies has let a corner of her modesty fall away.

Stanza IV is also difficult because of puns, and the difficulties
are not confined to the last line.

> Moillerat, per saint Ylaire,
> Son d'una foldat confraire,

Qu'entr' els es guerra moguda
Tals que cornutz *fa* cornuda,
E cogotz copatz *copada*,
Puois eis la coa de braire.   (19–24)

Husbands, by Saint Hilary, are confederates in one folly: for war has been declared among them such that the horned man has the horned woman, and the injured cuckold the crested lark, and then the 'tail' stops complaining.

He puns on *cornutz* and *cornuda*: the *cornutz* is the horned cuckold; the *cornuda* is so called because she is correspondingly deceived by her own husband, but the word is probably also meant in a sexual sense.[1] *copar* means 'to strike down, injure':[2] the injured cuckold takes the *copada*, who is both 'injured' because of her husband's deceit, and 'struck down' by the *copatz*. But *copada* is also the name of a bird, 'crested lark',[3] and this is humourously linked with the image of cuckoldry. *Coa*, 'tail' could mean 'remainder': no one could complain, since all are included in the 'ronde'. But it may also have a sexual sense.[4] This play on words is another example of Marcabru's use of *colors*, and does not need to be explained by the *qufl*.

In the remaining stanzas the last lines are not difficult. Marcabru blames the folly of adulterous husbands (stanza V) concluding, 'E ieu sui del dich pechaire' (30), 'And I am a sinner for saying so'; if the fool is burned in the furnace, 'Non sui malmeire ni laire', 'I am not culpable or criminal, I am not to blame' (stanza VI);[5] stanza VII ends with the vilifying of *Proeza* by 'Duc e rei et emperaire' (42); in stanza VIII the poet sees how 'Amors es

---

[1] Cf. Arnaut Daniel, ed. Toja, I and appendix, the *sirventes* of Turc Malec: 'Non es bona dompna el mon / Sim mostrava lo corn el con / Tot atretal cum il se son / E pois m'apellava: Raimon, / Cornatz m'aissi sobrel redon . . .'.

[2] *SWB* i. 286: *copar* (*colpar*) 'treffen, verwunden; abschlagen'.

[3] *SWB* i. 356: 'Haubenlerche'.

[4] *acoatar*: Rayn. ii. 419: 'unir, accointer'; cf. Marcabru XVIII. 37–8: 'Ab diables pren barata / Qui fals' Amor acoata'; *concoa, concoeira* 'concubine' (Rayn., loc. cit.); *cauda* L & S 303, III 'membrum virile'. This sense might be intended in Marcabru XVIII. 31–6: 'Greu sera mais Amors vera . . . Doussa.us er com chans de lera / Si sol la coa.l troncatz' (but cf. Dejeanne and Lewent, p. 334).

[5] Dejeanne: *mal meire* from *mal merir*, 'être coupable, pécher' (*PD* 245). Lewent, 'Beiträge', pp. 319–20 suggests 'unglücklich' for *Non sui m.*, and emends to *si.n laire*, 'wenn ich darüber schelte'; this is rejected by G. Bertoni, 'Lewent', p. 498 n. 1, in favour of Dejeanne.

cujaire', 'how Love is self-deluding'. The *tornada* may appear obscure:

> Desirat per desirada[1]
> A nom qui.n vol amor traire.   (55–6)

The one who wishes to elicit love from here is called 'Desired by the Desired'.

Marcabru has just described the home of true love, surrounded by branches so that it is protected from strangers (stanza IX). The imagery is reminiscent of the *hortus conclusus*,[2] and *Desideratus* was a name for Christ.[3] It cannot be said for certain that Marcabru means that the only true love is Christian love; but whatever his exact meaning, the imagery is Christian.[4] This *tornada*, the only part of the song which seems to be deliberately enigmatic rather than rhetorically complex, points to Christian symbolism rather than Arabic influence.

4. 'Trobar braus'

Just as Marcabru composes in ways which are followed in later songs of the *trobar clus*, so he is the model for the style later known as *trobar braus*. Raimon de Miraval links the two:[5]

> Anc trobars clus ni braus
> Non dec aver pretz ni laus;

The closed or rough style should never have fame or praise.

---

[1] MS. *desiraire*, but the rhyme requires *-ada*.

[2] Cant. 4: 12 ff.; cf. Errante, p. 185, and Robertson, 'Five poems', p. 551.

[3] Aggaeus 2: 8: 'Et veniet Desideratus cunctis gentibus'; cf. Robertson, loc. cit. and also F. J. E. Raby, *The Oxford Book of Medieval Latin Verse* (Oxford, 1959), no. 59:

> Beata mater munere,
> cuius supernus artifex
> mundum pugillo continens
> ventris sub arca clausus est.
> Benedicta caeli nuntio,
> fecunda sancto spiritu,
> desideratus gentibus
> cuius per alvum fusus est.

[4] Roncaglia, *CN* xxix (1969), 22–6 also points to the Christian imagery here and besides this shows that *el Deseado* was the official surname of Sancho III (*desiderabilis Sancius*) whose birth, not before 1133, had long been desired by his father Alfonso VII of Castile. Marcabru was at the court of Castile and must have composed the song to celebrate the promise of marriage between Sancho and Blanche, still children. *Desirat* would have been seen as a *senhal* generally recognized for Sancho, and Roncaglia equates *desiraire* with his father, and *blanch' amistat* with Blanche who is 'drawn from' the *hortus conclusus*, or geographically speaking, from the region of Navarre. If, as the rhyme seems to require, *desirada* should replace *desiraire*, this would seem to refer to Blanche rather than Alfonso.   [5] Ed. L. Topsfield, XXXI. 1–2.

The *trobar braus* is satirized by Uc de Saint-Circ:[1]

> Guillems Fabres nos fai en brau lengage
> Manz braus broncs brenx, bravan de brava guia,
> E rocs e brocs qe met en son cantage,
> E fils e pils e motz d'algaravia;

Guillem Fabre creates for us in harsh language many harsh, spiky prongs, roughening in rough fashion, and rocks and thorns which he puts into his singing, and files and pestles and words of gibberish.[2]

Marcabru deliberately chooses harsh rhymes: *ucs* ('Al departir'), *issa* (XXX), *usca* (XI), *esc*, *esca* (XIV), *atz*, *utz*, *es* (XXXIX). He 'shouts and clamours' about *Malvestatz*:

> Per so sospir, car mouta gens ahura
> de malvestat c'ades creis e pejura:
> so m'en somon qu'ieu sia guerrejaire,
> c'a lieis sap bon quan m'au *cridar ni braire*.[3]

For this reason I sigh, that many people predict that evil will continually increase and grow worse; this urges me to wage war on it, for they like to hear me shout and clamour.

The starling, messenger to the poet's lady of little reputation, does not sing sweetly but 'brai e crida' (XXVI. 13); ironically his voice is 'made clear': 'Tant ha sa votz esclarzida' (14), and the lady greets it as discordant noise: 'Auzels, . . . per cui / Fas tal brui / Ho cal(s) amor(s) tensa?' (19–22); 'Bird, . . . for whose benefit are you making such a noise, and what kind of love is he quarrelling about?'[4] In Marcabru's opening stanzas, frogs croak, owls hoot: 'la rana chant' el vivier' ('Al departir', 5), 'Bel m'es quan la rana chanta' (XI. 1), 'E s'esforsa si la rana / Lonc la fontanilha, / E.l chauans ab sa chauana, / S'als non pot, grondilha' (XXI. 9–12); even the nightingale cries and shouts, 'E.l rossinhols crid' e brama' (XI. 5), and birdsong is mingled, or 'adulterated',[5] with cries: 'E l'auzel desotz la verdon / Mesclon lur(s) critz ab lo chanton' (II. 7–8).[6] Even the sound of water suggests pain and complaint: 'la douz gem e la fonz bruig' (VIII. 2).

---

[1] Ed. A. Jeanroy and J.-J. Salverda de Grave, XXVIII. 1–4. MS.: v. 1 *lignage*, v. 4 *de galgaravia*.

[2] From *pilar*, 'pound, crush' (*PD* 294), *pilo* 'pestle' (Rayn. iv. 538)?

[3] 'Aujatz de chan', 5–8.

[4] Text emended by Lewent, 'Beiträge', p. 431: 'Auzels, ui / Ditz, per cui / Fas . . . ?'

[5] On *mesclar*, see Topsfield, *NMi*, vol. lxix, no. 2 (1968), p. 285. *Mesclanhas* means 'quarrels, brawls' in XLI. 12; cf. also XXXVI. 35, *IK*.

[6] This is linked with Marcabru's imagery of birds as representing quarrelsomeness or empty noise, see pp. 36–7.

By his harsh sounds, Marcabru poetically rejects the smooth language associated with deceiving flatterers.[1] He may also be protesting against a contemporary smooth style of poetry, such as Cercamon sometimes adopts:

> Plas es lo vers, vauc l'afinan
> Ses mot vila, fals, apostitz,
> E es totz enaissi bastitz
> C'ap motz politz lo vau uzan;
>
> (Jeanroy, III. 31–4)

The *vers* is smooth, I refine it without any vulgar, false, misplaced word, and it is entirely constructed so that I use only polished words in it.[2]

This belongs to courtly praise of the lady, where no improper word is used and social values are harmonious and unquestioned. Marcabru sees the world as upside-down, false, and discordant; his harshness disrupts illusions of harmony. This is, perhaps, the stylistic division at Marcabru's time: one between *braus* and *plan*; not essentially an aesthetic division, although Marcabru evidently preferred the colour of a rough style, but a division in attitudes to society.

To sum up, Marcabru's view of *eloquentia* is one of suspicion, but this is the suspicion of an educated writer himself well versed in Rhetoric. His own poetic *eloquentia* is *trobar naturau*, the art of composing according to the truth and an understanding of the natural moral order of things. Although he never mentions the *trobar clus* his work anticipates this style in all its major aspects, just as it also provides a model for the *trobar braus*.

In Marcabru's disciple Peire d'Alvernhe, eloquence in both rough and smooth styles becomes not an expression of social criticism or an object of suspicion, but a prized attribute of the courtly poet.

---

[1] See pp. 8–9.

[2] Mölk, p. 55, observes that *plan* here means 'smooth', not 'simple' (Jeanroy). Cf. Jaufré Rudel, II. 30–1; 'Tramet lo vers, que chantam / En plana lengua romana' (*CEMRSUXae; ABDIK* plan et en l.r., Sa plazent l.r.).

2

PEIRE D'ALVERNHE, FIRST OF THE 'VULGARES ELOQUENTES'[1]

DANTE ranks Peire among the 'antiquiores doctores' in his *De Vulgari Eloquentia*, and Peire is the earliest troubadour he mentions.[2] According to his Provençal biographer, Peire was 'lo meillor trobator del mon, entro que venc Girautz de Borneill'.[3] He admired and imitated Marcabru:

> Chantador, lo vers vos fenis:
> aprendetz la comensansa.
> Marcabrus per gran dreitura
> trobet d'altretal semblansa . . .[4]

But whereas Marcabru, if skilled in rhetoric, distrusted eloquence and rarely drew attention to his own unless to emphasize its overriding moral purpose, Peire frequently boasts of his eloquence and regards eloquence as a courtly attribute.

1. *Eloquence and courtliness*

The song 'Rossinhol, el seu repaire' (I) combines a lightness of touch and lyrical quality with a highly conscious rhetorical craftsmanship in which the poet's own artistry is cleverly mirrored in the nightingale.[5] Sent as a messenger to the poet's lady, the nightingale is full of courtly qualities: he is *guai* (16), *de bon aire*

---

[1] Unless otherwise stated texts are quoted from Del Monte's edition. Peire's career is dated 1158–80 (R. Zenker, *Peire*, pp. 24–40; Del Monte, p. 9).

[2] *DVE* I. x. 3. Giraut de Bornelh's career is thought to have begun about 1165: see p. 88.

[3] Del Monte, p. 13. The biographer may have been persuaded by Peire's own boasts of his poetic superiority (XI. 1–6; XII. 79–82).

[4] See p. 29.

[5] The freshness and delicacy of this song have been described by R. Lejeune, 'Thèmes', pp. 74–88; she also suggests that Marcabru's *estornel* songs (XXV, XXVI) may have followed this one as a parody, though Marcabru could be parodying an earlier song in the same genre: see E. Müller, p. 25.

(21), and he responds, as the courtly lover himself would do, to the sight of the lady's beauty with a spontaneous outburst of song:

> Quan l'auzeletz de bon aire
> vi sa beutat aparer,
> dous chant comenset a braire,
> si com sol far contra.l ser;   (21–4)

When the nobly born little bird saw her beauty appear, he began to sound a sweet song, as he is wont to do at evening;

but immediately his powers of reflection are necessary: he falls silent, thinking about the manner of speech which will best persuade the lady of his message:

> pueis se tai
> que no brai,
> mas de liei s'engenha,
> co.l retrai
> ses pantai
> so qu'ill auzir denha.   (25–30)

then he fell silent so that he did not sing but reflected on a plan concerning her: how he should relate to her with composure what she might deign to hear.

As the lover's *plaidiaire* or advocate (51) the nightingale broaches his speech with discreet modesty, putting himself in the lady's power:

> 'Sel que.us es verais amaire,
> volc qu'ieu en vostre poder
> vengues sai esser chantaire,
> per so que.us fos a plazer.   (31–4)

The one who is your true lover desired that I should come here to be a singer in your power, in order that this might be pleasing to you.

Tactfully he mentions the lover's desire, reminding the lady of the joy she would feel at accepting such a worthy lover and rapturously anticipating her agreement, before drawing back with *mezura* for fear of excessive presumption:

> E si.l port per que.s n'esclaire,
> gran gaug en devetz aver,
> c'anc hom no nasquet de maire
> tan de be.us puesca voler.
> Ie.m n'irai
> e.m mourai

> ab gaug, on que.m venha . . .
> No farai,
> quar non ai
> dig qual plag en prenha.   (41–50)

And if I bear news to him which will cause him to rejoice, you ought to have great delight, for never man of woman born might wish you so much good. I will go forth and depart with joy, wherever I may come . . . No I will not, for I have not told him what agreement he may conclude.

With a delicate image of white petals falling on to dark wood, the nightingale reminds the lady that love must be enjoyed before it is too late:

> que tost chai
> blancs en bai
> cum flors sobre lenha;
> e val mai
> qui.l fag fai
> ans qu'als la.n destrenha.   (55–60)

For white on dark quickly falls, as blossom on the branch; and it is better to act before being constrained to do so.

The nightingale's eloquence is successful and the lady sends word that she is pleased with his *parladura* (67). She bids him report on her compliance with the lover's wishes, *en dreg lengatge*, and the nightingale returns, full of *mezura*, learning, and eloquence:

> 'Dous auzels, vas son estatge
> m'iretz, quan venra.l matis,
> e diguatz l'en dreg lengatge
> de qual guiza l'obedis.'
>   Abrivatz
>   n'es tornatz,
> trop per gran mezura
>   doctrinatz,
>   emparlatz
> de bon' aventura.   (111–20)

'Sweet bird, when morning comes you will go straight to his dwelling for me and tell him in true language in what way I obey him.' Swiftly he returned from thence, excellently and most temperately taught, eloquent with good fortune.

Not only does Peire use a conscious rhetoric, he gracefully reminds his audience of this: he indicates that eloquence, control, *mezura*, *doctrina* are not only compatible with delicacy of sentiment and expression and spontaneity of feeling, but are essential to a truly courtly way of conducting and expressing oneself.

2. *'Vers entiers'*

Peire's term for a perfectly composed song is *vers entiers* (XI. 4). What does he mean by 'whole' songs? To what extent is his poetic ideal a moral one, to what extent is it aesthetic? What special attributes does he ascribe to *vers entiers*?

Peire admired Marcabru; while he does not follow Marcabru's term *trobar naturau* he was probably familiar with it,[1] and the idea of a *vers entier* can be traced, verbally at least, to Marcabru's distinction between thinking which is *entier* or *frait*,[2] and to his condemnation of poets who make words 'entrebeschatz de fraichura'.[2] However, we have already observed in the poem 'Rossinhol' that Peire's view of eloquence differs from Marcabru's and in the song in which Peire praises his own *vers entier* he sets himself apart from all other poets, past and present.

Both Köhler[3] and Del Monte[4] see Peire's concept of *vers entiers* as being moral as well as aesthetic. Köhler attempts to explain it in the light of scholastic aesthetics; Del Monte, in relation to Peire's concept of courtly joy. Köhler quotes Thomas Aquinas who says that the *integritas sive perfectio* of a work of art depends on the unity of *pulchrum* and *bonum* in it, and works lacking this unity he terms *diminuta*.[5] This terminology Köhler identifies with the terms *entier* and *frait* in the troubadours' poetry. In the light of this, he concludes that Peire's song 'Sobre.l vieill trobar' claims to reconcile stylistic perfection in courtly poetry with the highest moral truth, and that for the first time the courtly world is expressing decisively its moral autonomy.[6] Del Monte, emphasizing that similarity of terminology in Aquinas and Peire does not necessarily imply similarity of concepts,[7] modifies Köhler's interpretation by transposing the terminology of Aquinas to the

---

[1] See p. 29. [2] See p. 10.
[3] pp. 21–7. [4] *Peire*, pp. 111–17.
[5] p. 22 and p. 235: 'Pulchritudo habet similitudinem cum propriis Filii. Nam ad pulchritudinem tria requiruntur. Primo quidem, integritas sive perfectio; quae enim diminuta sunt, hoc ipso turpia sunt. Et debita proportio sive consonantia. Et iterum claritas: unde quae habent colorem nitidum, pulchra esse dicuntur.' (*Summa theologica*, I. 39. 8.)
[6] p. 23. [7] *Peire*, p. 113.

plane of Peire's concept of *jois*. Aquinas claimed that the *pulchrum* of a work, with its *debita proportio sive consonantia, claritas,* and *integritas,* leads the reason (*ratio*) to understanding (*cognitio*) of higher truths; Del Monte equates Peire's *ratio* with his *sen,* his *cognitio* with the *ioi d'amor.* The latter, he says, is the source of knightly virtue or *cortezia,* but is attainable only through complete surrender to the lady with the 'absoluteness' belonging to the feudal ethic; hence *entier* comes to mean 'in genuine integrity and spiritual absoluteness' and *frag* describes one who has 'broken this integrity and spiritual absoluteness, denying true and complete self-surrender'. Hence the fault of which Bernart Marti accuses Peire in his song 'D'entier vers far',[1] is that of 'dissimulation of and incoherence in his own (true?) feelings'.[2]

However, even if it can be assumed that the ideas expressed by Thomas Aquinas were current in the middle of the twelfth century, there is no reason to think that Peire was influenced by them either directly or indirectly. His use of the term *entier* may be quite vague and mean simply 'perfect'. If his ideas are to be linked with learned literary theories, there are other examples of the term *integritas* in a literary context which could have influenced Peire at least as easily as some unspecified source he might have shared with Aquinas. In the context of Rhetoric, Quintilian discusses *brevitas integra* which, when badly imitated, can lead to obscurity: 'brevitas integra . . . est . . . pulcherrima, cum plura paucis complectimur, quale Sallustii est: "Mithridates corpore ingenti, perinde armatus": hoc male imitantes sequitur obscuritas';[3] *integritas Latini sermonis*[4] means simply the correctness of Latin language; in Rabanus Maurus' *De clericorum institutione,*[5] *integritas lectionis* is the full significance of a text once all the meanings, literal and figurative, have been understood. Any one of these concepts could conceivably have influenced Peire. Clearly it is

[1] Ed. Hoepffner, V; see p. 67. [2] *Peire,* p. 113.

[3] VIII. iii. 82.

[4] Cicero, *Brut.* xxxv. 132: 'incorrupta quaedam Latini sermonis integritas'.

[5] PL ciii. 385 (based on Augustine's *De doctrina Christiana*): 'Deinde de ignotis translatibus, in quibus subtilitas et utilitas lectionis habetur, postea vero de ambiguis signis, propriis atque translatis, quibus ad purum elicitis, et secundum veritatem inventis, firmitas et *integritas* lectionis generatur.' ('The text in its established and complete form is produced by bringing out the meaning, firstly of obscure metaphors in which the subtlety and point of the text is contained, and secondly of ambiguous indications, literal or figurative, and selecting these for their purity and finding out about them according to the truth.')

crucial to return to the text of his song. Unfortunately it is very difficult and exists only in two manuscripts, *EV*; I have re-edited it.[1]

I   Sobre.l vieill trobar e.l novel
      vueill mostrar mon sen als sabens,
      qu'entendon be   aquels c'a venir son
      c'anc tro per me   no fo faitz vers entiers;
      e qui non cre   qu'ieu.n sia verdadiers,   5
      auia dese   con estau a razon.

II   Qu'ieu tenc l'us e.l pan e.l coutel
      de que.m platz apanar las gens
      que d'est mestier   s'an levat *u*n pairon,
      ses acordier   que no.s rompa.l semdiers;   10
      qu'ieu dic que n*i*er   si mostr'els faitz non *ni*ers,
      c'a fol parlier   ten hom lui el sermon.

III   C'a un tenen ses mot borrel
      deu de dir esser avinens;
      quar qui trassaill   de Maurin en miron   15
      entre.l mieg faill   si no.s pren als ladriers,
      com del trebaill   que*c*s motz fatz trezagiers,
      qu'en devinaill   met l'auzir de maison.

IV   E qui que.n frima ni.n fragel,
      pos qu'es mos trobars tan valens,   20
      . . . .
      qu'ieu soi raitz   e dic que soi premiers
      de digz complitz,   vensen mos fatz guerriers,
      que.m levon critz   qu'ieu no m'en tenh pron.

V   Donx com qu'ill sion d'un tropel,   25
      menton tot gent er per las dens,
      qu'ie.m sen sertans   del mieils que aqui fon,
      ensegurans   de mon chant e sobriers
      ves los baisans   e sai que dic, qu'estiers
      no vengua.l grans   don a trop en sazon.   30

---

[1] In addition to the texts of Zenker and Del Monte, see J. Coulet, and Dejeanne, *AdM* xvi (1904), 341-7.

VI   Quar er m'abelis e m'es bel
       qu'el mieu ioi s'enans lo iovens;
       e s'ieu ren *d*ic   que lur an environ,
       aisi m'en gic,   c'uns gaugz mi creis dobliers
       d'un dous espic   qu'es ioios consiriers,   35
       don m'an amic   huoimais li mal e.ill bon.

VII   D'aisi.m sent ric   per bona sospeison,
       qu'en ioi m'a*f*ic   e m'estau volentiers;
       e ab ioi pic   e gaug mos deziriers,
       e ab ioi pic   e gaug vueill: Dieus lo.m don.   40

VARIANTS

1. *E* . . . l vieill trobar . . . vel; *V* viell. 2. *E* vueill m . . . r mon sen als . . . ns.; *V* vul. 3. *E* quentēdon . . . aquels cavenir . . . ; *V* ceil que avenir so. 4. *E* c. t. per . . . o fo f. ve . . . ntiers; *V* per mi. 5. *E* equi . . . re quieu en sia; *V* queu sia. 6. *E* . . . stau arazon. 7. *E* cantel; *V* tejn, couteil. 8. *E* plas; *V* gentz. 9. *E* q. daquest; *E* en p., *V* capairo. 10. *E* acordar; *V* acordiers. 11. *E* ner, vers; *E* mostron *V* dic dese emostrels f. novers. 12. *E* e afol parlar, al s.; *V* cafol parler. 13. *E* Cazun t. sen moc b.; *V* Da un t. ses mot boreil. 14. *V* avinentz. 15. *E* tras al demaurin; *V* car; demauri emiro. 16. *E* ladrers. 17. *E* quieis; *V* trebail queix mot fas messatgiers. 18. *E* devinar, damaion; *V* divinar, demaiso. 20. *V* pus, valentz. 22. *V* eu son iratz edic queu sol primers. 23. *E* guerrers; *V* ditz, vezen, gerriers. 24. *E* crim, que ieu; *V* crim canc no fon vertadiers. que eu metex nomen pusc tener pro. 25. *V* Doncs cans quil sia. 26. *V* dentz. 27. *E* sertas; *V* sertas, miels ques equefo. 28. *E* enseguratz; *V* esegurat d.m.c. a sobriers. 29. *E* dic estiers; *V* vas los bauzas. 30. *E* grat; *V* vengral gratz be ma trop ab sazo. Stanzas VI–VII in *E* only. 32. *E* iois enans. 33. *E* aic. 34. *E* giec. 37. *E* ricx. 38. *E* masic.

I. On the old and the new art of composing I want to show my wisdom to the knowledgeable, so that those who are yet to come may fully realize that a truly whole song was never composed until by me; and if anyone does not believe that I am truthful in this matter, let him forthwith hear how reason justifies it.

II. For I have the experience and the bread and the knife with which it pleases me to feed (get the better of) the people who have raised up a model for themselves in this profession, without recognizing that a task should not be left half-finished; for I say that he is appearing to be dark (true) in deeds which are not dark (true), so that he is considered as a foolish speaker in what he says.

III. For he ought to be pleasing by speaking consistently without any dark word, since whoever takes a leap in imitation of Maurin falls down mid-way if he does not cling to the sides, as he makes all the words certain to cause toil, so that the whole audience is set to guessing.

IV. And whoever may quiver and tremble at this, since my composition is so full of worth . . . I am the root, and I say I am the first in the use of complete expressions, vanquishing my foolish opponents who raise an outcry against me because I pay no attention to them.

v. Therefore however they may band together they are now quite simply lying in their teeth; for I feel confident about the best that ever was, self-assured about my song and superior to those on the decline; and I know what I am saying, for in no other way is the grain forthcoming, of which there is much in due season.

vi. For now it pleases me and delights me that youth may advance in my joy; and if I say anything that crosses them, I now refrain from this, because one joy is increased twofold for me from a sweet ear of corn which is joyous reflection, and for this reason from now on both good and wicked people will have me as their friend.

vii. Therefore I feel noble through fine hopes, for I attach myself to joy and willingly remain with it; and with joy I chisel and gauge my desires, and with joy I desire both pick and gauge: God grant this to me.

NOTES

The text is re-edited from the MSS., *EV*. As *E* is the most complete, the last two stanzas being missing from *V*, *E* is taken as the base.

1. *Sobre.l vieill trobar e.l novel:* what is the 'old' and the 'new' poetry? Coulet suggested that Peire was attacking Marcabru and the *trobar clus*, but this view was rejected by E. Hoepffner (*R* liii (1927), 130) and Jeanroy (*Poésie lyrique*, ii. 37ff.). C. Appel (*Deutsche Literaturzeitung* (1901), col. 2964) suggested that he might be attacking Bernart Marti, but Del Monte rejects this idea (p. 112). 'I bring things never said before' is a *topos* (see Curtius, pp. 85 ff.), and Peire is claiming to be the best poet and blaming his detractors in a boast of superiority which was not necessarily provoked by a specific incident or troubadour, although if my version is correct he does seem to have a particular rival in mind [*pairon*, v. 9]. In view of Bernart Marti's response it does not seem to me entirely improbable that he was the rival in question.

7. *E cantel.* This, the 'piece' or 'hunk of bread', repeats the idea of *pan*. The poet says he has all the different things necessary to a superior composer: the practice (*l'us*), the material (*pan*), the instrument or technique (*coutel*).

8—12. The main difficulty of this stanza is the syntax: to whom does *lui* (v. 12) refer? Zenker does not translate vv. 9–12. Del Monte takes *lui* to refer to *pairon* (v. 9), translating : 'Che io possiedo l'esperienza e il pane e il coltello con cui mi piace nutrire le genti; perchè in questo mestiere hanno innalzato a modello, senza il patto che non si cambi via, colui che io dico che si mostra triste nei fatti non tristi, sicchè si considera un folle parolaio lui e il (suo) discorso.' (p. 111.) The syntax here is awkward and doubtful: one would expect not 'en pairo ... qu'ieu dic' but 'en pairo ... cel don ieu dic'; and if *capairo* (*V*) were the correct reading instead of *en pairon* (*E*) this construction would be impossible. Yet the sense seems to demand this. I tentatively suggest changing *en pairon* to *un pairon*, and, following *V*, adopting *mostr'els* instead of *mostron*.

8. *apanar* is a pun on *pan* (7) and has the double meaning of 'feed' and 'steal from' (*SWB* i. 67; Rayn. iv. 409–10, who quotes G. Riquier, 'Aital vos pana, / Et aital vos engana'). Peire 'steals' from his rival the position of being the best poet.

9. *pairon:* 'patron, modèle' (*PD* 274; see Del Monte, p. 114). The alternative reading, *capairo* (*V*) (*PD* 64 'chaperon, coiffure; chaperon, couverture de tuiles, de maçonnerie en dos d'âne, placée sur le haut d'un mur'), might mean that people have 'raised their hats' in appreciation of some poet (any who challenges Peire's position) without recognizing that his skill is incomplete. Köhler, p. 140 renders *capairo* arbitrarily as 'Nichtskönner'. Coulet, p. 784: 'have entered combat'.

10. *que no.s rompa.l semdiers:* Del Monte (pp. 114 ff.) interprets this in the light of the following lines from 'L'airs clars' (VI): 'qui de gaug a dezirier / (ben) tengua a dreyt so semdier' (21–2), 'dov'è perspicuo che *tener so semdier* significa "proseguire nella propria via, perseverare nel proprio sentimento" . . . *Romper lo semdier* significherà quindi "interrompere la propria via, non perseverare nei propri sentimenti".' Peire has not yet mentioned any theme of personal sentiment, however; he is discussing his poetic skill. *que no.s rompa.l semdiers* is probably a variation of the *topos*: 'a work begun must be brought to a proper conclusion', which could apply to various situations: both the single-minded pursuit of joy (VI. 21–2), and, here, the successful achievement of one's poetic aims. (For this *topos*, cf. Marcabru, 'D'aisso' 7–9: 'C'assatz es lait / s'intratz en plait / don non sabretz a lutz issir' (see p. 20), Raimbaut d'Aurenga XXIV. 14: 'Car si ieu vos o avia mogut, e no.us o trazia a cap, tenriatz m'en per fol.') The foolish poets have attempted too difficult a task; they have undertaken more than they are capable of completing.

11. *qu'ieu dic que nier si mostr'els faitz non niers:* nier and niers, adopted by Del Monte, are suggested by *ner* in *E; vers* is the last syllable of the line in both MSS., and seems the more likely reading, except that it does not rhyme with *-iers*. If *nier(s)* is adopted, Peire means: the poet is obscure in what should be clear; if *ver(s)*, he appears to be truthful in things which are not true. In either case his critics are turning the facts upside-down. *V e mostr'els faitz* is corrupt, following *qu'ieu dic dese* which is unrhymed: perhaps *si mostr'*, which would not significantly alter the sense.

12. Del Monte reads *e.l sermo*.

13. *C'a un tenen:* Del Monte: 'coerente', *PD* 361: 'sans interruption, tout d'une fois'.
 Ses mot borrel: Zenker, p. 180: 'läppisch' (*borrel*) from Latin *burra*, 'zottiges Gewand'; Jeanroy (*Poésie lyrique*, ii. 39–40): either 'rugueux', from *burra*, or preferably 'de couleur sombre, terne', from *burrus* (cf. Rayn. ii. 271: *burel* 'brun'); Del Monte, p. 115: 'superfluo', from *burra* meaning 'waste, sweepings' (*quisquiliae*, quidquidcadiae). *E* sen moc borrel: Rayn. ii. 237: 'il s'en émut bagarre' makes no sense: conceivably *moc* = 'morve' (*PD* 249), 'without useless (obscure) rubbish', but the word would be rather strong. I hesitate between 'dark-coloured' and 'rubbishy'; the first fits with v. 18; the poor poet's dark-coloured words, which he cannot use properly, set the whole audience guessing; the second would indicate Peire's low opinion of his rival's style. In a poem attributed to Marcoat, 'Mentre m'obri eis huisel' (ed. Dejeanne, *AdM* xv (1903), 362, reprinted by A. Jeanroy, *Jongleurs*, (pp. 12–13), the author sings 'Un sirventes escubel' (2), 'a trashy *sirventes*'. (Dejeanne emends *escubel* to *escur bel;* but cf. *PD* 162: *escobar* 'balayer, nettoyer, purger; fustiger'; *escobilh* 'balayures, immondices'.) Peire might be referring to such a style, although 'Mentre m'obri' is 'trashy' because of its somewhat scurrilous subject-matter, and this is not implied by Peire.

15. *de Maurin en miron:* this has usually been taken as *de Mauri en Miro*, referring to undetermined places (see Del Monte, p. 115). Del Monte corrects to *de M-ari en Mi-ro* ('*mi ari*, da arire<*adridere*) . . . Mi-ro (da *roire*), intendendo: chi passa

saltando dal tema della buona accoglienza a quello della repulsa, della distruzione ecc.', which is over-ingenious. Although *Maurin* and *Miron* could be two places, it is also possible that *Maurin* is the name of a person, and that *miron* comes from the verb *mirar*, 'to admire, reflect, imitate' (*SWB* v. 284: 'beschauen, betrachten, ansehen, bewundern'; *se mirar* 'sich spiegeln, ein Beispiel, Muster nehmen'), to give 'in imitation of Maurin'. *Maurin* could be the hero of the Provençal *chanson de geste*, *Aigar et Maurin* (A. Scheler, *Aigar et Maurin. Fragments d'une chanson de geste provençale inconnue* (Bruxelles, 1877), to which Bertran de Born refers in his song 'Rassa, tan creis' (Stimming, XXXVII. 51). This epic survives only in fragmentary form, but it seems that Maurin's flaw was overweening pride: 'Orgueil en guerre et orgueil en gabar' (761), and ambition to own half of his overlord's kingdom (726–56). What end he came to is unknown, but he may have been an example of pride coming before a fall. *Trassalhir* means not only to 'spring' but also 'pass beyond the proper limits, commit a crime or sin' (*SWB* viii. 378: 'hinüberspringen, springen; hinwegspringen; schwinden; die rechte Grenze überschreiten; sich vergehen . . .'). Peire's meaning may therefore be: for whoever is overweeningly presumptuous, following the example of Maurin . . .

17. *trezagiers*: *PD* 371: *trazachier* 'sûr'; *V messatgiers*: 'as he makes all the words herald toil . . .'

17–18. See Del Monte's note, p. 116. Zenker does not translate: Köhler (p. 141): each word announces the poet's efforts as an artist, which forces members of the court to listen with intellectual concentration; Del Monte: 'chi s'esprime con parole non selezionate, pone l'intendere di casa nell'indovinare.' Peire is blaming poets who try to use words that are too clever, with the effect that every word becomes a labour for the listeners, who have to resort to guesswork.

21–2. Del Monte (p. 116) shows that there must be a gap in v. 21.

24. MSS. *crim*; Zenker's emendation.

29. *E* baisans; *V* bauzas. Del Monte adopts *V*, 'mentitori', which links with v. 26, 'menton tot gent . . .' *Baisans* implies that Peire's rivals are on the decline. The rhyme in vv. 27–30 in *as, ans*, is indicated by *sertas* (*EV* 27), and *baisans, bauzas* (29).

32. Del Monte: *s'enant la iovens. Iovens* is masculine (MS. *lo*). MS. *iois enans*. I take *s'enans* as 3rd ps. pres. subjunctive of *s'enansar*.

33. MS. *aic*: Zenker's emendation.
   que lur an enviro: see Del Monte's note. Schulz-Gora, *Literaturblatt* (1902), 73: 'wenn ich etwas sag, was sich auf sie (sc. *bauzas*) bezieht'; Del Monte: 'se io dico qualcosa in comune coi *bauzas*'. It is possible that *environ* should be *en viron*, from *virar* 'to turn', with the idea of 'turning against': 'if I say anything which might go against them'. This would link with v. 36: if Peire says anything which crosses his adversaries, he now renounces this: for from now on he will be friendly to everyone.

38. MS.: *asic*; Dejeanne's emendation, p. 347.
   asic may possibly be 1st ps. perfect: cf. *vic* in Marcabru XXXII. 4: 'De so qu'ieu vei e vic', which Anglade, *Grammaire de l'ancien provençal* (Paris, 1921), p. 303, gives only for the 3rd ps.

39–40. Del Monte: 'e con gioia e letizia sollecito i miei desideri e sollecito con gioia, e letizia voglio: Dio me la conceda.' In the notes, p. 117, he suggests alternatively: 'e voglio che io li solleciti con gioia e letizia: Dio . . .' (see his note for earlier suggestions). If the text is not corrupt, it seems likely that Peire is playing on words. In v. 39 *pic e gaug* seem to belong together: the construction according to Del Monte's version is odd and awkward. *Picar* can mean 'pick' (with pick-axe), 'sharpen', 'cut stone' (Rayn. iv. 534: 'piquer, piocher, frapper';

SWB vi. 309: '(mit der Spitzaxt) graben, behauen, (Mühlsteine) schärfen; picken': 'tailler la pierre'). Giraut de Bornelh uses it in an image of craftmanship: 'Fola res, e cel que picha / No vai l'obra melhuran / Cada pauc?' (Kolsen, XXX. 43): 'Foolish creature! and does not the man who chisels away gradually improve the work little by little?' *Gaug* means 'joy' but may also come from *gaujar*, *SWB* iv. 87: 'aichen, vermessen'. Peire seems to be playing on these meanings: 'and with joy I pick and gauge my desire, and with joy I desire pick and gauge (joy)' (or: 'and with joy I pick and desire joy'). This could be an image of the poet-artisan who works away at his song in the inspiration of joy and in the hope of joy: cf. Arnaut Daniel, ed. Toja, II. 12–14: 'Obre e lim / Motz de valor / Ab art d'Amor'.

The song is a literary *gap:* Peire claims he is the best and wisest poet in spite of rivals or detractors. Using a Rhetorical *topos* he comments on his wisdom, for the good speaker or poet must be a wise man;[1] and in referring to 'the old art of poetry and the new' he may again be using a *topos:* 'I bring things never said before'.[2] There is no indication that the old and new poetry refer to different styles: they mean 'all the poetry there is', including the 'new' which is Peire's own: the first *vers entiers*.

He claims to have all the attributes necessary to make him the best poet (7); these enable him to 'feed' people with his good poetry, or alternatively, as he is probably punning on *apanar*, to 'steal' from them the title of best poet. These people admire as their model a presumptuous poet, without realizing that his poetry is only half-complete. Because this so-called model poet is unable to complete the task he sets out to do, anyone who disputes Peire's position as the best poet (see vv. 5–6) talks like a fool, for the facts have been turned upside-down (11–12).

Stanza III contains the explanation of what Peire means by 'complete' poetry. The poet who has presumed too far in setting himself up as Peire's equal, without realizing that his 'path should not be broken', ought, Peire says, to make himself pleasing without any *mot borrel*: any 'dark', or 'rubbishy', word. For someone who 'leaps in imitation of Maurin', or who presumes too far, aspires too highly, falls down in the middle if he does not hold on to one side or another. The result of his using *motz borrels* is to make each word a labour in itself as the whole audience has to guess what he means.

[1] Horace, *Ars Poetica*, 309: 'Scribendi recte sapere est et principium et fons', Quintilian, Preface, p. 9; II. xvi. 11; II. xx. 5; XII. i. 1.
[2] See notes.

This stanza can be explained in terms of common Rhetorical ideas. It is a Rhetorical commonplace that a speaker or writer should not attempt a style which is beyond his capacities: in Dante's words: 'Et ideo confutetur illorum stultitia, qui arte scientiaque immunes, de solo ingenio confidentes, ad summa summe canenda prorumpunt; et a tanta presumptuositate desistant; et si anseres natura vel desidia sunt, nolint astripetam aquilam imitari.'[1] It is also a commonplace that the vice of the high style in Rhetoric is turgidness and obscurity: 'Gravitas ne turgida sit vel opaca'.[2] Peire's presumptuous rival is trying to compose in too high a style for his abilities, and falling into the vice of laboriousness and obscurity. He 'falls down mid-way' because he composes neither in one style nor the other; it would be better if he composed in a lower key and were content to be *avinens* in that. In medieval Rhetoric, 'charm' or the ability to please (*delectare*) is the property of the middle style.[3] *Mot borrel* therefore seem to be words proper to the high style: 'dark' words, or 'darkly coloured' words, similar to the 'bruns . . . motz' of Raimbaut d'Aurenga,[4] and the *colors* of Marcabru.[5] The alternative meaning for *borrel*, 'rubbishy', may possibly be present too, hinting at the inferior poet's choice of words which he thinks are sophisticated but are in fact worthless as they lead to obscurity.[6]

In stanzas IV–V Peire amplifies the theme of his superiority over his rivals and detractors. He is the 'root' of worthwhile composition (22–4) and confident that his poetry alone will produce 'grain' (30).

In the last two stanzas, which may possibly have been added later,[7] the theme is expanded to include courtly *joi*. Peire is pleased that youth follows his version of joy, and declares that its ennobling power makes him magnanimous even to his critics. In the final stanza he seems to bind up the two themes of joy and poetic skill, by 'picking' or 'chiselling' his desires through joy.

[1] *DVE* ii. iv. 11.

[2] Geoffrey of Vinsauf, *Poetria Nova*, 838 (ed. Faral, p. 223); cf. *Rhet. ad Her.* iv. x. 15: 'In hoc genus plerique cum declinantur et *ab eo quo profecti sunt aberrarunt*, specie gravitatis falluntur nec perspicere possunt orationis tumorem.'

[3] Lausberg, *Registerband*, 680–1; § 1079, 2a–b.

[4] See p. 148 ff.   [5] See pp. 21 ff.   [6] See notes.

[7] Del Monte makes this suggestion (p. 117) on the basis of these lines from Cerveri de Girona (ed. Riquer, C. 16–18): 'mey vers seran loncs com cil que fazia / Peyr' ab son gran, d'Alvernya, qui plazia, / car cascun an d'una cobla.s crexia.' Cf. Peire: 'no vengua.l grans . . .' (30) and 'd'un dous espic' (35).

Is this song concerned with the *trobar clus*? This is not stated, and terms such as *clus, serratz, escur* are absent. *Devinaill* (18) is no indication that Peire is referring to the *trobar clus*, since he says that it is through the fault of bad poets that the audience has to make guesses. *Nier* (11) is an uncertain reading; if it is correct, Peire may mean not only that his detractor is turning the facts upside-down, as they appear obscure when they are not: but also that the critic's poetry appears obscure when it ought not to do so. As this would again describe a fault, it is doubtful that *nier* refers to the *trobar clus*.[1] *Mot borrel* may, however, be linked with the 'bruns motz' of Raimbaut's *clus* song 'Cars douz', which would seem to indicate that 'Sobre.l vieill trobar', as its difficulty suggests, belongs to the *clus* tradition, and that therefore the *trobar clus* may be linked with the highest style of Rhetoric. This is I believe borne out by Peire's *clus* song 'Be m'es plazen';[2] however, at this point Peire is much more concerned to discuss style in the Rhetorical context of stylistic levels, than to define or describe the *trobar clus*.

Vers entiers in this song means therefore 'songs in which the (high) level of style is faultlessly maintained', and its opposite indicates works in which too high a style has been attempted, resulting in laboriousness and obscurity. It is an aesthetic and not a moral ideal.

Bernart Marti's attack on Peire's concept of *vers entiers* is most probably a direct response to this work. Blaming Peire for his 'fols vanars', Bernart declares he has no intention of composing a *vers entiers*: at least, not in the sense in which Peire uses the term; but his song will not be *frag* or broken either.

> D'entier vers far ieu non pes
> Ni ges de frag non faria;
> E si fatz vers tota via,
> En l'an un o dos o tres;
> Et on plus sion asses,
> Entier ni frag no so mia.[3]　　　　　(1–6)

I am not thinking of composing a 'whole' song, nor yet will I compose a 'broken' one; and still I continually compose songs, one or two or

---

[1] Del Monte's suggestion that *nier* means 'gloomy' (p. 115) is not supported by my interpretation, for the subject of joy and courtly attitudes does not appear until stanza VI. The main part of the song is solely concerned with stylistic technique.

[2] (VIII); see p. 77.　　　　　　　　　　　　　　　[3] Ed. Hoepffner, V.

three a year; and even if they were many more they are certainly not 'whole' or 'broken'.

Peire entirely misuses the word, for

> Aisso non creyrey ieu ges
> Que lunh(s) vers de leujairia,
> Don creys peccatz e follia,
> Per dreg nom entier agues. (7–10)

Thus I certainly will never believe that some frivolous composition or other that gives rise to sin and folly should rightly be called 'whole'.

A song which is beautifully bound up, 'melhs entrebesques' (16), but based on vanity, 'Qu'om de vanetat fezes' (17), is neither *entier* nor *frag* (18), but sheer nonsense based on falsehood:

> Foudat fai e nescies
> Qui vers fai de truandia.
> Pessa qu'entiers ni fragz sia?
> Que chanso ni sirventes
> Ni stribot ni arlotes
> Non es, mas quan lichairia. (19–24)

He who composes a *vers* of lies commits folly and ignorance. Does he think it can be 'whole' or 'broken'? For it is not a *chanso* or a *sirventes* or an *estribot* or an *arlotes*, but nothing but futility.

Someone who speaks in frivolities loses his personal integrity (25–30); Marti points to Peire's lack of integrity in his own life, when he promised himself to God as a canon but 'pueys si fraysses' when he changed his mind and became a 'fols joglares' and spoiled his 'entier pretz' (31–6). Such a song as Peire's is displeasing to God for it confuses good and evil in its inflated arrogance (*ufanaria*) (37–42), and telling lies in one's profession is evil, despicable, and churlish (43–8). *Fols vanars, grans laus, fols mentirs*, and being *ufanes*, 'puffed up', in one's speech, are Peire's crimes (49–54), 'E selh no par ges cortes / Qui.s lauza ni.s glorifia' (55–6). Peire has overstepped *mezura*:

> Pro sap e ben es apres
> Qui so fay que ben estia,
> Et es mager cortezia
> Que sos laus es pels paës
> Per autruy que per el mes,
> Qu'ab [al?] pobol par vilania. (67–72)

One who does what is seemly knows what is right and is well educated, and it is greater courtliness for one's praise to be spread abroad by someone other than oneself, for self-praise seems loutish even to the common people.

In other words, *vers* which are truly *entiers* are not only perfect from an artistic point of view: they depend on the good character and courtly qualities of the poet, and the truth of the poem. Peire has turned his work into a lie because it is a lie to say he is better than anyone else.

E. Köhler[1] sees Bernart's reply in more philosophical terms than this: he interprets Bernart's words as meaning that the art of poetry requires moral truth in order to be beautiful, so the arrogant claim to be the best poet implies the hubris of the claim to have exclusive knowledge of the truth. He thinks Bernart is defending a Christian view of poetry and protesting against the growing autonomy of secular values.[2] But Peire was not concerned with a special view of truth: his discussion was, until the very end of his song, purely concerned with style. Peire's fault is having made his song a lie through his arrogant boasting. Bernart does not blame him for claiming some exclusive knowledge of moral truth, but simply for being untruthful.

However, 'Lo fuelhs e.l flors' (V) contains a different emphasis from that of 'Sobre.l vieill trobar'. Here a moral element *is* present in his stylistic ideal. He stresses the unity of courtly joy, wisdom, and eloquence—a unity which was present in the nightingale. Joy, inspired by the delights of nature, and in turn inspiring the poet to seek ever greater understanding and wisdom (stanza I), is essential to the poet:

> Quar ses gaug grans sabers ni purs
> ni gienhs ginhos
> non er aut elegutz;   (11–13)

For without joy, great and pure wisdom and subtle genius will not be highly esteemed.

It brings him *entendemens*, 'understanding' (7), and makes him want to be more and more *sabens*, 'wise and learned'[3] (8–10): essential qualities of the poet even if they are worthless without joy. *Sabers* and *joys* are inseparable, for the people 'cuy falh

---

[1] p. 25.   [2] pp. 25–6; cf. Köhler p. 140.
[3] A. H. Schutz, 'Some Provençal words indicative of knowledge', *S* xxxiii (1958), 508–14, says *sabers* usually refers to a higher kind of wisdom than simple good judgement (*sens*), while *sciensa* denotes scientific knowledge of demonstrable nature.

sciens' e patz' (18) are also the ones who lack joy (19–20),[1] and the 'digz durs / d'omes iros' Peire combats with 'senatz sens' (27). Love makes him 'sapiens / . . . e mai melhuratz / d'autres sinc cens / d'amor enamoratz' (57–60), 'wise . . . and more improved than five hundred others enamoured of love'. This wisdom acquired through the joy of love ranks him greatest among all the 'esciens / de trobar ses fenhs fatz' (67–8), those 'expert in composing without foolish presumptions'.

While the wisdom acquired through the joy of love makes him one of the greatest poets, eloquence is equally important. This demands firstly *gienhs ginhos*, 'subtle creative ability',[2] the *ingenium* of Rhetoric.[3] Secondly, in the vocation, to which *bon'amor* (30) has called him, and in which it has granted him the ability to compose celebrated music and poetry, the poet must constantly improve himself:

> E sembla.m ben els ditz escurs
> et en razos
> de dir ses motz romputz;
> de que cove que mot mellurs
> tu, cuy det sos
> e motz far mentaugutz;
> que.l mai manens
> d'autruy part pert viatz
> bos covinens,
> pus no.y ren dels dos gratz.   (31–40)

And it seems good to me to speak without broken expressions in one's dark words and in one's themes; therefore it is fitting that you should greatly improve, you to whom (love) granted that you should compose melodies and verses of renown; for the richest man soon loses goodwill on another's part if he gives him no thanks for the gifts.

The improvement is both moral and poetic. In the second sense, the poet knows he must constantly practise his art if he is not to lose his natural talent. In Rhetoric it is a *topos* that the successful

---

[1] Del Monte, vv. 19–20; *envj encens / sobre.ls enamoratz:* 'desidero incenso sopra gl'innamorati'. E. Vuolo, *SM*, vol. 4, no. 2 (1963), pp. 614 ff., emends to *e.n vj en cens*, 'e ne vidi (ho visto) a centinaia fra gl'innamorati', i.e. 'di persone cui mancano sapienza (scienza) e pazienza'.

[2] Cf. p. 25.

[3] Lausberg, § 1152: 'Das *ingenium* (Quint. 10, 2, 12; 10, 1, 130) . . . ist die natürliche Begabung, die weder durch *imitatio* noch durch *ars* zu ersetzen ist (Quint. 10, 2, 12).'

speaker needs to train his *ingenium* by *exercitio*, guided by *iudicium* or good judgement, in order to achieve *scientia* or full knowledge of his art.[1] Peire's detractors lack *sciensa* (18) but Peire claims himself to be among the *esciens* of poetic composition (67), his *gienhs ginhos* being developed by constant self-improvement guided by *senatz sens* (27). Peire seems to have transposed Rhetorical ideas to a courtly environment.

Two key phrases concerning his style are *motz romputz* and *ditz escurs:* 'E sembla.m ben els ditz escurs / et en razos / de dir ses motz romputz' (31–3). Zenker thought *motz romputz* were words whose endings were deliberately changed for the sake of rhyme: 'ihre Endung ist ihnen gleichsam "abgebrochen" und durch eine andere ersetzt.'[2] Coulet followed this but emended *ses* to *sos*,[3] thinking that Peire meant that Love prefers a poet to use *motz romputz* in the *ditz* and *razos* of the *trobar clus*. Del Monte translates *ses motz romputz* as 'senza argomenti spezzettati', considering that Peire either means that the poet should be coherent and single-minded in his way of life, or uses *romputz* in the same sense as *frag* in Marcabru and Bernart Marti and means 'imperfect'.[4]

In 'Sobre.l vieill trobar' Peire said that the foolish poet 'broke his path', because he tried to sing in a higher style than his capabilities would permit, and produced meaningless obscurity rather than well-bound-up expressions. *Motz romputz* are probably the result of the same fault.

Quintilian discusses a similar fault: he says that phrases need to be carefully bound together to avoid interrupting the flow of sense: 'clausula cum praecedentibus cohaereat: quamlibet sit enim composita ipsa, gratiam perdet, si ad eam *rupta via* venerimus.'[5] The faulty linking of phrases in Rhetoric leads to a style that is disconnected (*dissolutus*), loose (*diffluens*), or fluctuating (*fluctuans*), and produces *dubium in sentencia* or the lack of *plenum*

[1] Isidore, *Etymologia*, II. iii. 2, *PL* lxxxii. 125, mentions three things needed for eloquence: 'Ipsa autem peritia dicendi in tribus rebus consistit, natura, doctrina, usu; natura, ingenio; doctrina, scientia; usus, assiduitate. Haec sunt enim quae non solum in oratore, sed in unoquoque homine artifice spectantur ut aliquid efficiat.' Cf. *Las Rasos de trobar*, ed. E. Stengel, p. 85 MS. *C* 39–42: '... et esgar los bos trobadors qom las han dichas qar null. gran saber non pot hom auer sas grant us si tot sap l'art.' Cf. also G. of Vinsauf, *Poetria*, 213–17, Faral, p. 203.

[2] p. 178.

[3] *AdM* xiv (1902) 379, followed by Köhler, p. 142.

[4] *Peire*, p. 56.

[5] IX. iv. 63; see Lausberg, § 1004.

intellectum et integrum.[1] In particular, the excessive use of ornament (*mala affectatio*) can lead to *corrupta oratio*.[2] Again it appears that Peire is expressing his own version of Rhetorical faults of style.

In Rhetoric *coniunctiones* or *coniuncta verba*, the means by which the style is correctly and elegantly bound up, can refer to the correct grammatical agreement between words,[3] or to the elegant linking of individual words and phrases.[4] Defective phrasing could result from poor rhythm or an inappropriate use of figures such as mixed metaphors or obscure or far-fetched images, or excessive conciseness. This theory may help us to understand what Peire means when he says one ought to speak without broken phrases 'els ditz escurs / et en razos'. Peire wants to bind up both words, *ditz*, and meaning, *razos*: he wants his expressions to be elegant and correct, and he also wants his meaning to be coherent. *Ditz escurs* are certainly not *obscure* expressions: not only is obscurity contrary to the idea of binding up words and meaning properly, and the fault which Peire condemned in 'Sobre.l vieill trobar', but there is no obviously intentional obscurity in the song. By analogy with Peire's discussion of the highest style in 'Sobre.l vieill trobar', *ditz escurs* are probably expressions which are dark with meaning or *colors* rather than obscure. Giraut de Bornelh says that his poetry is 'teeming with wisdom' as he makes it dark as ebony: 'c'aixi l'escur e.l n'ebejn, / mon trobar ab saber prejn.'[5]

In practice Peire has not taken the use of *colors* as far as Marcabru did in the *gap*: he does not bind together distinct layers of meaning. He does, however, suggest a double theme both explicitly and by the use of certain 'coloured' words. The theme is both literary and moral; these two aspects are visible separately, stanzas I–III mainly concerning the moral qualities of *joys* and *sabers*, stanza IV treating poetic vocation, stanzas V–VI again moral improvement, stanza VII the poet's resulting literary perfection. At the same time certain phrases suggest both moral

---

[1] See Quadlbauer, p. 51: 'sine firma ligatura et coniunctionibus . . . fluctuans: dubium in sentencia' (MS. Med. Laur. Plut. 90. sup. 87, 13th-century, fol. 43); p. 87: 'Hic versus non habet plenum intellectum et integrum' is said of the vice of failing to link phrases properly (MS. Med. Laur. Strozzi 38, 12th-century).

[2] Quintilian, VIII. iii. 56–7.

[3] Quadlbauer, pp. 49–50; Charisius defines a solecism as 'non conveniens rationi sermonis verborum iunctura'.

[4] Quintilian, IX. iv. 63, quoted on p. 71.

[5] 'Ans que venia', 55–6; see p. 119.

and literary qualities:[1] in stanza II *grans sabers ni purs* (11) suggests knowledge of both love and poetry. The *digz durs | d'omes iros* (24–5) are the slanderous remarks of the detractors, but also suggest the harsh style of certain moralizing poetry such as Marcabru's form of *trobar braus*.[2] In stanza V, where Peire describes his efforts to be *amoros* and *ben volgutz*, he says:

> quar si trop tens
> mi fes fals' amistatz
> ia.m sent tenens,
> de fina afinatz;   (47–50)

for if false friendship would make me too quarrelsome, I now feel secure, purified by pure friendship.

Again the moral effect of love is the dominant theme, but Peire also imples that his poetry is now refined and avoids polemic or criticism. As one of the 'esciens | de trobar ses fenhs fatz' (67–8) Peire knows how to avoid 'foolish presumptions' either in love or poetic style. *Romputz* can mean 'morally corrupt' as well as 'broken',[3] and Peire may imply that the poet should compose without morally as well as stylistically corrupt words. He does not bind together distinct layers of meaning through consistently used ambivalence, as Marcabru did in the *gap*; but he does imply the overlapping of poetic and moral values. In this light *escur* may refer to the 'wisdom' of depth of thought which his words contain. It may, however, simply imply the richness of technical artistry.[4]

In this poem, therefore, Peire's poetic ideal combines both aesthetic and moral elements which indicate that in this case Köhler and Del Monte are right to see 'wholeness' as the unity of formal and moral perfection (whether or not there is any influence of scholastic aesthetics).[5] This poem marks a change

---

[1] Rhetorical authors tended to link stylistic faults with moral vices (both called *vitia*): see Quadlbauer, §§ 25q, 43d, 56s, 72k, 78,8.

[2] See pp. 52–4.   [3] *SWB* vii. 376 ff., 8): 'gebrechlich, hinfällig'.

[4] This song is one of Peire's most elegant and polished. The versification is unique (see p. 222); rhymes are linked in sibilants but varied in vowel sounds: *urs, os, utz, ens, atz*, the rhythm varied through long and short lines; the sounds are bound together by rich alliteration: 'Lo *f*uel*hs* e.l *f*lor*s* e.l *f*rug*z* ma*d*ur*s* (1) *m'es* ioy*s* e gaug*z* m'a*d*utz (3), *per p*las e *p*er murs (4), mi *v*en e *v*oluntatz (8), de *m*ais en *m*ielhs (10)'; see M. Scholz, 'Die Alliteration in der altprovenzalischen Lyrik', *ZRP* xxxvii (1913), 385–426, and Zenker, pp. 70–1, who note alliteration as one of Peire's most frequent devices.

[5] I am inclined to think that this came about less through the influence of

from 'Sobre.l vieill trobar', a change which it is tempting to see as an important development in Peire's own thoughts on poetry,[1] and one perhaps brought on by Bernart Marti's attack on his integrity as the best courtly poet. It seems that Peire may be reinforcing an already aristocratic concept of poetry by justifying it in terms of the highest courtly values. All this is to say that the unity of formal and moral elements is an embellishment, rather than a necessity as it was for Marcabru. *Sabers* for Peire lends dignity to the poet and to his concept of a high poetic style; but he appears to have taken over this idea as a means of self-justification, rather than of probing into truth and falsehood as Marcabru had done. For Marcabru, eloquence was untrustworthy and consistently subordinated to moral truths. In Peire's work, eloquence is not only made respectable and harmonized with courtly ideals—the courtly poet is eloquent as well as courtly— but it can be seen virtually as an independent goal in itself, as in 'Sobre.l vieill trobar'. This emphasis on the aesthetic rather than the moral can be seen in Peire's development of the *trobar braus*.

3. 'Trobar braus'

For Marcabru, a rough style was a means of expressing moods of conflict and discord, and of rejecting the glib eloquence of the *lengua-plana*. It arose not from the demands of a genre but from the poet's attitude of mind. Peire attaches this style to the genre of blame: a genre which he tackles as a craftsman rather than a moralist. The best example of his rough style is the song 'Belh m'es qu'ieu fass' huey mays un vers' (XV). To be sure, the content is moral; but moral themes are merely a pretext. Eloquence is all. He seeks the maximum effect of shock and discord: through grating sounds,

> S'als malvatz no fos tan grans guaucx,
> avoleza ia no fora,
> et es tant adubertz lo traucx
> que sobre rocas laora,
> selh cuy iais cors, e martelha;
> qu'ayssi.ls ten enredatz lo retz

scholastic aesthetics than through the literary needs of courtly society which was looking for the highest expression of its social, moral, and aesthetic values.

[1] No chronological indications are available.

> non lur pot escantir lo setz
> ni.l crims: tan los rasc' iselha!;[1]   (25–32)

monosyllables,

> Hai! pretz, quon iest mutz, sortz e guers,   (9)
> e.l belh temps nos a del lag ters;   (3)

the accumulation of vituperative adjectives:

> Aquist engres, envers, estrait
> fals e flac filh d'avols paires,
> felo, embronc, sebenc, mal fait,
> sers ressis, nat d'avols maires . . .[2]   (33–6)

images suggesting harsh sounds: 'so que dedins mi gragelha' (8), 'what is grumbling within me', 'et ieu suy del castiar raucx' (19), 'and I am hoarse from reprimanding'. These are combined with images of distortion and disease:

> Hai! pretz, quon iest mutz, sortz e guers,
> e, proeza, co.us vey rota
> e menar de tort en travers,[3]   (9–11)
> tan lo rasc' iselha!   (32)
> don nays e bruelha.l   pustelha,   (40)

vice and ugliness (stanzas V–VI), and violence:

> q'una puta gens fradelha,
> que tir' e bat e pren a mors,
> vos an confondut e destors.[4]   (13–15)

What for Marcabru was a way of conveying moral conviction has become for Peire the means of displaying his *fin trobar*, for which the genre of blame offers a pretext and specific stylistic possibilities. His predominant interest in eloquence is confirmed by the conclusion, which is not a moral peroration but a boast and explanation of his stylistic skill:

> Peire d'Alvernha mot quera
> qi acomtos us' a concas:

---

[1] 'And if it were not such great delight to the wicked, vileness would never exist, and the chasm is so gaping that the man towards whom joy hastens labours and hammers upon rocks; for the net holds them so enmeshed, their thirst and their crime cannot be extinguished: they are so eaten up by scurvy!'

[2] 'These obstinate, perverse, rigid, false and flaccid sons of vile fathers, treacherous, sullen, despicable, deformed, feeble slaves, born of vile mothers . . .'

[3] 'Ah, reputation! how dumb, deaf and squinting you are; and prowess, how I see you broken and wandering crookedly and twistedly.'

[4] 'for a wanton, unscrupulous people, that tears and beats and puts to death, has confounded and destroyed you.'

e per aqui hom lo sabra,
car del fin trobar non roncas,
ans n'as ben la flor plus belha:
detorz e l'art e l'aparelh,
e no.i a motz fals que rovelh
ni sobredolat d'astelha.

On plus hom mos vers favelha,
fe que.us deg, on mais valon elh
e no.y a motz fals que y rovelh
ni sobredolat d'astelha.   (57–68)

Peire d'Alvernhe will seek a form of expression which uses ornaments
by the bushel-load, and by this (work) it will be made known: for you
are not snoring in vain expectation of fine poetry, but have indeed its
fairest flower: I deploy both the art and the tool, and in this (work)
there is no false word which rusts nor excessive planing away of
splinters. The more one performs my songs, by my faith, the more they
are worth, and there is no false word in them which rusts, nor excessive planing away of splinters.[1]

Peire seeks the maximum level of stylistic ornamentation in a
song which, he claims, is an example of the finest flower of *fin
trobar*, in which he combines theoretical mastery of his art (*l'art*)
and practical craftsmanship (*l'aparelh*). He makes no suggestion
that this style belongs to an inferior genre or is of a lower level
than the style of 'Sobre.l vieill trobar', even though the subject
of blame might be considered inferior to the subject of love and
joys.[2] The style here differs from the style of 'Sobre.l vieill trobar'
and 'Lo fuelhs' chiefly in texture: it is deliberately rough, it is
not planed too smoothly.[3]

[1] Del Monte emends v. 58 to 'qui acoint es*qui*us a concas': 'che faccia conoscere a
conche intere i villani'. For his reasons and previous suggestions, see *Peire*, p. 157. The
MSS. read: *z* qi acomtos us aconcas, *m* qia uns adoncas. The reading of *z* stands if we
take *us* as a verb whose subject is *mot* (57), and *acomtos* as a noun object derived from
the Latin *como*: L & S 385 = 1. *como* II trop. 'to deck, adorn . . . Esp. freq. of rhet.
ornament: non quia comi expolirique non debeat (oratio), Quint. 8, 3, 42; cf.:
linguae orationisque comendae gratia, Gell. 1, 9, 10.—Hence, *comptus* (*-mtus*), a,
um, . . . usu. of discourse, *embellished, elegant*: compta et mitis oratio, Cic. Sen. 9. 28
. . .' Cf. *PD* 5: *acomtir* v. refl. 's'orner, se parer', *SWB* 14: *acomtan* 'beredt': *achomp-
tans* eloquens, *Don. prov.* 42b, 22.

[2] The courtly man concentrates on joy, not criticism: cf. 'Sobre.l vieill trobar',
31–6; V. 14–30.

[3] Pollmann, '*Trobar clus*', p. 32, sees this poem as 'ein "trobar clus" vom Urtypus,
wenn man so sagen darf, ein "casteis" . . .' His theory of the existence of a genre
called 'casteis' in which a troubadour would covertly criticize society (pp. 8–22
and *N* xlvii (1963), 24–34), has been refuted by Mölk, pp. 45–9 and Topsfield,
NMi, vol. lxix, no. 2 (1968), 280–302. This song in any case bears no resemblance
to 'Be m'es plazen' which we know to be *clus*.

4. 'Trobar clus'

Peire is among the first troubadours, as far as we know, to have
used the term *clus*. He does so in the song 'Be m'es plazen' (VIII),
of which Del Monte's text is here reproduced.

I   Be m'es plazen
      e cossezen
    que om s'ayzina de chantar
     ab motz alqus
     serratz e clus   5
    qu'om no.ls tem ja de vergonhar.

II   D'aut chai em bas
      qui per compas
    no sap lo segle demenar;
     e ben hi falh   10
     qui tan trassalh
    que non hi puesc' a temps tornar.

III   Ben es auras
      totz crestias
    que ia nems si vol encombrar, 15
     ni sobre.l cays
     leva tal fays
    que corren no.l puesca portar.

IV   Qu'ieu sai e sen
      mon escien,   20
    e vuelh vos en tot castiar,
     per trop captens
     val hom mot mens
    e ten hom plus vil son afar.

V   Mais am un ort   25
      serrat e fort
    qu'hom ren no m'en puesca emblar
     que cent parras
     sus en puegz plas[1]
    qu'autre las tenh' ez ieu las guar. 30

VI   Quel reprochiers
      es vertadiers

[1] Del Monte has a colon after *plas*; see my translation.

que dels antics auzi comtar:
 lo ric al ric,
 e l'om mendic . . . :
quecx d'eis semblan troba son par.   35

VII   De tot can suelh
  amar, me tuelh
e so qu'ei amat desampar,
  qu'ieu non am re   40
  ni autre me
e cug me totz d'amor lonhar.

VIII   Qu'arreire temps
  ai amat nemps
e vuelh m'en atrazach layssar;   45
  non aura grat
  qui m'a amat
ni en cor m'avia d'amar.

IX   Qu'ieu ai un cor
  et un demor   50
et un talan et un pessar
  et un amic
  vas cui m'abric
et a cuy me vuelh autreyar.

X   Si mal m'en pren   55
  per eys mon sen,
cug a ma vida follejar;
  apres ma mort
  no.m fass' om tort
d'aquo qu'ieu ai ad oblidar.   60

XI   Daus manhtas pars
  me for' afars
en prendre o en gazanhar;
  fers e parvenz
  es mos talenz   65
vas m'amiga qu'eu tenc plus car.

XII   . . . .
   . . . .
  . . . .

amors de lonh,   70
tan gran besonh
qu'ai de tener e de balhar.

I. To me it is well pleasing and fitting that one should undertake to sing with certain locked and closed phrases, provided that one never fears lest one may dishonour them.

II. From high to low falls the man who does not know how to lead his life in moderation; and he certainly fails in this if he leaps forward so far that he cannot turn back in time.

III. Any Christian is surely mad if he wishes to overburden himself, or raises up such a load on his face that he cannot carry it while running.

IV. For I know and realize for certain and wish to advise you in all this: through undertaking too much a man is worth much less, and his conduct is considered more base.

V. I prefer a locked, strong garden, from which nothing can be stolen from me, to a hundred parcels of land high up on the open plain, where another might own them and I only look at them.

VI. For the proverb is true which I have heard told by the ancients: rich to the rich, and the man goes begging . . . : each man finds his equal among those of his like.

VII. I abandon all that I usually love, and all that I have loved I renounce; for I love no creature, nor does any love me, and I intend to separate myself entirely from love.

VIII. For in former times I have loved too much and I wish to renounce this forthwith; one who has loved me will receive no thanks, nor one who had it in mind to love me.

IX. For I have one heart and one dwelling and one desire and one thought, and one friend in whom I shelter and to whom I wish to promise myself.

X. If I am harmed through this judgement of mine I think I shall be mad my whole life; after my death let no one blame me for what I have to forget.

XI. From many sides I would be in a position to take or gain; fierce and visibly apparent is my desire for my beloved whom I more highly cherish.

XII. . . . distant love, which I have such great need to hold and give.

Zenker interpreted the poem as a farewell to the world before the poet enters a monastery,[1] Scheludko as a *de contemptu mundi*.[2] Köhler saw it as a spiritual withdrawal into a private world as Peire begins to turn away from courtly ethics to Christian ones.[3] Del Monte, whose text adds stanzas VI, VII, XI, XII to Zenker's,

---

[1] *Peire*, p. 211.   [2] *NMi* xxxviii (1937), 235.   [3] pp. 139–40.

sees the song as the abandonment of empirical loves and the surrender to his own spiritual solitude, to love for love's sake.[1]

The main problems of interpretation are these. What is the meaning of stanza I, especially of *motz . . . | serratz e clus* and the last line, 'qu'om no.ls tem ja de vergonhar'? Stanzas II–IV mean, in general terms, that pride must come before a fall and that one should not take on more than one can manage, but in what sense? What is the poet's *ort | serrat e fort* (26)? What kind of love is he abandoning in stanza VII? What is his new love: his *amic* (52), his *amiga* (66), his *amors de lonh* (70)? Is Peire deliberately esoteric, refusing to reveal his true meaning? Has he one meaning, or does he intend to suggest several equally valid ones, as the anonymous Provençal poet who says:

> Quar s'a trop sens una razos,
> Mout m'es meiller quan quecx es bos?[2]

Stanza I is the key to Peire's poetic method. Poets should undertake to sing with *motz . . . | serratz e clus*, expressions which are tightly packed and closely bound up, in other words in the way in which Peire boasts he composes in 'Sobre.l vieill trobar' and 'Lo fuelhs e.l flors': without 'breaking his path', without *motz romputz*. But poets should undertake this only provided 'qu'om no.ls tem ja de vergonhar' (6). Del Monte translates this line as 'sicchè non si esiti già a rispettarle'; Zenker, reading *que om tem ja de vergonhar*,[3] as 'die man zu verunstalten sich scheut': he thinks that Peire wants to write so artfully and with such dark and difficult words that the *joglars* will have to learn his songs by heart word for word and it will not be possible for them to reproduce them inexactly.[4] I see *om* in vv. 3 and 6 as the same person, that is, the poet who uses *motz . . . serratz e clus*: this poet should sing with such expressions only if he is not afraid of spoiling or shaming them.[5] Peire is once more referring to the vice of the highest poetic style: of failing to bind up expressions properly and becoming turgid or obscure.

Stanzas II–IV can be taken as an extension of this technical

---

[1] *Peire*, pp. 83–4.   [2] See p. 24.
[3] MSS.: *a*[1] com nols tengua de ver digar / *C* quom t. / *m* . . . nols tem ia de vergoin . . .
[4] *Peire*, pp. 119, 168, 210, followed by H. S. Chaytor, *From Script to Print*, p. 68. Mölk, pp. 104–6, combines the interpretations of Zenker and Del Monte, concluding that Peire finds in the *trobar clus* an esoteric style suited to his personal *amor de lonh*.
[5] *vergonhar*: *PD* 381: 'couvrir de honte, déshonorer, honnir; gâter, abîmer; avoir honte de; respecter; *v. refl.* avoir honte.'

introduction. The poet who presumes too far, who attempts a style beyond his capacities, will fall down in the attempt and show himself to be a fool, just as Peire says in 'Sobre.l vieill trobar':

> quar qui trassaill   de Maurin en miron
> entre.l mieg faill   si no.s pren als ladriers.[1]

In these stanzas, expressed in vague and general terms, other senses are possible also: a poet should not aspire to love too great a lady if he is unworthy; or a Christian should not excessively burden himself with worldly preoccupations; or a lover should not pay court to a large number of ladies.

Stanza V is clearly based on Marcabru's images in his *gap* of the same versification:

> Mos alos es
> en tal deves
> res mas ieu non s'en pot jauzir:
> aissi l'ai claus
> de pens venaus
> que nuills no lo.m pot envazir.[2]

Marcabru's image had two senses: the literary and the erotic. Peire's image also has a literary sense: by repetition of the word *serrat*, he links this stanza with the first one, thereby suggesting that his 'ort / serrat e fort' is his poetry, perfectly bound up so that no one 'can steal anything from it'. Marcabru expressed a similar stylistic ideal when he said that he knew how to bind up his theme and compose the *vers* 'si que autr' om no l'en pot un mot traire'.[3] Peire has said that he likes poets to compose well-bound-up poetry in the best style if they are capable of it, but not to attempt it if they are not; he himself prefers such poetry, which is strong and tightly locked so that each word is necessary to the whole, to 'a hundred parcels of land up on the open plain' which another might own. In other words, he prefers poetry in the highest style to what is common to all: in the words of Raimbaut d'Aurenga, 'So que es a toz comunal'.[4] The word *plas* in v. 29, as also perhaps *vil* in v. 24, remind one of Raimbaut's contempt for the common style or for a 'rima vil' e plana',[5] while Peire's following stanza, where he says that each man (or poet) finds his own level, suggests a specific allusion to the high

---

[1] See p. 60.   [2] pp. 21 ff.   [3] 'Aujatz de chan', v. 4; see p. 12.
[4] See p. 146.   [5] See p. 170.

style: 'lo *ric* al ric'.[1] Hence it appears most probable that Peire is here taking part in the controversy, waged principally by his contemporaries Raimbaut d'Aurenga and Giraut de Bornelh, over *trobar clus* and *trobar leu;* he prefers the *trobar clus*, which is the highest and most demanding style, to the style which is common to all, although lesser poets should not venture to try it.

Through 'coloured' words, however, he suggests other possible meanings through this image of 'un ort / serrat e fort': that he prefers the secret love of one special lady to a hundred open favours of other ladies; or that he prefers a special kind of love to the ordinary: either 'love for love's sake', as Del Monte proposes, or perhaps a Christian love.

The 'love' which he abandons in stanza VII contains similar 'colours': he may mean that he abandons all ladies except for one special one; or that he renounces all love of real ladies in favour of a spiritual one. On a literary level, *amor* here may mean popularity: he renounces the love of public praise and will not be grateful for it.[2]

Now Peire has one *amic* who shelters him; he chooses one *amiga* and rejects all other possibilities open to him; and he longs for an *amor de lonh*. These are intentionally inexplicit. *Un amic* could perhaps be a lady (cf. *midons*); it could conceivably be Christ; it could be the poet himself: from now on he will rely only on his own spiritual resources; it could also be another troubadour[3] to whom alone Peire now entrusts his poetry, now that he scorns popular approval. His *amiga* or beloved could be seen as a lady, as the Virgin, as love in the abstract, or as his poetry, and again *amors de lonh* can suggest various possibilities of rare, valuable love or poetry.

This song is an example of the use of *ditz escurs*: not obscure, but tightly-bound-up words and meanings, composed only by the best poets. Implicit in this poem is the idea that the poet of the most precious style is capable of the most precious love. Although Peire was clearly influenced by Marcabru's *gap*, his themes and treatment of them differ from his. Marcabru's erotic satire has been replaced by the theme of *amor de lonh*, and the literary theme in Marcabru's poem, concerning his dialectical

---

[1] See p. 180 ff.
[2] Cf. Raimbaut d'Aurenga in the *tenso* with Giraut, 15–21 (p. 146).
[3] Raimbaut d'Aurenga?

method and use of 'colours' in argument to baffle an opponent, has given way to the expression of a purely poetic method. While Marcabru bound together distinct layers of meaning through words having different figurative senses, Peire's themes are less distinctly separable: they are suggested not by the ambivalence of individual words but by the openness and vagueness of expressions. Whereas Marcabru used layers of meaning to sharpen the thoughts, Peire uses them to create a mood of almost mystical rarity. Moreover, Peire has moved far away from Marcabru's usual concern to clarify difficult thoughts; he has chosen an aristocratic concept of poetry for a small élite: perhaps even solely for himself.

Such a choice is only temporary, however, for in 'L'airs clars' (VI) we find Peire singing a *vers non-clus.*

> L'airs clars e.l chans dels auzelhs
> la flors fresc' e.l fuelha
> que s'espan per los brondelhs
> — e.l vertz herba bruelha —
> mi mostra d'esser ysnelhs
> q'un vers non-clus cuelha,
> tal que.l sos sia novelhs,
> que.l chant qui ia.s vuelha;
> per qu'ara chanten cavallier,
> que chans aporta alegrier,
> e pert de son segle lo mays
> qui seguon sazo non es guays.   (VI. 1–12)

The clear air and the song of the birds, the fresh flower and the leaf which unfurls on the twigs—and the green grass sprouts—indicates to me that I should be swift to gather up a non-closed song, so that its melody should be new, and that whoever so wishes may sing it; for knights are singing, as song brings mirth, and he who is not gay according to the season loses the best part of his life.

Non-clus here must refer to meaning rather than form, since the binding up of form is as elegant, polished, and ornate as it is in 'Lo fuelhs e.l flors': again the rhyme scheme is unique,[1] rhymes chosen for musical balance, patterns, and contrast, with masculine and feminine rhymes alternating in the *pedes*, sometimes linked closely in sound (stanza I *elhs, uelha;* III *ens, ensa;* IV *a, erma*), sometimes contrasted (stanza II *iers, eza;* V *au, eya*). Peire does not use words in this song to suggest different meanings, and this

---

[1] Frank, 253, 1 (see p. 222).

may be the reason for calling it *non-clus*. But the term *non-clus* probably tells us less of the nature of the *trobar clus* than that Peire is now finding it necessary, as a result of public pressure, to reassure his audience that they will be able to understand and enjoy his song. By about 1170[1] he is joking about his incomprehensibility, claiming to be master of the troubadours, 'ab c'un pauc esclarzis sos motz / c'a penas nuils hom los enten' (XII. 83–4).[2] Once *clus* has become a controversial term, it may be a general one to cover any poetry, whether esoteric or not, that some people find hard to follow.

In conclusion, we can say that for Peire *clus* poetry is composition in the highest form of *eloquentia*, and for it to be perfect or *entier* the words and meanings must be perfectly bound together without any *motz romputz* in either themes (*razos*) or richly coloured expressions (*ditz escurs*). Such a concept of poetry can be found in Marcabru,[3] although he avoids using this to set himself above other poets in eloquence, as Peire does.

In the song 'Be m'es plazen' and in his *vers non-clus*, Peire clearly plays a part in the troubadours' controversy over *trobar clus* and *trobar leu*. But he never actually refers to these as such, as specifically formulated styles, probably because they have yet to be so formulated by Giraut de Bornelh and Raimbaut d'Aurenga. What is striking in Peire's *clus* and *non-clus* poetry is the fluidity of his technique: three songs in which Peire calls attention to his command of the highest style vary in their degree of difficulty, for 'Sobre.l vieill trobar' makes fairly clear sense once its context is understood, which it would have been by those interested in matters of eloquence; 'Lo fuelhs e.l flors' is quite clear, even if double meanings are sometimes suggested; while 'Be m'es plazen' deliberately leaves itself open to many different

---

[1] See *Peire*, p. 129.

[2] Köhler, pp. 141–2, comments that Peire composes a *vers non-clus* for *cavalier* which puts them in a gay mood, essential for life at court, but says that true courtly *ioy* demands dark poetry. But this whole song concerns the nature of joy, alternatively *gaug* and *ioy* (vv. 21, 25, 33, 37, 49, 59). Pollmann's interpretation ('*Trobar clus*', pp. 32–3) is constrained to support the theory that the *trobar leu* expresses courtly, joyful, non-dualistic attitudes, and the *trobar clus* critical, dualistic ones. He stresses Peire's references to *joy* (8–12) in this song and he thinks this is why it was called *non-clus*. But he also perceives in it dualistic elements, concluding that the poem is not therefore a pure *vers non-clus*. Yet it is the first if not the only troubadour song to be so called!

[3] 'Aujatz de chan', 1–4; see p. 12.

interpretations and suggests a dark, mysterious mood. His *vers non-clus* corrects a tendency to become dark or even esoteric and to compose for his personal satisfaction, but in style it resembles 'Lo fuelhs e.l flors' or perhaps Peire's *braus* song 'Belh m'es' (XV), composed in the highest style without using different layers of meaning. Peire does not go nearly as far as Giraut de Bornelh in attempting a *non-clus* style; he avoids esoteric tendencies without seeking a positive simplicity.

5. Peire and Rhetoric

Peire's *trobar clus*, or his concept of *vers entiers*, is based, as we have seen, on medieval Rhetoric: a poet should not presume to compose in a style above his capabilities; if he does mistakenly try to achieve the high style he may fall into the vice of obscurity; he ought therefore to seek to 'please' with a lower style without darkly coloured words; a poet requires ability, discipline, and knowledge of both the theory and practice of his art; he should bind up his words and themes properly; and he himself can compose perfectly in the highest style, using ornaments 'by the bushel-load'. Peire, whom his biographer described as 'Savis hom . . . e ben letratz',[1] must have had a fairly detailed knowledge of Rhetoric.

The way in which he adapts this knowledge to his own style and concept of courtliness, and the particular details which are important to him, show that Rhetoric plays a different role in his poetry from the one it does in Marcabru's, even though many of Peire's ideas, such as the perfect binding up of words and themes, and the use of levels of meaning, can be traced to Marcabru. The latter distrusted eloquence and emphasized above all the importance of truth and clear thinking; Peire makes eloquence one of the main qualities of the courtly poet. Marcabru discusses Rhetoric in terms of argument and legal issues, of defining and persuading. Peire sees eloquence in terms of stylistic levels and aesthetic perfection. Marcabru's ideas accord with the Augustinian tradition of Rhetoric, where the truth of what one is saying is considered more important than the way it is said, and they seem to have been influenced also by debating techniques. This debating element is not noticeable in Peire's songs, and while he stresses the importance of *sabers*, this is used to give dignity to

[1] *Peire*, p. 12.

his poetry and unify stylistic and courtly ideals, and Peire is more interested in the techniques of eloquence itself than in a deeply felt moral purpose: an attitude which is present in the medieval arts of poetry and the Rhetorical tradition based on Horace.[1] Peire has no dualistic concept of eloquence as Marcabru had: he never suggests that it could be used for the wrong ends, and for him the bad poet is one who is technically poor or, secondarily, uncourtly. Marcabru draws on Rhetoric for argument, debate, definition, and persuasion; Peire, for the perfection of the highest style, its craft, and its aptness as the expression of courtly ideals.

6. Peire and Dante

Dante quotes none of Peire's songs, but mentions him as one of the 'antiquiores doctores'. One reason for his recognition of Peire's artistic worth may be that Peire combines a special knowledge of eloquence with courtly ideas of love and joy. Peire may also be the earliest troubadour whose style exemplifies those qualities which Dante praises in the De Vulgari Eloquentia.

From an artistic point of view, the most famous of Peire's works seems to have been the song 'Deiosta.ls breus iorns e.ls loncs sers' (VII). Its melody survives, and in the Vida the biographer declares that Peire 'trobet ben e cantet ben. e fo lo primiers bons trobaire que fon outra mon, et aquel que fez los meillors sons de vers que anc fosson faichs e.l vers que ditz: Dejosta.ls breus jorns e.ls loncs sers.'[2]

In a new way it combines a theme of wise and contemplative love with a deliberate mingling of rough and smooth sounds, a stately rhythm, and a rhetorically ornate but clear style, anticipating the style of some of the songs of Arnaut Daniel.[3]

Among the early troubadours a rough style mainly characterizes moralizing poetry: in Marcabru, Bernart Marti, Peire himself:[4] while love poetry usually has mainly smooth sounds: in Cercamon, Jaufré Rudel, the two songs of Marcabru's which

---

[1] For an account of the different Rhetorical traditions in the Middle Ages: the Augustinian, the Horatian, and the Virgilian, see Quadlbauer.

[2] Del Monte, Peire, p. 13. The reading may be 'que anc fosson faichs el vers', meaning that the song was famous because of its music; but sos is plural, which suggests that the biographer is praising Peire's melodies in general, and 'Deiosta' in particular as a complete composition, words and music.

[3] See pp. 202–5. Toja, Arnaut Daniel, pp. 7–11, dates Arnaut's career from about 1180.

[4] See pp. 52–4, 74–6 and Bernart Marti, II (especially 43–8).

most closely approach a courtly attitude,[1] and Peire's most conventionally courtly song of homage to a lady, 'Ab fina ioia
comenssa' (III). In 'Deiosta.ls breus iorns' Peire mixes the two:
rough or hard sounds: *b, br, cs, nc, tz* (stanza 1) give a slight
abrasiveness and richening of texture to harmoniously smooth
sounds, in the way that Dante advocates through the use of
vocabula pexa atque yrsuta,[2] and these rough sounds reflect in a
new way the poet's theme and mood, suggesting not blame and
discord but intellectual and moral effort.

> Deiosta.ls breus iorns e.ls loncs sers,
> qan la blanc' aura brunezis,
> vuoill que branc e bruoill mos sabers
> d'un nou ioi qe.m fruich' e.m floris;
> car del doutz fuoill vei clarzir los garrics,
> per qe.s retrai entre.ls enois e.ls freis
> lo rossignols e.l tortz e.l gais e.l pics.   (1-7)

At the time of the brief days and the long evenings, when the white
air darkens, I wish my knowledge to branch and sprout of a new joy
that ripens and blossoms for me; for I see the oaks grow lighter as the
sweet leaves fall away, and cause the nightingale and the thrush and
the jay and the woodpecker to retreat from the snows (vexations) and
the cold.[3]

The influence of Marcabru's 'Pois la fuoilla' is evident,[4] but
Peire has transferred Marcabru's vocabulary and moral imagery
to love poetry. The poet's mood of contemplation and inward
growth is also reflected in the rhythm of the long ten-syllable
line (vv. 5-7), which Dante praised as the best because of its
stateliness and capacity for holding thought,[5] and which appears
only this once in Peire's surviving songs.[6] 'Deiosta.ls breus iorns'
may mark the beginning of a new eloquence anticipating Dante
himself.

[1] Cercamon, I, II, III; see the remarks on II. 31: 'Plas es lo vers', on p. 54.
Cercamon's moralizing poems are also smooth-textured, as are all of Jaufré's
songs. Marcabru, in XXVIII and 'Cortesamen vuoill comensar', temporarily seems
to be arguing his ideas within a conventionally accepted framework of *cortezia*
rather than by standing outside society and criticizing it; these two songs are smooth-
textured. 'Cortesamen' is sent to Jaufré Rudel (v. 38).

[2] *DVE* II. vii. 2-4; see Bowra, pp. 459-74.

[3] In v. 6 the MSS. hesitate between neus CN^2R, enueis *EIK*, enuis *V*, nois *X*;
perhaps a pun is intended.

[4] See p. 36.   [5] *DVE* II. v. 3.

[6] 'Sobre.l vieill trobar' can be seen as having ten-syllable lines with internal
rhymes, or as Frank's version indicates:
    a b c d c e c e c d   8 8 4 6 4 6 4 6 4 6 (843, 1; see p. 222).

3

GIRAUT DE BORNELH, MASTER
OF THE TROUBADOURS[1]

PEIRE merely touched on the controversy over *trobar clus* and *trobar leu*: he never used the term *leu*, he composed one *vers non-clus*, and in his satire on the troubadours jokingly said that hardly anyone could understand him. Giraut de Bornelh is the focal poet of this controversy. In different songs he boasts of his ability to compose in the *trobar clus*, defends it against demands for a simpler style, yields to these demands, formulates the 'new' *trobar leu*, and defends this against supporters of the *clus* style. While Giraut does not 'invent' the *trobar leu*, since clear, light songs existed already in the songs of Cercamon, Peire, and Bernart de Ventadorn,[2] Giraut appears to be the first to formulate and defend it theoretically.

Different reasons have been advanced for Giraut's change from *clus* to *leu*. Vossler[3] thought that Giraut originally imitated Marcabru and Peire in the *trobar clus*. but discovered that this did not suit his temperament. J.-J. Salverda de Grave[4] did not accept that Giraut ever did finally change styles: 'En effet, rien ne nous autorise à admettre, pour Giraut, une conversion à la Moréas de la poésie hermétique à un art plus intelligible'; his reservations reflect the problem that in spite of Giraut's apparent switch in theory, it is often very hard to tell in practice which songs belong to which style. U. Mölk[5] recognizes a development in the troubadour's attitude to style, which is indeed apparent from the way in

---

[1] I use the edition of A. Kolsen and the corrections of Jeanroy, Bertoni, A. Stimming, Lewent, and J.-J. Salverda de Grave (see Bibliography). Kolsen (ii. 284–6) dates Giraut's career from 1165 to 1199.

[2] Bernart's career may not have begun much earlier than Giraut's; according to Delbouille, 'Les senhals littéraires désignant Raimbaut d'Orange et la chronologie de ces témoignages', *CN* xvii (1957), 49–73, Bernart's earliest datable song was composed in 1171, and his career probably began about 1160 (p. 72).

[3] Vossler, *Die göttliche Komödie*, ii, 439. He thought that Giraut only imitated his models superficially, in form rather than in mood or attitude of mind.

[4] *Observations*, p. 83. He quotes LXVIII. 1–13 as evidence that Giraut composed in both styles at once (see p. 95 in this chapter), but Giraut only says he intends to be clear rather than too dark or ornate; he does not mention two styles. [5] pp. 119 ff.

which Giraut praises certain of his songs for their *clus* style without mentioning any stylistic controversy,[1] defends the *trobar clus* in others against demands for a lighter style,[2] then in others defends *leu* against *clus*.[3] Whether Giraut's attitudes changed permanently or not is another question. Mölk reasonably considers that after composing early in his career in the manner of Linhaure' (XXIX. 55–6), Giraut was impelled, being dependent on patronage, to change his style to suit his audience.

A more complex problem is presented by the distinction in practice between *clus* and *leu*. As Salverda de Grave points out,[4] 'A quelques exceptions près, il nous est donc impossible de distinguer les poésies obscures des autres, et ce qui, pour nous, constitue l'obscurité des vers de Giraut, n'était donc pas toujours caractéristique du *trobar clus*.'[5] If Giraut changed from one style to another, why is it so difficult to tell them apart in his poems? Kolsen suggested that Giraut wanted above all to be clear, and that external influences caused him to compose certain songs in the dark style; later he tried to free himself from these influences, without complete success.[6] Salverda de Grave also thought that Giraut was unable to escape from his learned background, and that he regarded clear poetry as the result not of relaxed inspiration but of an effort even greater than that required to compose in the *trobar clus*.[7] Such an effort, he argues, depends on the poet's mood which must be serene and inspired by the lady's favour.[8] The relative clarity of a work would then depend partly on the degree to which he escapes from his learned background, partly on his mood. E. Köhler thinks the poet's mood is the important factor, though in a more complex way. He claims that Giraut's style becomes dark when his mood is complicated, and not

---

[1] III and XXVII; see pp. 117–31. [2] XXVI; see p. 93.
[3] IV, V, XXVIII, XL, XLVIII, LVIII, LXVIII. [4] *Observations*, p. 81.
[5] Cf. Scheludko, *Arch. Rom.* xv (1931), 143, who notices the same problem.
[6] A. Kolsen, *Guiraut von Bornelh, der Meister der Trobadors* (Berlin, 1894), p. 42.
[7] *Observations*, p. 86: 'Giraut se rendait compte que la poésie d'amour doit être autre chose que des artifices de mots, et pourtant il ne réussissait pas à se soustraire à son ambiance claustrale. L'idée de se laisser aller et de s'abandonner à son inspiration ne lui venait pas, la poésie étant, pour lui, par essence, un art ... et voilà pourquoi la "clarté" ne peut être pour lui que le résultat d'un effort plus grand que celui que demandait la poésie "difficile" '.
[8] *Observations*, pp. 84, 85–6: 'les poésies "claires" exigeaient un plus lourd travail. ... Or, cet effort plus grand ne lui était possible que quand il était libre de tout souci.' Vossler, op. cit., p. 440, thinks Giraut lapses into obscurity from moodiness and negligence.

serene as demanded in the highest poetry; and that composing
in the dark style is a way for him to purge himself of feelings
which obstruct a mood of joy; the *trobar clus* has, he thinks, the
purpose of removing the barriers standing in the way of joy by
means of the poet's immersing himself in a compressed, oracular
language.[1] A light song, he argues, demands a serene mood, which
is the exception: so the light style becomes the most valuable
result of poetic effort.[2] The argument that obscurity results
from the poet's mood is doubtful, partly because any statement
the poet makes to this effect may be a conventional *topos*,[3] partly
because Giraut's grave, sententious style does not give the impression of depending on fluctuations of mood; and when Giraut
says that a light-hearted mood is needed for the light style, this
means that this style was to *express* such a mood, according to
the taste of the audience, not that it was the result of a personal
state of mind.[4] Probably it is Giraut's learned background which
explains the vagueness of practical distinction in his works
between *clus* and *leu*. Scheludko wondered whether the troubadours
ever really thought in terms of two opposing styles, or whether it
was in fact a question of the different treatment they gave to the
same basic style.[5] While this may seem a startling idea if one com-
pares Marcabru with Bernart de Ventadorn, it may apply to
Giraut's case, as we shall see when we come to discuss his stylistic
theory in the light of medieval Rhetoric.

1. 'Trobar clus'

What does Giraut mean by *trobar clus* and *trobar leu*?

He mentions the term *clus* once only,[6] when he turns from
trobar clus to *trobar leu*:

---

[1] pp. 145–6. [2] Ibid., p. 145. [3] See Dragonetti, pp. 21–4.

[4] Köhler quotes two passages: XX, stanzas I–II, and XVII, stanza I, to support
this view. In the first Giraut pretends he cannot sing a 'chansoneta plana' because of
his mood, but this is a conventional formula for he does, in fact, compose one which
is simple and smooth. In XVII, he turns from moralizing to gaiety because moralizing
is no use; but there is no suggestion that gaiety is reached through the purging of
a complex mood. [5] *Arch. Rom.* xv (1931), 143.

[6] Kolsen's text of XXVI. 46–9 reads: 'Mas pero l'altr' an, / Can perdei mo gan, /
M'anava chantan / Plan e clus ades'. *Plan e clus* he translates as 'in beiden Dichtweisen'
('einfach und dunkel'). Only 2 of 14 MSS., *RSg*, have *clus*, the rest *plus* (*ABDIKM
NTUa* plus, *C* pus, *Q* peic). *Plan e plus ades* is therefore probably the correct reading:
'smoothly and ever more so'; cf. Salverda de Grave, *Observations*, p. 88: 'je fais
des chansons claires, et toujours davantage.'

> Ja, pos volrai clus trobar,
> No cut aver man parer
> Ab so que ben ai mester
> A far una leu chanso;   (IV. 15–18)

I do not, if I wished to compose in the closed style, think I should have many an appearance; so I am indeed obliged to create a light *chanso*.[1]

He gives no indication that the *trobar clus* involved intentional obscurity; he rejects it simply because it is not clear to everyone, 'tuch no.n son parsoner' (10), and because he wants all to appreciate his *leu chanso*: 'Que l'entenda tota gens' (5).

Clarity is more important than the interlacing of words:

> Qu'eu cut c'atretan grans sens
> Es, qui sap razo gardar,
> Com los motz entrebeschar.   (19–21)

For I think it is just as clever to preserve one's theme as to interlace the words.

These lines are usually taken to mean: 'For I think it is just as clever to keep to what is reasonable as to interlace the words artificially',[2] but by the expression *razo gardar* Giraut probably means that he needs to keep his *razo* or theme intact.[3] For Marcabru, *motz entrebeschar* meant the confusion and entanglement of meaning in a pejorative sense;[4] Bernart Marti[5] and Raimbaut

---

[1] *man parer*: Jeanroy, *AdM* xix (1907), 389–90, gives *maint parier*, 'je ne crois pas avoir beaucoup d'égaux'; Salverda de Grave, p. 83: 'je ne crois pas trouver un bon accueil général.'

[2] Kolsen: 'glaube ich doch, dass in vernünftiger Weise zu dichten von ebenso grossem Verstande zeugt wie die Worte überkünstlich zu verknüpfen'; Lewent, 'Zum Text', p. 3: 'Denn ich glaube, dass es (sc. das leichte Dichten) von ebenso grossem Verstande zeugt für diejenigen, der sich die Vernunft seines Urteils bewahrt, wie die überkünstliche Verknüpfung von Worten'; Salverda de Grave, p. 83: 'd'ailleurs, je suis d'avis qu'il est aussi raisonnable de savoir rester intelligible que de se livrer à des tours de force de paroles.'

[3] See pp. 12 ff.   [4] See p. 10.

[5] Ed. Hoepffner, III. 60–1: 'C'aisi vauc entrebescant / Los motz e.l so afinant', 'for thus do I interlace the words and refine the music'. This interlacing of words probably refers not only to their elegant formal connection, but the way imagery is used to suggest emotional and physical threads of meaning:

> L' esparviers ab bel semblant
> Va del pueg ves leis volant:
>   La longua trencada,
>   Pren lai sa volada.

d'Aurenga,[1] however, use this expression for the skilful binding
up of phrases and meanings, and this also seems to be Giraut's
intention here. The skilful interlacing of words is not excluded,
but coherence is the first consideration. This is just what Peire
said in 'Sobre.l vieill trobar',[2] although Peire was trying to dis-
courage presumptuous poets from aiming at the grand style,
while Giraut sees this from another point of view: that interlacing
the words so often does lead to obscurity that it is better to
concentrate on clarity first.

Veiled expressions, or *motz cobertz*, are rejected on the same
grounds as *clus:*

> Be.l saupra plus cobert far;
> Mas non a chans pretz enter,
> Can tuch no.n son parsoner.   (IV. 8-10)

I could certainly make it more veiled, but a song does not have a
perfect reputation when not everyone can share in it,

or in the song 'No posc sofrir' (XL), where he says that although
he formerly composed with veiled or locked words he now makes
sure they are clear:

> E vos entendetz e veiatz
>   Que sabetz mo lengatge,
> S'anc fis motz cobertz ni serratz,
> S'era no.ls fatz ben esclairatz.
>
> E sui m'en per so esforsatz
> Qu'entendetz cals chansos eu fatz. (XL. 71-6)

And you who know my language hear and may see whether, if ever

> En breu m'es (com) fils de lana
> Lo fortz fres e la capsana
>   Qui que.s grei,
>   So.us autrei,
> Tota.l rengua ab correi.
>   C'aisi vauc entrebescant
>   Los motz e.l so afinant:
>   Lengu' entrebescada
>   Es en la baizada.   (51-63)

'The fine-looking hawk takes flight towards her from the hill-top: the thong severed,
it wings towards her. Swiftly the strong curb and the tether are to me as woollen
thread, the whole rein and the bridle too, I assure you—whoever may object; for
thus I interlace the words and refine the music: the tongue is interlaced in the kiss.'

The 'bridle' is the lover's control of his sensual desires: cf. Marcabru, VIII. 36-9,
'De sol la paor ai faich fre / Que majormen aura faich me / Plus fort d'un caval
arabit.'

---

  [1] 'Cars, bruns e tenhz motz entrebesc!' See p. 148.   [2] See pp. 65-6.

I composed veiled or locked phrases, I do not now clarify them well. And in this I have made a special effort, for you can hear what kind of *chansos* I compose.

Again, there is no suggestion that *cobert* means 'intentionally obscure'.[1] Giraut makes a special effort to make himself clear, so that his audience may more readily appreciate his skill.

In the last quotation *serratz* was used in a negative context, together with *cobertz*. In 'La flors del verjan' (XXVI), however, Giraut praises his *menutz motz serratz* and defends, in clear language, the merits of the *trobar clus*. People have told him, he says, that he ought to sing in a light style, but he believes that a song is worth more if it is rich and full of meaning that emerges gradually the more people think about it.

> Mas era diran
> Que, si m'esforses
> Com levet chantes,
> Melhs m'ester' assatz.
> E non es vertatz;
> Que sens e chartatz[2]
> Adui pretz e.l dona
> Si com l'ochaizona
> Nosens eslaissatz;
>   Mas be cre
>   Que ges chans ancse
> No val al comensamen
> Tan com pois, can om l'enten. (XXVI. 18–30)

But now they will say that it would be much better for me if I forced myself to sing in an easy style. And this is not true, for meaning and richness bring and bestow reputation, just as unbridled meaninglessness quarrels with it. But I well believe that a song is never worth as much at the beginning as it is later, when it is understood.

Giraut is careful to distinguish between a style which is full of meaning, and one which is obscure because it has no sense, just

---

[1] It is misleading to translate *cobert* or *serrat* by 'obscure' (see Salverda de Grave, p. 83, XL. 73: 'couverts et obscurs', IV. 8: 'je saurais bien la rendre plus obscure'). *Cobert* means 'covered' (*SWB* i. 268), *serrat* 'locked' or 'tightly packed' (*SWB* vii. 614).

[2] MSS. (according to Kolsen): *ABNQTUa* echartatz, *IK* ecardatz, *Sg* e clardatz, *CR* e tardatz, *D* e caritatz, *M* acordatz. Rayn. and *SWB* do not attest *echartar* or *ecardar* meaning 'écarter'. It is, therefore, doubtful that Giraut meant 'obscure, remote', or that this passage shows, as Mölk suggested, that the *trobar clus* required a single obscure level of meaning into whose remoteness alone the *bel saber* of an élite audience extends (p. 121). The probable reading is *sens e chartatz*.

as Peire blamed poets who became obscure in their over-
ambitious pursuit of the high style.[1] Those who blame him for
wanting his theme to unfold gradually, Giraut continues, are
those who would find some reason to complain about anything.

> E donc a que.m van
> Tot jorn chastian?
> Qu'enquer planheran,
> S'eu ja joi cobres,
> Car no serai pres!
> Car s'eu jonh ni latz
> Menutz motz serratz,
> Pois en sui lauzatz,
> Can ma razos bona
> Par ni s'abandona;
> C'om ben ensenhatz,
> Si be.i ve
> Ni mo drech chapte,
> No vol al meu escien
> C'a totz chan comunalmen.   (31–45)

And so why are they constantly blaming me? For they will still be
complaining that I am not close to (possessing) joy even if I might ever
have obtained it. For if I join and lace finely locked words together, I
am subsequently praised for this when my fine theme appears and
yields itself up; for a well-educated man, if he sees correctly in this
matter and champions my right, will not in my opinion want me to
sing to everyone communally.[2]

Giraut does not say he wants to *exclude* certain listeners; this is not
a defence of a deliberately hermetic style. If he does not want to
sing 'a totz . . . comunalmen' this is because he does not want to
have to bring down the level of his style in order to make sure
that it is within everyone's grasp. The less intelligent listeners are
not excluded; they are left behind. The means of presenting a

---

[1] See pp. 65–6.

[2] The meaning of vv. 33–5 is uncertain; those who blame Giraut may complain
because he does not immediately take possession of any joy within his grasp: that
is they expect their desires to be instantly gratified, just as they want to understand
the song straight away; or else they complain that he has no joy even if he has, and
complain about his song because they know nothing about it. Salverda de Grave,
p. 87: 'Plus tard, si je suis heureux en amour, on se plaindra que je sois loin (parce
que, alors je pourrais de nouveau faire des vers gais (?))'. He translates vv. 39–40 as
'si le contenu paraît bon et ne coule pas à l'aventure (?)'. Mölk, p. 120, thinks the
om ben ensenhatz in. v. 41 is Raimbaut d'Aurenga; Giraut may be thinkingof Raimbaut, but he is also appealing to the general public by singling out his supporters as
ben ensenhatz.

fine theme by gradually revealing it is to bind it up in *menutz motz serratz. Serrar* means 'to lock' or 'to lock together' in the sense of 'press, compress'. The troubadour Lanfranc Cigala describes the dark style as one compressed 'by a tightening band':

> E pres mais, qui qu'en ais s'apil,
> Clars digz ab obra polia,
> Qu'escurs moz ab seran lia;
> E no.m par qu'aia tant d'onor,
> Si tot la cui' aver maior,
> Cel qui son chant ser' e lia,
> Qon cel que.l fai ab clardat agradiu;[1]

And I value more, whoever may support a different opinion, clear expressions with polished work, rather than dark words with a tightening band; and it does not appear to me that one who tightens and binds his song has as much honour, even if he thinks he has greater, as one who makes it pleasing through clarity.

Menutz motz serratz are words which are tightly locked together, compact, or concise. They may not be immediately accessible to all, but they are not intentionally obscure.

The same is true for *dichs escurs*. In the light style Giraut planes away the *dichs escurs* of his song:

> Vauc un chantaret planan
> De dichs escurs
> C'us non i remanha.   (XXVIII. 3–5)

I plane a little song smooth of dark expressions so that not a single one remains.

Since he wants to make this song 'leu entenduda' (9) *escur* might seem to mean simply 'obscure'. But elsewhere, in 'De bels dichs menutz frais' (LXVIII), he tries to avoid expressions which are not simply *escur* but *trop escur:*

> Trop volgra mais donar
> Mos gais sonetz joios
> Ab bels dichs et enters,
> Entendables e plas,
> Que trop escurs ni sobrestorias.   (LXVIII. 9–13)

I should far prefer to present my gay, joyous melodies with fine and complete expressions, intelligible and smooth, than with words that are too dark or over-embellished.[2]

---

[1] F. Branciforti, XII. 13–19. Cf. *SWB* vii. 614: *se serrar* 'dicht aneinander rücken, Arm an Arm schliessen'.

[2] Salverda de Grave, p. 72, emends *sobrestorias* to *sobrestojan*, 'obscur', from *estojar,*

Giraut uses *enter* and *escur* in the sense that Peire did: *enter* means 'without faults of style', *escur* means 'rich in sense or embellishment', and Giraut does not want to spoil his style by overloading it. He and Peire are looking at the same style, only from a different point of view: Peire wanted to make his style as rich as possible within the limits of *vers entiers*; Giraut, forced to adopt a less elevated style to suit his audience, justifies it by saying that anything more elaborate would be faulty; in other words he still sees his style in terms of the high style, although it may be less ornate than Peire's (at least in theory). In his light songs Giraut may wish to plane away rich expressions entirely (XXVIII) or to tone them down (LXVIII). In his possibly most obscure and difficult song, 'Ans que venia',[1] he 'darkens' his style in a positive way, to fill it with *saber*:

> E qi.n parra greus l'apenres
> de mon chantar, no s'en laixe,
> si no.l soi del dir esc*a*s:
> c'ap fin coratge l'essejn,
> sitot mosejnh*e*r n'Aimars
> se cuia que faz ab ojn;
> c'aixi l'escur e.l n'ebejn,
> mon trobar ab saber prejn.[2]   (49–56)

And if anyone finds it difficult to learn my song, let him not abandon the attempt, even if I am not niggardly towards him in my language; for I teach it with a sincere heart, although my lord Sir Aimars considers that I compose with unguent; for I colour it darkly and thereby make it black as ebony, this composition of mine pregnant with wisdom.[3]

The idea of 'darkening the style with wisdom' is opposed to being *escas*, 'miserly', in language, and this confirms that *escur* means, in such a context, 'rich in meaning and language'[4], as it

---

'cacher, enfermer dans un étui'. Kolsen gives no variant to *sobrestorias;* Salverda de Grave says the MS. reads *sobrestorian*, but in any case the rhyme requires *-as*. *Estoriar* means to 'depict' (*SWB* iii. 332), so Kolsen's translation 'übermässig geziert' is acceptable.

   [1] See p. 117.
   [2] This passage shows that Scheludko (*Arch. Rom.* xv (1931), 146) was incorrect to think that *escur* was always pejorative.
   [3] See notes on this text, p. 121.
   [4] This may be equivalent to *ric*. Cf. Peire Vidal, ed. A. S. Avalle, III. 1–5: 'Ajostar e lassar / Sai tan gent motz e so, / Que del car ric trobar / No.m ven hom al talo, / Quant n'ai bona razo.' 'I know how to couple and lace words and music together so gracefully that no one can compete with me in the precious, rich style, when I

does for Peire d'Alvernhe (p. 72). *Far ab ojn* may mean 'to compose with flattery' since *onher* has the sense 'to flatter';[1] it may have a second meaning, 'to make cloudy or obscure',[2] which would indicate that Giraut was defending himself against charges of obscurity by stressing his wisdom and fundamental coherence. *Essejn* may mean 'teach': the poet teaches people his song. Perhaps a second sense is implied: Giraut 'ensigns' his style or 'fills it with signs' (*senhs*) or 'oblique implications'.[3]

To such 'signs' he draws attention in the song 'Si.m sentis fizels amics' (XXVII), pointing out that not everyone can follow the full subtlety of his meaning:

> Mas, per melhs assire   Mo chan,[4]
> Vauc cerchan   Bos motz en fre
> Que son tuch chargat e ple
> D'us estranhs sens naturals
> E no sabon tuch de cals.   (XXVII. 50–4)

But, in order to seat my song the better, I seek out fine, tractable words which are all loaded and full of several unfamiliar senses, and not everyone knows which ones.

The meaning of *estranhs sens naturals* can be discovered only by examining the song as a whole;[5] but it seems that just as Marcabru was full of *gignos sens* and *cent colors*,[6] so Giraut seeks to fill his words with several meanings. These are 'strange' or

have a good theme for it.' Here *ric* and *car* are synonymous. *Car* can apply to the *clus* style, as in 'Cars douz' of Raimbaut d'Aurenga (see pp. 147–56), and cf. my note on *sens e chartatz* in Giraut, p. 93. Giraut may also be alluding to *trobar ric* when he mentions Linhaure's manner of composing: 'E pero veiatz en l'escolh / Linhaure vers de trobador / E no.m n'aiatz per gabador, / Si tan *rics motz* me passa.l cais' (XXIX. 55–8): 'And yet behold a troubadour vers in the style of Linhaure: and do not think of me as a braggart if such a lofty claim passes my lips.' Although scholars (see p. 2) have used *clus* and *ric* to make a convenient distinction between two styles, the one dark in meaning, the other clear but ornate, the troubadours seem to have been much vaguer in their terminology.

[1] *SWB* v. 489.

[2] Kolsen, *Giraut de Bornelh*, ii. 21: 'vgl. dazu *uncta aqua* (Horaz), "unreines, trübes Wasser" (Georges unter ungere IIa).' He interprets: 'dass ich ihn nur trübe und nicht völlig dunkel mache' (ibid. i. 15). If *ab ojn* means 'cloudy' then Giraut means Aimars thinks he is obscure, but he is full of wisdom. *Unctus* can mean 'rich, copious ('unctior . . . splendidiorque consuetudo loquendi', Cic. *Brut.* xx. 78); Aimars may think Giraut is over-ornate.

[3] Cf. Marcabru's *gap*, p. 26.

[4] Salverda de Grave, p. 87: 'pour donner à mes vers plus de poids'; but cf. *SWB* i. 90, and Bernart de Ventadorn, ed. Appel, XXVII. 5–6 'bos motz assire / en est so'.

[5] See p. 125.   [6] See pp. 21–8.

'unfamiliar', or different from the obvious literal sense, and at the
same time *naturals* or 'genuine'.[1] The words he chooses are well
under control, *en fre*: that is, they avoid *nosens eslaissatz* (XXVI. 26)
or incoherent nonsense.

Giraut then sees the *trobar clus* as a style in which words are
'closed' and 'tightly locked' (*clus, serratz*), where the density or
compactness of expression may lead to oblique or compressed
meaning. Such words are tightly bound up or *entrebeschatz*, so
they become *cobert* ('veiled') or *escur* ('rich in sense and language').
The *trobar clus* is by no means an obscure style; on the contrary,
it is full of meaning and reveals the theme gradually, making the
song more and more valuable the more it is heard. Words may
be used in unfamiliar senses, but a balance must be maintained
which avoids sparseness on the one hand and incoherence or
obscurity on the other. Even when Giraut turns away from the
trobar clus he does so not because he considers it deliberately
obscure or exclusive but because not everyone can share in it; an
effort is needed to make it clearer and more accessible.

Pollmann[2] rejected Köhler's[3] identification of the *trobar clus*
with *ornatus difficilis* on the grounds that *clus* poets sought obscurity, which would have been a fault of style in the context of
ornatus difficilis; hence he considered that the two stylistic ideals
were diametrically opposed to one another. But both Giraut and
Peire blame obscurity and want their style to be rich in coherent
meaning, even if this meaning is to be revealed only gradually.
Giraut's view of the *trobar clus* and the terminology or imagery
with which he describes it are similar in several respects to the pre-
cepts of Geoffrey of Vinsauf in his *Poetria Nova*. There is no question of Geoffrey's having influenced Giraut since the *Poetria*
was written, according to Faral,[4] about 1210; but Geoffrey must
have reproduced ideas which were current in the twelfth-century
teaching of Rhetoric.[5]

In his *trobar clus* Giraut binds together *menutz motz serratz* from
which his fine *razo* gradually appears. Geoffrey teaches how to
compress a theme within narrow limits by the devices belonging

---

[1] They really belong to the words. There is no reason to think that Giraut thinks
of *natural* in the sense that Marcabru did (see pp. 28–54).

[2] '*Trobar clus*', p. 45.   [3] pp. 133 ff.   [4] Faral, pp. 28–9.

[5] Mölk, pp. 177 ff. argues that *ornatus difficilis* was a term invented by Geoffrey
and cannot therefore have influenced the troubadours, but that the theory of *locutio
simplex* and *locutio figurata* which led up to it may have done so.

to abbreviation: these include not only means for avoiding unnecessary words but devices for implying meanings which are
not explicit, and Geoffrey stresses that these are designed not to
veil meaning, but to reveal it from its obscurity:

> Vel manus artificis multas ita conflet in unam,
> Mentis ut intuitu multae videantur in una.
> Hac brevitate potes longum succingere thema,
> Hac cymba transire fretum. Narratio facti
> Eligit hanc formam verbi, quae facta modeste
> Non superinfundat nubem, sed nube remota
> Inducat[1] solem. Concurrant ergo, sed apte,
> Emphasis, articulus, casus sine remige liber,
> Unius in reliquo nota callida, vincula dempta
> Clausarum, sensus multarum clausus in una,
> Ejusdem verbi repetitio nulla. . . .   (700–10)

Let the craftsman's skill effect a fusion of many concepts in one, so
that many may be seen in a single glance of the mind. By such con-
cision you may gird up a lengthy theme; in this bark you may cross
a sea. This form of expression is preferable for a factual account, in
order not to enshroud facts discreetly in mist, but rather to clear away
mist and usher in sunlight. Combine these devices, therefore, when
occasion warrants: emphasis, articulus, ablative absolute, deft implication of one thing in the rest, omissions of conjunctions between
clauses, fusion of many concepts in one, avoidance of repetition. . . .[2]

The idea of bringing out meaning from darkness and revealing
one's theme is central to Giraut's view of the *trobar clus*; the term
clus itself, with its idea of binding meanings together, is suggested
by Geoffrey's phrase *sensus multarum clausus in una*.[3] This passage is
concerned with brevity in a factual account, but similar ideas
appear in the section on *ornatus difficilis*:

> Praescriptis formis quaedam pictura coloris
> Et quiddam gravitatis inest, quae nascitur inde
> Quod res in medium facie non prodit aperta,
> Nec sua vox deservit ei, sed vox aliena,
> Et sic se quasi nube tegit, sub nube serena.   (1046–50)

---

[1] Faral, inducet, but inducat in *BCD*.

[2] Translated by M. F. Nims, *Poetria Nova of Geoffrey of Vinsauf*, (Toronto, 1967),
p. 41.

[3] Lausberg, *Registerband*, indicates that *claudere* [*cludere*] in Rhetoric refers to
similar functions: (a) the rounding off of a sentence or clause (as in Raimon de
Miraval, ed. Topsfield, XXXI. 7. 'Ab bels ditz clars e gen claus', 'with fine, clear
words elegantly rounded off'); (b) in irony, where implied meaning is enclosed in
the speaker's mind: 'cum aliud in pectore reclusum, aliud in lingua promptum
habemus' (Rufianus), etc. The latter recalls Marcabru's *gap*.

In the figures given above there is a common element of adornment
and weightiness, arising from the fact that an object does not come
before us with an unveiled face, and accompanied by its natural voice;
rather, an alien voice attends it, and so it shrouds itself in mist, as it
were, but in a luminous mist.[1]

Just as Giraut fills his style with *estranhs sens*, Geoffrey says that
expressions of the *ornatus difficilis* appear with a *vox aliena*.[2] The
meaning is veiled; but it shines through 'sub nube serena'. The
object or idea *(res)* which does not present itself openly, but 'se quasi
nube tegit', seems to correspond, at least in theory, with Giraut's
motz cobertz. This idea is not confined in Geoffrey's treatise to
abbreviatio but also appears in *amplificatio*, where in order to
lengthen a theme the writer is advised: 'Nec plane detege, sed
rem / Innue per notulas' (229–30), 'Do not unveil the thing fully
but suggest it by hints.'[3] Similar imagery and vocabulary, suggesting the unlocking of meaning, appear in Geoffrey's treatment of
the subject of obscurity and how this must be avoided:

> Sic tamen esto gravis ne res sub nube tegatur,
> Sed faciant voces ad quod de jure tenentur,
> Quae clausum reserent animum sunt verba reperta
> Ut quaedam claves animi: qui vult aperire
> Rem clausam, nolit verbis inducere nubem. . . .
>
> (1063–7)

Yet be weighty in such a manner that your subject is not hidden under
a cloud; rather let the words pay fealty to their rightful lord. Words
are instruments to unlock the closed mind; they are keys, as it were, of
the mind. One who seeks to open what is closed does not set out to
draw a cloud over his words. . . .[1]

Just as Geoffrey advocates the veiling of meaning only to the
extent that the sense must shine through and not be hidden, so
Giraut wants his *razo* to 'appear and yield itself up' without his
singing 'a totz . . . comunalmen' or on the other hand singing
nosens eslaissatz. The principle behind the use of figurative expressions which conceal or veil meaning is, according to Isidore,[4]
to keep the listener alert and make sure the subject is not cheap-
ened by being expressed too nakedly or bluntly: '(tropi) ad ea,

---

[1] Nims, p. 54.
[2] Cf. Lausberg, § 562, Cicero, *De Or.* iii. xxxviii. 155: 'quod enim declarari vix
verbo proprio potest, id tralato cum est dictum, illustrat id, quod intellegi volumus,
eius rei, quam *alieno verbo* posuimus, similitudo.'
[3] Nims, p. 24.
[4] See Lausberg, § 552, p. 283 (Isid. i. xxxvii. 1–2) and also § 556.

quae intellegenda sunt, propterea figuratis amictibus obteguntur, ut sensus legentis exerceant et ne nuda atque in promptu vilescant' : '(tropes) are veiled with respect to the things which are to be understood, by means of figurative garments, in order that the perceptions of the reader should keep alert and that (these matters) should not become cheap by being naked or publicly exposed.'

In Giraut's view of the *trobar clus*: of compact style, of *estranhs sens*, of veiled meaning which is revealed indirectly, he seems to be expressing his own version of ideas found in medieval Rhetoric. The faults of style he mentions also have Rhetorical counterparts: Giraut avoids being *escas* in his speech, which corresponds to avoiding the vice of aridity or meagreness;[1] excessive ornamentation—words which are *sobrestorias*—leads to the vice of the high style which is obscurity.[2]

2. '*Trobar leu*'

Giraut is most probably the 'inventor' of the *trobar leu*. That is to say he is the first to define a 'light' style as opposed to the *trobar clus* and to give it a title. Peire calls a song *non-clus* but never mentions the term *leu;* Bernart de Ventadorn never uses the expression nor discusses the clarity of his style; but Giraut defends the *trobar leu* in seven songs and points out his intelligibility in others.[3] While Bernart remains poet of the most limpid style without theorizing about it, Giraut 'invents' a new theory of style in reaction to the *trobar clus*, to its growing unpopularity,

---

[1] Lausberg, § 1097 i g), p. 520; Geoffrey, *Poetria*, v. 1877.

[2] See p. 66. Giraut also uses *bos motz en fre*, an image used by Geoffrey when discussing the proper use of hyperbole: 'Currat yperbolicus, sed non discurrat inepte / Sermo: refrenet eum ratio placeatque modestus / Finis, ut excessum non mens nec abhorreat auris.' (1013–15.) 'Give hyperbole rein, but see that its discourse does not run ineptly hither and yon. Let reason keep it in check, and its moderate use be a source of pleasure, that neither mind nor ear shrink from excess.' (Nims, p. 52.) As Marcabru was full of signs and Giraut perhaps 'fills his song with signs' (*c'ap fin coratge l'essejn;* see p. 161; also *estranhs sens* may be = *senhs*), so Geoffrey says the writer may reveal his meaning through oblique signs: 'Talibus egregium sententia nacta colorem / Non detecta venit, sed se per signa revelat. / Lucet ab obliquo, non vult procedere recte / In lucem.' (1580–3.) 'Thought, finding excellent adornment in such devices, does not appear unveiled, but makes itself known by signs. It shines with an oblique ray and chooses not to advance directly into the light.' (Nims, p. 72.) Cf. Lausberg, *Registerband*, p. 811 and § 568, 5); § 573, 1).

[3] He defends *leu* in IV, V, XXVIII, XL, XLVIII, LVIII, LXVIII; he mentions clarity in XVII, XLIX, LI.

and tries to formulate a learned justification for the style he thought his public wanted.

Leu has many meanings, including 'light', 'quick', 'sprightly', 'easy', 'flighty'.[1]

In 'A penas sai comensar' (IV), where he appears to undertake a *leu chanso* for the first time, *leu* means 'easy to sing' and indicates a style intended for everyone to understand and enjoy, which keeps the theme clear while the words are bound up.

I
> A penas sai comensar
> Un vers que volh far leuger
> E si n'ai pensat des er
> Que.l fezes de tal razo
> Que l'entenda tota gens   5
> E qu'el fassa leu chantar;
> Qu'eu.l fatz per pla deportar.

II
> Be.l saupra plus cobert far;
> Mas non a chans pretz enter,
> Can tuch no.n son parsoner.   10
> Qui que.s n'azir, me sap bo,
> Can auch dire per contens
> Mo sonet rauquet e clar
> E l'auch a la fon portar.

III
> Ja, pos volrai clus trobar,   15
> No cut aver man parer
> Ab so que ben ai mester
> A far una leu chanso;
> Qu'eu cut c'atretan grans sens
> Es, qui sap razo gardar,   20
> Com *l*os motz entrebeschar.[2]

I hardly know how to begin a *vers* which I want to make light, and indeed I have been thinking since yesterday about how I might compose it on such a theme that all people may understand it, and how I might make it easy to sing; for I compose it purely to entertain.

I should certainly know how to make it more veiled; but a song has an incomplete reputation when all are not able to share it. Whoever else may be angry about this, I am pleased when I hear people vying with each other in repeating my melody hoarsely and clearly, and when I hear it carried to the well.

I do not, even if I wanted to compose in the *clus* style, think I should have many an appearance, so I am indeed obliged to make a light

[1] Rayn. iv. 58; *SWB* iv. 372.
[2] v. 6, Kolsen: 'fass' a leu'; correction Lewent, p. 2.

chanso; for I believe that it is just as clever to know how to preserve one's theme as to interlace the words.[1]

The notion of *leu* being 'easily understood' is repeated in 'Tot suavet' (XXVIII), where Giraut praises his 'chansos leu entenduda' (v. 9). In 'Razon e loc' (XVII) *leu chantar* corresponds to singing in a gay mood and forgetting moralizing attacks on the *baros*:

> Razon e loc
> E cor e sen
> E grat de Mo-Senhor e mais
> Agr' eu, si pogues avenir
> En un leu chantar conge,
> Que.m dones jai,
> Ab que.m partis d'un fol esmai
> Que solh menar,
> Can cudava.ls baros rengar
> A cobrar cortz e messios;
> E car non i posc avengar
> E vei que no.m seria pros,
> Lais lo trebalh,
> Que.m sol grevar,
> E torn a mas gaias chansos.   (XVII. 1–15)

Theme and occasion and heart and mind and thanks from My-Lord and more I should have, if I could manage to compose a light, gracious song which might give me joy, if only I could quit a foolish care which I used to pursue in imagining that I could discipline the barons to procure assemblies and free spending; and since I cannot succeed in this, and I see that it will be profitless for me, I abandon the difficult task which used to burden me, and turn to my gay songs.[2]

Giraut is anxious to stress that the *trobar leu* is no less difficult or valuable than the *trobar clus*. In 'Si sotils sens' (LI) his *leus chans* is 'valens ni chars' (III. 11), epithets which Linhaure gives to the *trobar clus* in their *tenso* (LVIII. 21), 'So que plus char es ni mais val'. *Leu* refers to the appearance of the finished work and not to the effort which has gone into it:

> Be deu en bona cort dir
> Bo sonet qui.l fai,
> Per qu'eu retrairai
> Un levet e qui l'apren,

---

[1] See pp. 90–1.

[2] Although Giraut turns here from moralizing poetry to light-hearted songs, moralizing attacks cannot simply be equated with *trobar clus*. 'Ans que venia' contains no more blame than the average courtly song in which the *lauzengiers* are attacked.

Parra d'ome no-chalen;
C'aissi com si no.m chalia,
Fatz leugers sonetz,
Per que.l plus greus semblans sia
Leus e bos afaire.   (XLIX. 1-9)

He who composes a noble melody ought well to repeat it in a noble
court; therefore I shall perform an easy one, and to him who learns it
it will appear to be the song of a carefree man; for just as if I had no
cares I compose sprightly airs, so that its most earnest aspect is light
and cheerful.[1]

He stresses that his style seems carefree, but takes great effort to
compose:

Leu chansonet' e vil
M'auri' a obs a far . . .
Qu'eu dic qu'en l'escurzir
Non es l'afans,
Mas en l'obr' esclarzir.   (XLVIII. 1-10)

I ought to compose a light, ordinary little song . . . [yet] I say that the
effort lies not in darkening but in clarifying the work.

Leu then means 'easy to sing and understand', 'light and entertaining', and 'giving a carefree impression'; but Giraut stresses
that it is as difficult to compose and as valuable as the *trobar clus*.

Leugier is sometimes synonymous with *leu* but has a different
range of meaning. It can mean 'light, carefree':

C'aissi com si no.m chalia,
Fatz leugers sonetz;   (XLIX. 6-7)

the same sense is indicated in 'A penas sai' (IV) where Giraut
wants to compose a *vers* which is *leuger*.[2] But *leugier* does not
necessarily apply to the *trobar leu*; in 'Si.l cor' (XVI) it describes the
sotil style:

Si.l cor no.m ministr' a drech
E mal so grat no l'afranh
En un chantaret sotil,
No m'es vis qu'era s'afranha,
Si no m'esfors' atz,
En aitals motz peceiatz.

---

[1] Lewent, p. 68, reads (8-9) *sembla sia*: 'Deshalb scheint das schwerste (Lied)
eine leichte und gute Arbeit zu sein'; Salverda de Grave, p. 56: 'pour que la plus
difficile semble être facile et agréable à faire.' (*a* a faire, *ABCDIKMNQ* per faire,
RSgV afaire.)

[2] See p. 102.

> Ja fo que.m n'entremetia
> Plus qu'era no fatz,
> Car melhs me lezia,
> C'a penas om conoissia
> Mos leugiers dichs veziatz
> Sotils e menutz soudatz. (XVI. 1–12)

If my heart does not serve me aright and I do not bend it against its will to (compose) a subtle little song, I do not think it will now force itself into words so well pieced together unless occasion obliges me. There was a time when I undertook this more that I do now, for I had more opportunity, at a time when people hardly knew my agile and cunning expressions, subtly and minutely soldered.[1]

Leugier then refers to the poet's lightness of touch and agility, rather than to clarity and ease of comprehension.

Giraut also terms the light style *levet*, meaning 'light, easy',[2] as *leu*; but it may also have pejorative overtones. In 'La flors del verjan' (XXVI) Giraut describes as *levet* the light style which the public demands but which he as yet despises:

> Mas era diran
> Que, si m'esforses
> Com levet chantes,
> Melhs m'ester' assatz.
> E non es vertatz .... (XXVI. 18–22)

But now they will say that if I forced myself to sing in an easy way, it would be much better for me. And this is untrue ....

In defending the *trobar leu* against Linhaure's criticism he seems to adopt an apologetic, pejorative tone to forestall criticism:

> Seign' en Lignaura, no.m coreill
> Si qecs s'i trob' a son talan.

---

[1] In v. 11, *ABDIKNRSga* read *veziatz*; only *C* has *euersatz* (Kolsen *enversatz*). Kolsen thinks Giraut refers to the *trobar clus*, and translates: 'sodass man meine frischen . . . Aussprüche kaum verstand.' Salverda de Grave, p. 66, suggests 'des paroles mises en pièces (?)' for *peciatz*; they are not 'broken' in the sense of *frag*, but probably 'finely pieced together': see my remarks on p. 139. He reads v. 1 as *Si.l cor no'm lus er tan drech* (Si c *B*; non *ABDSg*; m.a)nistra *a*; esta a *R*; luz era *N*²; lus aras *DIK*; luser tant *B*; lug tant *AN*): 'Si le cœur n'est pas maintenant pour moi une bonne étoile' (p. 124), 'Si je ne suis pas maître de mon cœur et si je ne puis pas l'amener malgré lui à une chanson "subtile", il me paraît qu'aujourd'hui il pourrait, sans y être forcé (*L*: *si non es forsatz*), se résoudre à faire des vers . . . (?) (Voir . . . p. 66). Autrefois j'en faisais plus que maintenant, car j'en avais plus l'occasion, au point qu'on distinguait à peine mes légères chansons . . .' (pp. 83–4). This ignores the negative *No m'es vis* (v. 4). The first six lines seem to me to be an elaborate expression of the *topos* 'I lack inspiration, but the occasion forces me to sing'.

[2] *SWB* iv. 388.

    Mas eu son jujaire d'aitan
     Qu'es mais amatz
     E plus prezatz
    Qui.l fa levet e venarsal;
    E vos no m'en tornatz a mal.[1]

My lord Sir Lignaura, I do not object if everyone composes for himself according to his own taste; but I prefer to judge this way: that a song is better liked and more highly estemed if one makes it easy and commonplace; and do not take me wrongly in this.

Venarsal, which Appel thinks is derived from *verna*, 'domestic slave',[2] can mean 'low, menial', as in the examples which Levy quotes (*SWB* viii. 680):

     Tals es savis et ab gran sen
     Que torna leugeiramen fals,
     E tals es vils e vernassals
     Que torna leu cortes e pros;

One man may be wise with great learning and readily turn false, and another may be common and menial and easily turn courtly and noble;

     Vill sirventes leugier e venassal
     Vueilh de vill motz en vill raçon bastir,

I want to construct a low *sirventes*, frivolous and menial, with low words on a low theme.[3]

It can be synonymous with *leu* or *leugier* in the sense of 'frivolous', 'thoughtless':

     Si as alcuns lausats,
     Guarda non digues mal,
     Car seras ne blasmats
     De lieu sen venertzal,

If you have praised anyone, take care not to speak evil, for you will be blamed for a light and frivolous mind.[4]

So it appears that Giraut intentionally exaggerates the 'humility' of his new style to forestall the blame of critics who might really regard it as common and worthless.[5] The defensively pejorative use of these terms may have been especially provoked by Raim-

---

[1] Ed. Pattison, XXXI, stanza II.   [2] *Arch.* xcvii. 187.
 [3] Levy comments: 'Rayn. übersetzt "bouffon". Das ist sicherlich falsch; aber der Sinn des Wortes mag weniger freundlich gemeint sein als bei Giraut de Bornelh.'
 [4] Levy: '— "Hoc vide, ne rursus levitatis crimine damnes" (Cato)'.
 [5] The same sense for *levet* is present in XLIV. 3–5; see pp. 103–4.

baut d'Aurenga's scathing remarks about the new style.[1] The best rendering of *levet* seems to be 'easy'; Giraut does not think his style is easy to compose in but he wants to give the impression of ease, and at the same time imply an ironic sense.

Giraut uses the decidedly pejorative epithet *vil* to shock his listeners into thinking about his new style:

> Leu chansonet' e vil
> M'auri' a obs a far
> Que pogues enviar
> En Alvernh' al Dalfi.
> Pero, s'el drech chami
> Pogues n'Eblon trobar,
> Be.lh poiria mandar
> Qu'eu dic qu'en l'escurzir
> Non es l'afans,
> Mas en l'obr' esclarzir.   (XLVIII. 1–10)

I ought to compose a light, menial little song which I could send to the Dauphin in Auvergne. Yet, if it could find Sir Ebles on its way there, it could well announce to him that I declare that the hard work lies not in darkening a composition but in clarifying it.[2]

Again Giraut speaks disparagingly of his style in order, he hopes, to draw attention to its virtues:

> E tu ja.t fas conoissens? —
> Eu oc. — E donc non entens
> C'us motz fatz fass' aprendens
>   E ses maestria? —
> Si fatz be, mas tot es sens! —
> Per que volh que tota gens
>   Li port garentia.   (V. 15–21)

And do you consider yourself discriminating?—Yes I do.—And do you not then realize that I am making you learn certain foolish, artless words?—You are indeed, but this is entirely wise!—Because I want all people to bear witness to her.[3]

The simple style is better able to publish his lady's reputation. *Motz fatz . . . E ses maestria* are the opposite of words chosen in a different style[4] where he claims they are so delicate and smooth no

---

[1] See pp. 170–3.
[2] Giraut may be punning on *vil* meaning both 'low' and 'sprightly'; cf. XII. 7–8 'Que plus sui salhens que leupartz / E vils non es chabrols ni cers.'
[3] Stimming: 'Jawohl, da alles verständig ist' (19).
[4] See p. 138, XXV. 4–7: 'Qu'el mon non a / Doctor que tan prim ni plus pla / Lo prezes / Ni melhs l'afines'.

doctor could improve on them, and the opposite of those expressions for which he is praised in the *Vida*: 'los sieus maystrals digs'.[1] Giraut's biographer, with his clerical bias,[2] probably liked the learned side to Giraut's poetry, but learning was not always praised: the biographer of Guiraut de Calanso said that Guiraut 'Ben saup letras, e suptils fo de trobar; e fez cansos maestradas desplazens e descortz d'aquella saison. Mal abellivols fo en Proensa e sos ditz, e petit ac d'onor entre.l(s) cortes.'[3] *Maestria* can mean 'artificiality', as in the *Vida* of Maria de Ventadorn:[4] 'Et onret la Deus de bel plazen cors avinen, ses maestria'. In boasting of his *motz . . . ses maestria* Giraut seems to be disclaiming a learned approach to style, although such an approach is still apparent in his selfconscious 'artlessness' and his emphasis that this does not detract from his *sens*.

It is sometimes thought that *trobar leu* is the same as *trobar clar*;[5] however Giraut uses *clar* only to describe a singing voice: 'Mo sonet rauquet e clar' (IV. 13).

Plan applied to diction meant 'smooth' for Marcabru and probably also for Cercamon and Jaufré Rudel.[6] This may be its meaning for Giraut though it is usually linked with clarity:

> Aital chansoneta plana
> Que mos filhols entendes
> E chascus s'i deportes,
> Fera, si far la saubes;   (XX. 1–4)

I should compose such a smooth little song as my godson might understand, and everyone might take delight in, if only I knew how to do so;

> Trop volgra mais donar
> Mos gais sonetz joios
> Ab bels dichs et enters,
> Entendables e plas
> Que trop escurs ni sobrestorias,   (LXVIII. 9–13)

I should much prefer to give my gay, joyous melodies, with fine, complete expressions, comprehensible and smooth, than with ones which are too dark or over-embellished.

[1] Kolsen, ii. 1–2.
[2] He relates how Giraut went to school in winter, and praises his celibacy and his gifts to the Church.   [3] J. Boutière and A. H. Schutz, p. 212.
[4] Ibid.; cf. *SWB* v. 5: *maestrat* 'kunstvoll, geschickt . . . auch im üblen Sinne . . . "fenchas, falsas, maestradas" (*Brev. d'Am.* 17546)'.
[5] Panvini, p. 11, calls Giraut a 'sostenitore convinto e zelante del *trobar clar*'.
[6] See p. 54 n. 2.

Sometimes Giraut polishes his style and yet does not clarify it enough for some people:

> Era, si.m fos en grat tengut,
>   Preir' eu ses glut
> Un chantaret prim e menut
>   Qu'el mon non a
> Doctor que tan prim ni plus pla
>   Lo prezes
>   Ni melhs l'afines;
>   E qui.m crezes
>   C'aissi chantes,
>   Polira,
>   Forbira
>   Mo chan
>   Ses afan
>   Gran.
> Mas, a lor veiaire,
> Car no.n sabon gaire,
> Falh, car no l'esclaire
>   D'aitan
> Que l'entendesson neis l'enfan.   (XXV. 1–19)

Now, if this were considered favourably for me, I should capture without lime a delicate, finely worked little song, such that no doctor in the world might take one so delicate or so smooth, or refine it better; and if anyone might believe that I should sing in this way, for him I should polish and adorn my song without great toil. But, in their opinion, since they know very little on the subject, I fail, because I do not clarify it to the extent that even children might understand it.

Since Giraut 'polishes' his song, *plan* suggests its smoothness; at the same time polishing it is apparently intended to make it clearer, even if some people are so stupid that they still cannot understand it. The way in which *plan* may come to mean 'clear, plain' is indicated by the following passage:

> Vauc un chantaret planan
>   De dichs escurs
>   C'us non i remanha.
> C'aissi leu, si s'era plas,
> Poiri' entre.ls Chatalas
>   Passar en Proensa;
> Que chansos leu entenduda
> Lai val e lai s'esvertuda.[1]   (XXVIII. 3–10)

---

[1] Salverda de Grave, p. 43: 'et là elle agit (sur les cœurs)'; cf. p. 67 *se esvertudar* 'se ranimer, prendre des forces' (OF *soi esvertuer* 'se ranimer').

I plane a little song of dark words so that not one remains. For in this way, if it were so planed, it would be able to pass easily among the Catalans and through to Provence: for there a song easily understood is valued and grows in influence.

Giraut clarifies his song, not by composing it spontaneously in a clear style, but by planing away all the dark expressions.

In short, Giraut sees the *trobar leu* as easy to sing and understand, light and entertaining, with an appearance of ease and carefree grace (*leu, leugier*). He describes its simplicity in deliberately pejorative terms: easy (*levet*), common (*venarsal*), menial (*vil*), foolish and unlettered (*fatz, ses maestria*). It is also smooth and polished, with obscurity planed away (*plan*).

After some hesitation[1] Giraut gives in to the pressure of his audience and turns to a light style. To the general public he justifies the change by stressing that his style is light, entertaining, easy to sing and understand, and not too learned; to potential critics, and supporters of the *trobar clus*, he argues that a *leu* song is more popular and just as hard to compose successfully as a song of the *clus* style.

The *tenso* between Giraut and Linhaure includes some of these arguments but a full discussion is hampered by Giraut's deferential attitude to Linhaure and his unwillingness to disagree with him too outspokenly. The arguments run as follows: Linhaure asks Giraut why he blames the *trobar clus* and whether he values what is common to all (I);[1] Giraut thinks everyone should compose according to his taste, but that a song which is 'levet e venarsal' is more popular (II); Linhaure argues that indiscriminate praise is worthless (III), to which Giraut replies that Linhaure seems afraid of applause, which is the chief end in singing (IV). Linhaure says he sings for his own satisfaction, not for applause, and seeks only to compose the best poetry (V);

> C'anc granz viutatz
> Non fon denhtatz:
> Per so prez' om mais aur que sal,
> E de tot chant es atretal;   (32–5)

For a thing of great commonness was never a thing of great worth; for that reason gold is more valued than salt, and with any song it is the same.

---

[1] In XXVI. 18–30 he defends the *trobar clus*.

[2] I follow Pattison's edition, *Raimbaut d'Orange*, XXXI. It is now generally recognized that Linhaure is Raimbaut d'Aurenga: see Kolsen, *Guiraut von Bornelh, der Meister der Trobadors*, Berlin, 1894, pp. 44–51, and Pattison, p. 23 n. 36.

Giraut's answer is not clear, and could mean that he takes just as much trouble over composing a light song as Linhaure does over a *clus* one, and is just as concerned in case a bad singer should spoil it, or that he prefers a humble person to sing it rather than someone of rank, or that it is better to sing a simple song as a poor singer will not spoil it as easily as he would a difficult one. Pattison thinks Giraut is trying to close the argument humorously.

> 'Lingnaura, fort de bon conseill
> Etz fis amans contrarian
> E per o si n'ai mais d'affan.
>   Mos so levatz,
>   C'us enraumatz
> Lo.m deissazec e.l diga mal,
> Que no.l deing ad home sesal.'   (36–42)

'Lignaura, excellent adviser, you are a very argumentative lover, and for that reason I am indeed more dismayed (than ever, as to whether or not I should follow your advice). Let a hoarse-voiced singer garble and sing badly my lofty tune, as I do not judge it fitting for a person of higher rank.' (Pattison).

'Giraut says that his poems are fitting only for the very lowest classes, not being good enough for those who have the slightest pretensions to rank.'[1] Possibly he also plays on *levatz* meaning

---

[1] Pattison takes D^a as base but emends E to *Etz* in v. 37 (which is unnecessary: 'L., a true friend (lover) who contradicts is full of good advice'). The variants are as follows:
36. *E* Linhaure, *R* Linaure; *R* cosselh. 37. *ER* Es, D^aN^2 E; *R* sis; D^aN^2R aman. 38. N^2 per so; *ER* sim ual; *R* may; *E* denfan, N^2R dafan. 39. *R* Me sō l. 40. *E* Cuns. 41. *ER* lonh (*R* luenh) de sagen nim digua (*R* nin diga), N^2 deissaçec. 42. *E* A cui nol deiz hom sesa, *R* A cuy hom no deya sensal, D^a Qe; D^a deig.
Kolsen takes *ER* as base: 'Linhaure, sehr gut meint es ein treuer Freund, wenn er widerspricht; ist mir also mein erhobener Gesang *mehr* Mühe wert, so möge ein Heiserer ihn mir immerhin verunstalten und denen schlecht vortragen, welchen ich als Dienstmann nicht etwa einen Tributgesang schulde!' He explains that Giraut means well when he contradicts; his song, sung in a loud voice because it is comprehensible, is worth more trouble; therefore, let a poor singer sing it badly only for himself and his like, for to Giraut's patrons it should be sung with a fine voice. (i. 377.)
Jeanroy (*AdM* xxi (1909), 363–8) thinks Giraut means that an elevated (*levatz*) song causes more anxiety than a simpler one since there is more fear that it will be garbled. Bertoni thinks Giraut wants to close the controversy and is saying that this argument is causing him more anxiety than a song of his being garbled: 'Linhaure! io so bene che un amico fedele è pieno di buone intenzioni quando redarguisce. Tale voi siete; siete molto benevolo a mio riguardo, benchè mi contradiciate sul

both 'lofty' and 'lightened': he would prefer his song, which is both valuable and 'made *leu*'[1]; to be sung by a humble singer rather than a sophisticated one.[2] Jokingly resorting to the word-play of the *trobar clus*, he would seek to amuse Linhaure and end the discussion. This would lead into the next stanza when Linhaure says: 'Giraut . . . Non sai de que.ns anam parlan . . .'.

D. Scheludko[3] claimed that all the distinctions between *trobar clus* and *trobar leu* could be explained by medieval Rhetoric. While the troubadours may use arguments taken from Rhetoric to support their own views of style, they adapt them for their own purposes within a secular literature; they do not simply repeat what was taught in the schools; and a correspondence between statements made by the troubadours and medieval Rhetoric does not of itself give a complete 'explanation' of their ideas. Yet his view applies most aptly to Giraut's stylistic theory.

When Giraut claims that he likes to hear his song 'carried to the well' (IV. 14), he seems to transpose into a medieval situation the Rhetorical precept which urges suitability of style to audience:

> Cum doceas artes, sit sermo domesticus arti:
> Quaelibet ars gaudet propriis. Sed sint sua verba
> Limitibus contenta suis: cum veneris extra
> In commune forum, placeat communibus uti.
> In re communi communis, in appropriatis
> Sit sermo proprius.[4]

When you are teaching the arts, let your speech be native to each art; each delights in its own idiom. But see that the idiom is kept within its own borders; when you come out into the common market-place

trovar chiuso. Epperò, mi fa male levare la voce contro di voi. Vedete? Questo mio canto, levàtovi contro, mi cagiona più d'affanno di quello che mi cagionerebbe un giullare arrochito (rauco) che me lo guastasse, disabbellendolo e dicendolo male, uno di quei giullari, a cui non occorre dare paga o ricompensa.' (*RLR* liii (1910), 520.)

Salverda de Grave thinks Giraut means his light song gives him more trouble to compose than an obscure one, and cares not if a hoarse *joglar* ruins it because he owes it to no man as tribute (p. 119).

---

[1] Cf. p. 104.

[2] Cf. IV. 12–13 'Can auch dire per contens / Mo sonet rauquet e clar', and Pattison's comment, op. cit., p. 176.

[3] *Arch. Rom.* xv (1931), 145.

[4] Geoffrey of Vinsauf, *Poetria Nova*, 1087–90. This doctrine has grown out of the distinction between *civiles quaestiones* and *quaestiones artium propriae*, general and specialized questions (see Lausberg, § 48 and § 55), in which appropriate language should be used; the use of *verba artium propria* (Quintilian, VIII. ii. 13) is one way of

it is desirable to use the common idiom. In a common matter, let the style be common; in specialized matters let the style be proper to each.[1]

The 'well' is Giraut's equivalent for the 'common market-place', though it is figurative: he still composes for a courtly audience, but for a wider section of that audience than poets of the *trobar clus* do.

Just as Giraut has certain reservations about discarding the *trobar clus*, emphasizing that he could compose in that style if he wanted to: 'Be.l saupra plus cobert far' (IV. 8), 'Ja, pos volrai clus trobar' (IV. 15), so Geoffrey in his *Poetria Nova* reminds the writer that even if he knows all things and is capable of lofty eloquence, he should think of his listener rather than his own abilities:

> Utere consilio; licet omnia noveris, unus
> Major in hoc aliis: in verbis sis tamen unus
> Ex aliis; nec sis elati, sed socialis
> Eloquii. Veterum clamat doctrina: loquaris
> Ut plures, sapias ut pauci. Nec tamen ex hoc
> Vilescis: sermone potes simul esse facetus
> Et facilis.   (1078–84)

Take counsel: it may be you know all things—you are greater than others in this—still, in your mode of expression be one of those others. Be of average, not lofty, eloquence. The precept of the ancients is clear: speak as the many, think as the few. You do not demean yourself by observing this precept; you can be at once elegant and easy in discourse.[2]

In both Geoffrey and Giraut the tension is present between the inclination to use one's most sophisticated skills, and the need to bend these to be appropriate to one's listeners. Geoffrey's words, 'loquaris / Ut plures, sapias ut pauci', find an equivalent in Giraut's words, 'E donc non entens / C'us motz fatz fass' aprendens / E ses maestria? — / Si fatz be, mas tot es sens!' (V. 16–19.)[3] Giraut's are transposed to a courtly situation: he wants everyone to sing his lady's praises.

Giraut stresses the outward appearance of ease of his *trobar leu*, and at the same time the hard work needed to achieve this

---

committing the vice of obscurity, through *improprietas* (Lausberg, § 533). Köhler, pp. 147–51, argues that Giraut draws his arguments in favour of the *trobar leu* from 'popular sources' combined with the Augustinian concept of *sermo humilis*.

[1] Nims, p. 55.   [2] Ibid. Cf. Scheludko, *Arch. Rom.* xv (1931), 146.
[3] See p. 107.

ease. Geoffrey says that even in the *stilus gravis*, *gravis* and *levis* must be combined: it must be *gravis* in thought or *inventio*, *levis* in clarity and ease:

> Egregie sic verba locas; sic verba locata
> Pervia mentis erunt oculo. Sed verba locare
> Res onerosa quidem studio. Modus iste loquendi
> Est gravis estque levis: gravis est inventio verbi,
> Mens levis inventi. Sic se contraria miscent,
> Sed pacem spondent hostesque morantur amici.
> Est ibi temperies quaedam. Ne sit leve verbum,
> Vile vel illepidum: trahit a gravitate leporem
> Et pretium. Gravitas ne turgida sit vel opaca;
> Praestat ei levitas lucem reprimitque tumorem:
> Altera castiget reliquam. Sic ergo loquaris,
> Sic grave iunge levi, ne res haec detrahat illi,
> Sed sibi conveniant et sede fruantur eadem
> Pacificetque suam concors discordia litem.   (830–43)

In this way you use words in distinctive places;[1] when the words are used in such places they will be clear to the mind's eye; to place them so, however, requires both labour and skill. This mode of expression is at once difficult and easy: finding the word is difficult; its relevance, once found, is easy. Thus contrary qualities mingle, but they promise peace, and, enemies once, they stay on as friends. There is a certain balance required here: the word must not be trivial, crude or awkward; it derives charm and value from its seriousness of meaning. Its seriousness, however, must not be pompous or obscure; ease[2] of comprehension renders it luminous and checks bombast. Each quality must temper the other. Let this be your mode of expression then: combine seriousness and ease[2] in such a way that the one does not detract from the other; let them be in accord with each other and enjoy the same dwelling; let harmonious discord reconcile their differences.

Just as *levitas* is at times an essential part of the *stilus gravis*, so Giraut emphasizes that his style is both *leu* and by no means less valuable than the *trobar clus*.

It seems that Giraut regards *clus* and *leu*, as Scheludko suggested,[3] as different aspects of the same high style: *clus* the high style refined and ornamented to the utmost of the poet's capacity, *leu* the high style tempered to suit the audience. While at the

---

[1] Geoffrey is discussing the metaphorical use of verbs, in the section on *ornatus difficilis*. Cf. Horace, *Ars* 47–8, 'Dixeris egregie notum si callida verbum / reddiderit iunctura novum.' Nims, pp. 45–6, reads 'You may transpose verbs very effectively in this way, verbs so transposed will be readily visible . . .'.

[2] Nims: 'easiness'.   [3] See p. 90.

extremes these two are different, the degree of difference will depend on the degree to which the poet has in mind the need for clarifying the meaning or ornamenting the style, and varying shades of clarification and embellishment are possible between the two extremes. This I think is the reason why it is not easy to distinguish between *clus* and *leu* in Giraut's works.

This does not necessarily apply to other troubadours. Giraut is the keenest theorist among the troubadours; he is especially concerned to define, classify, justify his styles, and he uses a Rhetorical framework in which to do so: yet he may be imposing this framework on styles which existed before his time and which developed in their own way, independently of Rhetoric or of Giraut's concept of it. This is indicated by Giraut's methods of composition: his form of *trobar clus*, relying mainly on embellishment, is different from that of Peire d'Alvernhe, or Marcabru or Raimbaut d'Aurenga, where the interweaving of meanings is most important.

Peire d'Alvernhe's biographer says that Giraut was the first troubadour to compose *chansos*: 'Canson no fetz [Peire], qe non era adoncs negus cantars appellatz cansos, mas vers; qu'En Guirautz de Borneill fetz la primeira canson que anc fos faita.'[1] The distinction between *vers* and *chanso* is now usually regarded as a chiefly musical one,[2] but it is possible that the term *chanso* appears with the emergence of the *trobar leu*.

Before the middle of the twelfth century *vers* is the common

---

[1] Boutière and Schutz, p. 163.

[2] J. H. Marshall, 'Le vers au XIIIe siecle: genre poétique?', *Revue de langue et de littérature d'oc*, xii–xiii (1962–3), 55–63, says that by about 1250 *vers* denoted a didactic or moral poem; before 1150–60 it was the almost exclusive name for any lyric poem. After 1150 the terms *vers* and *chanso* run concurrently, while more exact terms, such as *tenso* and *sirventes*, emerge to describe special genres. Marshall says that Raimbaut d'Aurenga is the first troubadour to distinguish between *vers* and *chanso* (in Pattison, IV, XVIII, XXX), although he notices Giraut's song 'A penas sai comensar' (IV) too (see below). After this time some troubadours speak of the *vers* as if it represents higher poetic values than the *chanso*, but the troubadours themselves seem confused, for Aimeric de Peguilhan refutes an assumption among his contemporaries that the genres are differentiated by their use of masculine and feminine rhymes.

Marshall thinks the *vers* was not a particular genre, but follows the theory of J. Chailley, 'Les premiers troubadours et les versus de l'école d'Aquitaine', *R* lxxvi (1955) 212–39, that *vers* originated from the liturgical *versus* at S. Martial de Limoges. During its evolution, Marshall suggests, the stanzaic forms of the *vers* ceased to resemble those of the *versus*, so the more general term *chanso* came to be used instead. He considers that by about 1160 the term *vers* was linked with what was archaic, and was for this reason prized by certain poets.

name for a lyric song;[1] while *chanso* exists as early as the *Chanson de Sainte Foi*,

> Canczon audi q'es bella 'n tresca,
> Que fo de razo Espanesca,[2]

there is no reason to suppose this refers to a lyric. Bernart de Ventadorn, whose career probably does not begin much earlier that Giraut's,[3] uses the term *chanso* in seven songs and *vers* in eleven,[4] without apparently distinguishing between the two. Giraut does, however, seem to make a distinction.

Not one of his *vers*, so called by name, is described as *leu, levet, leugier,* or *plan*.[5] On the other hand nearly all of the songs which he calls *chansos*, or diminutively *chansonetas*,[6] contain remarks about their lightness or clarity:

> Ja, pos volrai clus trobar,
> No cut aver man parer
> Ab so que ben ai mester
> A far una *leu chanso;*   (IV. 15–18)

> ... si pogues avenir
> En un *leu chantar* conge;   (XVII. 4–5)

> Vauc un chantaret planan
>   De dichs escurs ...
> Que *chansos leu entenduda*
> Lai val e lai s'esvertuda;   (XXVIII. 3–10)

> Aital *chansoneta plana*
> Que mos filhols entendes;   (XX. 1–2)

> *Leu chansonet' e vil.*[7]   (XLVIII. 1)

In the song 'A penas sai comensar' (IV), which marks a turning-

---

[1] See p. 115 n. 2.   [2] A. Thomas, p. 3 vv. 14–15.
[3] See p. 88 n. 2.
[4] *Chanso*: IV. 61; VI. 24, 62; VIII. 1, 53; X. 51; XVIII. 32; XXVIII. 67; XXXIII. 44; *chansoneta*: XVI. 49; *vers*: I. 1; VI. 24; VIII. 2; XIII. 6; XV. 50; XXI. 57; XXII. 7; XXIII. 57; XXVI. 36; XXIX. 8; XXXI. 58. (Ed. Appel.)
[5] IX. 12; XVIII. 46; XXII. 5; XXIX. 67; XXXII. 3; XXXIII. 10; XXXV. 7; LX. 73; LXII. 46. In IV and XL both terms appear: see below.
[6] *chansos*: IV. 18; XVII. 15; XXVIII. 9; XXXI. 78; *chansonetas*: XX. 1; XLVIII. 1.
[7] Giraut also calls three songs *sonetz*: XLIX. 7; LXVIII. 10; LIII. 1. *Sonet* is probably a diminutive of *son*, 'melody'. Two of these mention clarity: XLIX. 1–9; LXVIII. 10–13. In IX. 23; XXX. 23–4; XL. 41–2, *chanso* and *vers* refer to songs in general, or the songs of other poets.

point in Giraut's attitude to *clus* and *leu*,[1] he regards the idea of a *vers leuger* as a contradiction in terms:

> A penas sai comensar
> Un vers que volh far leuger;   (IV. 1–2)

once he has managed to make it *leuger* it has become *una leu chanso* (v. 18).[1]

'No posc sofrir' (XL) presents some ambiguity. The composition is called *vers* (v. 30), yet Giraut ends by saying he has made his words 'ben esclairatz', 'Qu'entendetz cals *chansos* eu fatz' (73–6). It is possible that he is using *vers* and *chanso* indiscriminately now, at a time sufficiently removed from the original controversy for the terms to have become vague. Yet, if I am right in thinking that Giraut consciously opposed the light *chanso* to the weightier *vers*, it would be strange for him to forget this when referring once more to the *clus-leu* controversy. I would suggest tentatively that he is indicating a compromise: what kind of *chansos* is he now singing? They have the weight and richness of *vers*, but are 'ben esclairatz'.

3. Composition in the 'trobar clus'

We have now reached the point where we can examine Giraut's methods of composition, and see in what way these correspond with his theories and how far his practice resembles that of other troubadours. His most obviously *clus* poem is 'Ans que venia'; it is one of Giraut's most difficult songs and is preserved only in *V*.[2]

I
> Ans que venia.l nou*s* frug*z* tendres
> ni.l sobrefaix brondels baixe,
> prec mon coragg' e l'amas
> vas un' amor e l'asejn.
> Sitot lo m'avi' espars   5
> per mantas contradas lojn,
> viul qu'era.s vir e s'atejn
> d'autr' obr' e d'autre captejn.

II
> E son aixi fresc*s* e tendres
> que per mal pas ni per raix*e*,   10

---

[1] See p. 102.

[2] The editions of Kolsen and Salverda de Grave (*Observations*, Appendix) are based on the reading of C. A. F. Mahn, *Arch.* xxxvi (1894), 416, so I have re-edited it from the MS.

si be.m va len ni de pas,
no.m laix a virar l'engejn
si que plus de mos afars
puscha tornar a nos*o*jn,
que lai vir la forz' al gejn   15
o.ls huils a.l coratge tejn.

III   E si *m'i*est amics, n'ofend*r*es
ni.t pes, qui que tenc o daixe,
zo qu'eras ves ni veiras:
c'Amors mi coz' e.m destreyn;   20
e si.m n'er estrayns ni pars
eras pus sai vir e p*o*jn
covenra c'al seu sejn rejn,
e.ls autres torn e*n* desdejn.

IV   Car d'una filla dos gend*r*es   25
pot hom greu far, no s'abaixe
vas l'un, de quascu se ras;
si gran forza non empejn
qu'aillors mi faz amics cars,
e sai, si fin' es, esojn   30
mos tresvolers: no.i retejn
mas que.l me vend' o m'enpejn.

V   E si.l malvatz crup-en-sendres
s'enardis qu'en lais s'eslaixe,
vils sia tengutz o bas;   35
c'aixi desfil' e destejn
desaffrenatz domneihars,
qui.l pretz no.i garda ni.l s*o*jn;
e s'eu a mos precs av*e*jn
no vendra be qui be.m pejn.   40

VI   Per trussar ni per diven*d*res
no.m destric que non engraixe
si.l sieus cors delgatz e gras
m'es de pres, c'aixi revejn,
si be.m n'ave greus parlars —   45
car ges monges de Cadojn
no.s fion en entresejn,
c'a ver nisi m'en depejn.

VII   E qi.n parra greus l'apend*r*es
de mon chantar, no s'en laixe,   50

si no.l soi del dir esc*as*:
c'ap fin coratge l'essejn,
sitot mosejnh*e*r n'Aimars
se cuia que faz ab ojn;
c'aixi l'escur e.l n'ebejn,   55
mon trobar ab saber prejn.

VIII   Can l'autre s'en van eu vejn,
              si Dies la.m salv' e la.m sejn.

I. Before the tender new fruit appears and the over-burden bends down branches, I implore my heart and gather it in and direct it towards one love. Although I had scattered it throughout many distant lands, I desire it now to turn back and commit itself to other work and other conduct.

II. And I am so fresh and tender that I do not allow my mind to waver because of obstacles or difficulties, even if I only proceed slowly and gradually; so that I can ignore most of my preoccupations; for I direct my energy to the task on which I fix my eyes and heart.

III. And if you are a friend to me, may what you now see or are about to see not offend or grieve you, whoever may be in favour of it or not: for Love burns and constrains me; and if it was formerly remote and distant from me, now, since I turn and aspire towards this lady, it will be fitting for me to conduct myself beneath its ensign and scorn all others.

IV. For a man cannot make two sons-in-law from one daughter: if he is not inclining to one, he has deprived himself of both; such great force does not impel me to make myself beloved by another lady, and if this one here is noble—may she excuse my excessive desires—I make no reserve but that she should sell me or give me in pledge.

V. And if the evil cinder-squatter is so bold as to rush headlong into lays, let him be held vile or base; for unbridled wooing unravels and discolours one who pays no heed in this to reputation and caution; and if I achieve the object of my entreaties, one who paints my likeness will make no sale (because my outward appearance will dissimulate my feelings).

VI. In ill treatment and fasting it does not hurt me that I do not prosper, if her svelte and comely person is near me, for thus do I thrive—even if this makes me tongue-tied, for even the monks of Cadonh do not trust to sign language alone, so that in this I depict myself as a real simpleton.

VII. And whoever may find it difficult to learn my song, let him not abandon the attempt, even if I am not miserly towards him in my speech: for I teach it (fill it with signs) with a sincere heart, although my lord Sir Aimars considers that I compose with unguent; for thus do I colour it darkly and make it black as ebony from this, my composition teeming with wisdom.

VIII. When others go, I come, if God saves and blesses her for me.

MS.: 1. nou frug. 2. dels brondels (extra syllable). 10. raire. 12. lengin. 14. anosejn. 17. sinnest; no fendes. 22. epuin. 24. e. 25. genres. 27. uas luna de quascu seras. 34. laixeslaixe. 38. sejn. 39. aujn. 41. diuenres. 49. lapenres. 51. escos. 53. mosejnhar. 58. saluu elam s.

NOTES

Stanzas I, II, IV show that the first line of the stanza is -endres; the rhyme in the sixth line is -ojn, as in stanzas I, IV, VI, VII.

2. *brondels*: Kolsen, 'Strauch' (ii. 19); Salverda de Grave, p. 115; 'rameaux'; cf. Appel, *Chrest.*, 30. 3: *branc e brondelh son nut*.

3. Kolsen, *plei* (for *prec*).

4. *asejn*: Kolsen: 'bringe es zur Vernunft' (note, i. 11: 'ich kläre es über die Liebesangelegenheiten auf, mache es dazu geeignet'). Jeanroy, *AdM* xix (1907), 389–90, is followed by Salverda de Grave, 'vers lequel je le dirige', from *assignare*, 'diriger, adresser'. Possibly both meanings are intended.

7. *s'atejn*: Kolsen: *s'arenh*, 'einrichte'; Salverda de Grave: *vir, e m'atenh*, ' . . . et je m'attache à agir' (p. 115). But see *SWB* i. 96: *se atener*, 'sich entscheiden'. Giraut wants to decide on the right kind of love: cf. Marcabru, XLII. 1–6: 'Quan l'aura doussana bufa . . . Ladoncs deuri' hom chausir / Verai amor ses mentir', and Peire d'Alvernhe, IX. 1–6.

9. Kolsen: *Et enaissi frescs es tendres*, 'Und so neu ist die Zuneigung (?)'; Salverda de Grave, p. 115, points out that *tendres* as an adjective has different sense in stanzas I and II.

10. Kolsen: 'trotz Gefahr und Qual', taking *malpas* as 'gefährlich zu passierende Stelle' (Gloss. ii. 211), and *raisse* from *raisar, raisos* (Rayn. v. 50: 'tourmenté, désireux', *SWB* vii. 10: 'soucieux'). Salverda de Grave: 'à cause du mauvais chemin et du mauvais temps', following Mistral: *reissa, raissa*, 'pleuvoir à verse' (*SWB* vii. 10). This would mean Giraut remains constant in spite of adversities.

12–14. Salverda de Grave: 'je ne laisse pas de changer mon esprit d'autrefois, de façon à ce que mes anciennes affections me deviennent aussi indifférentes que possible.'

15. Kolsen: *fors' e.l genh*. Salverda de Grave: *Que lai vir a forza.l genh*, 'car je force ma pensée vers l'endroit . . . .' The poet's *genh* is 'what he has in mind'.

17. Kolsen, Salverda de Grave: *si m'est. no fendes*: Kolsen, *no.n tendres*; Salverda de Grave, *n'ofendes*, 'ne t'en offense (?) pas'. *SWB* v. 464: *ofendre*. I take *ofendres* as imperfect subjunctive with the subject *zo qu'eras ves*: 'might what you now see . . . not offend' or 'would that . . . did not offend'.

18. Kolsen: *qui que t'en so d'aisse*; Salverda de Grave: *teng' o laisse*, '"dans aucun cas" (Littéralement: "qui que ce soit qui tient ou laisse" (?))' *daisar = laisar*, see Rayn. iv. 12, *SWB* ii. 2.

21. Kolsen: 'und war ich bisher darin (in Liebessachen) spröde und zurückhaltend'; Salverda de Grave: 'et si (jusqu'à présent) Amour m'a été hostile et s'est tenu loin.'

22. Kolsen hits on the reading of *V* in his emendation of Mahn's reading *sai iurn estuin*, to which Salverda de Grave's comments relate.

23. *sejn*: Kolsen, 'Winke'; Salverda de Grave, 'd'après ses indications'. *Senh* can mean 'sign, mark, signature' (*PD* 340) and suggests Love's 'trademark'; 'ensign' is strictly *ensenha*.

25–9. *Car d'una filla . . . greu far* comes from a proverb, 'D'une fille deux gendres' (see Jeanroy, *RC* (1908), no. i, p. 150, or 'Len ne puet faire d'une fille deus gendres' (J. Morawski, *Proverbes*, p. 55, no. 1515). Kolsen's text and translation ignore the proverb: 'Car de filhas a dos gendres, / Pot om greu far no s'abaisse / Vas l'un que chascu ser as? — / Si grans forsa no m'empenh / C'alhors me fass' amics chars. —' 'Da es zwei Arten Frauen gibt (?), kann man deshalb schwer umhin, sich mit der einen stets zugänglichen (?) (Art) [note: 'der einen, die du jeden Abend (zur Verfügung) hast' (?)] einzulassen? — Wenn grosse Charakter-stärke mich nicht dahin bringt, mir anderswo *wertvolle* Freunde zu erwerben.' Jeanroy emends:

> 'Car d'una filha dos gendres
> Pot om greu far. — No *t*'abaisse
> Vas l'una de cal seras! —
> Si grans forsa no m'empenh
> C'alhors me fass' amics chars
> E, s'aissi fin' e ses sonh
> Mostre.*m* voler(s), no.i retenh
> Mas qu'*ilh* me vend' o m'empenh.'

'Car avec une seule fille il est difficile de faire deux gendres (c.-à-d. un seul amant ne peut servir deux femmes). (Puis le poète se fait adresser la parole par un interlocuteur imaginaire.) — "Ne t'abaisse pas vers une femme dont tu seras (deviendras) la propriété!" — (Le poète répond:) "A moins qu'une force irrésistible ne me pousse à me faire l'ami d'une autre, et si, fidèle et sans m'op-poser d'obstacles, elle montre qu'elle m'accepte, je ne retiens rien (de moi-même) sauf ceci qu'elle me vende ou me mette en gage."' (See Kolsen, ii. 20.) Salverda de Grave reads v. 27: 'Vas l'una de qu'a.scu seras', 'Car avec une seule fille on peut difficilement faire deux gendres (et un homme ne doit pas appartenir à deux femmes) sans s'abaisser envers l'unique à qui tu serviras de bouclier (sc. protecteur); une si grande force (qu'est mon amour pour elle) m'empêche de chercher d'autres amantes, et si elle (sc. ma dame) est si parfaite, qu'elle me pardonne alors mes autres amours (antérieures). . . .' His version of v. 27 is improbable. *Tresvolers* probably means 'excessive desires', but for this lady, not for past loves.

v. 27 contains an extra syllable, and the simplest to eliminate is *a* in *una*. *Un* and *quascu* seem to be antithetical, as *aillors* and *sai* (29–30), and *una* and *dos* (25). I suggest that 25–7 contain one idea: 'Since a man can hardly make two sons-in-law from one daughter, if he does not incline to (choose) one of them, he has lost both', taking *se ras* from *raire* (*SWB* vii. 8–9: *raire alcun de*, 'jmdm (einen Besitz) schmälern'. If the prospective father-in-law does not make up his mind which suitor to take, he will lose both, and Giraut also sees his ultimate profit in fidelity to one lady. This is the theme of the song. He continues: 'Strong temp-tation does not induce me to make myself beloved elsewhere.'

28. *empejn*: Salverda de Grave: 'empêche'; but *PD* 139: 'pousser, heurter'.

34. *lais*: this can be pejorative, suggesting an inferior type of song and by extension 'rumours': cf. *SWB* iv. 307: 'Que.l gelos braus janglos di lays, / Que sabra tot nostra voler' (*Prov. Ined.*, p. 287, v. 6).

40. I follow Salverda de Grave.

41–8. See Salverda de Grave.

49. *qi = cui*.

51. Kolsen: 'wenn ich ihm auch zu viel dichte'; Salverda de Grave: 'Je suis dis-posé à la répéter souvent.' Giraut is indicating the richness of his style: see p. 96.

53. Kolsen: 'Si tot Mo-Senhor no m'ars'; Salverda de Grave: 'Si tot Mos Senher

no m'ars', following Mahn. Giraut composes a *planh* to *mossenher n'Aimars* (77.
19), whom Kolsen identifies with Ademar V, Viscount of Limoges, 1148–99
(ii. 271).

54. Kolsen, note p. 15 (vol. i): 'dass ich ihn nur trübe und nicht völlig dunkel
mache'; Salverda de Grave: '"de chic" (Littéralement "avec de la peinture,
comme une chose peinte, non réelle"), donc "que je ne l'aime pas"'; but this line
does not refer to the lady. *Onher* means 'to flatter' (*SWB* v. 489): Giraut seems to
be protesting that he is sincere (v. 52) in spite of Aimars's belief that his words are
pure flattery. *Ab ojn* may also mean 'with obscurity' or 'with too much richness':
see my remarks on p. 97.

55. Kolsen: *l'escur com ebenh*; Salverda de Grave: *? e l'ebenh*. To follow the MS. we
must suppose (as Salverda de Grave) the existence or formation of a verb
ebenhar, and that *n'* refers to *fin coratge*, or the manner in which Giraut is composing.

57. Salverda de Grave: 'Là où d'autres renoncent à un amour non répondu, moi
je persiste.'

K. Vossler[1] saw this song as an example of superficial and
arbitrary darkness, crowded with confused, half-thought-out
images and incomprehensible allusions. It is certainly difficult,
but even if all the obscurities have not yet been resolved it is
uncertain that Giraut intended to be obscure.

While Giraut leads us to expect depth of meaning in his
trobar ab saber prenh, his theme proves simple and commonplace:
a decision to be faithful to one lady. Underneath the rhetorical
language are troubadour *topoi*: the poet wants to be morally
fruitful, and after scattering his attentions he turns to a single
dompna and a new way of life (stanza I);[2] his youthful outlook
(v. 8) gives him patience, single-mindedness, and *mezura* (stanza
II);[3] this is a result of Love's power over him (stanza III);[4] he
accepts the need for fidelity and submission (stanza IV);[5] the
boorish, slanderous rival should not be heeded for he will not
care for the lady's reputation as the poet does (stanza V);[6] his
lady's presence sustains him in spite of hardships, but he appears
foolish because he is unable to tell her of his feelings (stanza VI);[7]
he boasts of his literary skill (stanza VII),[8] and ends on a note of
perseverance and hope (stanza VIII).[9]

[1] *Die göttliche Komödie*, ii. 439.
[2] Cf. Marcabru, XLII, stanza I, and pp. 36–7.
[3] Ibid. XXXVII. 24: 'Jois, Sofrirs e Mesura.'
[4] Bernart de Ventadorn, XLII. 47; XVII. 2; XXII. 52.
[5] Giraut, LXVIII. 71–2; XVI. 49–52; XLV. 76–80.
[6] Ibid. LIX. 47–8; LXIX. 33–6; LXIV. 37–48.
[7] Ibid. II, stanza II; Bernart de Ventadorn, XVII. 37–40.
[8] Cf. all Giraut's boasts quoted in this chapter.
[9] Giraut, VI. 3–4; XXII. 7–8; XLIV. 54–64.

These *topoi* could have been expressed in the *trobar leu*. Unlike Marcabru's themes, which demanded complex treatment because of devious thoughts, a paradoxical state of mind, the process of bringing truth out from darkness, Giraut's theme is straightforward but overlaid with rhetorical embellishment.

This consists in devices for amplification and circumlocution, the variation of commonplace ideas, and implied additional meanings. Simple ideas are extended or turned round by periphrasis: 'qu'aillors mi faz amics cars' (29) means simply 'that I should woo another lady'; 'e s'eu a mos precs avejn / no vendra be qui be.m pejn' (39–40), simply 'if I am successful I will be discreet'. Statements are varied acording to *conversio*:[1] 'si be.m n'ave greus parlars' rather than 'si be no sap a lei parlar' (45), *expolitio*: 'no.m destric que non engraixe . . . c'aixi revejn' (42–4), understatement: 'si no.l soi del dir escas' (51), metonymy: 'Per trussar ni per divendres' (41), literally 'through being trampled underfoot, and Fridays', meaning 'through hardships and fasting'. In stanza III ideas are amplified by repetition in synonymous or antithetical pairs: 'n'ofendres / ni.t pes', 'tenc o daixe', 'ves ni veiras', 'mi coz' e.m destreyn', 'estrayns ni pars', 'vir e pojn', 'seu . . . autres'. In stanza I the metaphor 'per mantas contradas lojn' (6) means simply 'in many ladies'; it has none of the allusiveness of the *amor de lonh* theme of Jaufré Rudel or Peire d'Alvernhe[2] and is removed from the context of such love.

Giraut embellishes the style with compound words such as *sobrefais* (2), *tresvolers* (31), *crup-en-sendres* (33), by rhetorical devices such as apostrophe (17 ff.), the (commonplace) personification of *Amors* (20), a proverb (25–6), comparison (46–7), and *licentia* (31–2)[3] when he pretends to make conditions under which he will agree to love the lady, but gives as the 'condition' that she should treat him as her personal property. Above all he enriches the style through images and words suggesting more than one meaning. The image of the fruit weighing down the branches (1–2) suggests moral fruitfulness; the poet 'implores' his heart, 'gathering it in' as if he were harvesting it; and by the word *asejn* he suggests both the theme of wisdom, linked with moral

---

[1] See Faral, p. 245. [2] Cf. Peire, II, VII, VIII.
[3] *Rhet. ad Her.* IV. xxxvii. 49: *licentia* or 'frank speech' may be used *adsimulatione*, 'with pretence', because the speaker pretends he is about to be too frank but says what the listener wants to hear.

fruitfulness (*sen* as 'wisdom'), and the idea of controlling or 'directing' his heart (*sen* as 'direction'), which leads into the theme of the poet controlling his emotions. In the second stanza the poet's state of mind, 'frescs e tendres', is linked with the themes of fruitfulness but the emphasis moves from heart to mind (*engejn*, *gejn*) as this takes control. Words are used metaphorically and ambivalently. *En lais s'eslaixe* (34) suggests both the poor singing and the slanderous rumours of the uncourtly man. *Desfil' e destenh* (36) depicts his character as a piece of cloth which has become unravelled and discoloured; as poetic craft is often described in terms of weaving (*entrebeschar*) and colouring (*colorar*) it is implied that his songs will also be 'unravelled' and 'discoloured'. The equivocal use of *tendres* in stanzas I–II links the poet's state of mind with moral fruitfulness. *Sejn* appears in a number of forms: *asejn* (4), *entresejn* (47), *essejn* (52) meaning 'teach' but possibly also suggesting the 'signs' or implied senses with which the song is filled,[1] *sejn* (23) meaning the lady's 'sign' or 'ensign'; this seems to be a key word and, in this song where Giraut claims he makes his style darkly coloured, may suggest the variety of 'signs' or 'implications' present in it. Similarly Giraut plays on the word *penh*, meaning 'paint' and suggesting misleading appearances: *empejn* 'impel' (28), *enpejn* 'impound' (32), *pejn* 'paint' (40), *depejn* 'depict' (48).

In his use of shades of meaning Giraut ostensibly follows Marcabru: 'Dels plus tors sens / sui ples e prens, / de cent colors per mieills chauzir';[2] but Giraut makes no attempt to weave together different layers of meaning: he simply chooses words which will individually suggest meanings, applies 'colours' to his style to enrich it with individual details. He does not unfold his meaning gradually, as Marcabru did, for in Giraut's song each stanza amplifies one basic theme of single-minded fidelity to one lady. Marcabru used 'colours' to express a moral searching for truth, a complex state of mind, or the many ideas filling his mind at once. Giraut is closer to the prescriptive Rhetoric of the medieval arts of poetry, which theoretically advise gravity of thought but in practice are mainly concerned with the technical execution of embellishment. The 'darkness' or 'colour' of Giraut's song results not from complex thought, but from a roundabout way of expressing simple ideas and from a play on words. This is

[1] See p. 97.   [2] See p. 21.

probably because Giraut has tried to apply to a conventional love song addressed to a lady techniques more suited to moralizing poetry, where some truth is to be communicated or some conflict worked out.

Giraut has taken over the theory of 'coloured' composition from earlier poets but in his case this form of composition has lost some of its point and become merely ornamental. In the poet from whom we learn the most about *trobar clus* from a theoretical point of view, the style is already on the decline.

In 'Si.m sentis fizels amics' (27) Giraut claims to fill his composition with *estranhs sens naturals*. The text is Kolsen's.[1]

I
   Si.m sentis fizels amics,
   Per ver encuzer' Amor;
   Mas er m'o lais per paor
   Que.m dobles l'ant' e.l destrics.
  Mas aitan posc dire, Ses dan,   5
   C'anc d'engan Ni de no-fe
   No.m membret, pos amei be,
   Per c'ai sofert de grans mals;
   C'aissi s'aven als leials!

II
   E can no grana l'espics   10
   Si com pareis a la flor,
   Cudatz que plass' al senhor?
   Ans l'en creis ir' e genzics
  E par que consire De l'an
   Enavan, Can sap e ve   15
   Que sos afars no l'ave;
   Qu'eu vi c'us jorns ferials
   M'era melher c'us nadals.

III
   E vi ja, mentr' era rics   20
   Segon lo tems qu'era cor,
   Que.m teni' a dezonor
   Mans plachs don er sui abrics.
  Car vencutz sofrire Que blan
   Sofertan, Car no.s recre,
   So que plus li desconve,   25
   A segon que s'es egals
   L'amors e l'amics chabals.

[1] MSS.: *ABCDIKMNQRSgVac*; base *CMRSgVa*.

IV   E qui se fenher' enics
         Per espaventar l'os lor?
         Can plas volers no.i acor,   30
         Pauc li val precs ni chanzics.[1]
    Per so fai bo rire   D'aman
         Que l'afan   D'amor soste
         E no.l sap lonhar de se,
         Pos ve que.s vira venals;   35
         Es lo donc amors aitals?

V   Cudatz, joves ni antics,
         Pos en sa bailia cor,
         Tri de dos mals lo menor?
         No fera.l reis Lozoics!   40
    Deu s'om donc aucire   Preian?
         Drech n'ai gran;   Qu'eu sai e cre,
         Mas que non o dic per me,
         C'als verais amics corals
         No vai enan lor chaptals.   45

VI   Oimais semblara prezics
         Mos chans e, si Deu azor,
         Trop a, no vitz trobador
         Cui menhs noz' anta ni trics.
    Mas, per melhs assire   Mo chan,   50
         Vauc cerchan   Bos motz en fre
         Que son tuch chargat e ple
         D'us estranhs sens naturals
         E no sabon tuch de cals.

VII   No m'en chal; c'ab us mendics,   55
         Lonh de pretz e de valor,
         M'irasc que.s fan gabador
         L'ora que lor falh afics.
    Car ses bo sofrire   Per tan,
         Car no van   Egal ab re,   60
         Son si brau e ses merce
         C'us mazans n'issira tals;
         'Parlem nos, fan cilh, sivals!'

VIII   E pos no m'i val chastics
         C'ades no sian peior,   65
         Ges no m'a tan de sabor

         ────────────
         [1] See p. 129, n. to v. 31.

Lor solatz com dels Galics.
Deus los denh maldire;   C'antan
Per un gan —   De que.m sove?
Pero si.s fara jasse! —   70
Mogron m'ist no-fezat fals
Tal guerra, pois fo mortals.

IX   Amia, d'aisso.m sove
C'anc, depos que.m fis comtals
No m'avenc pois tan grans mals.   75

X   E tu ni tos chans que vals
Giraut, lonh dels Proensals?

I. If I felt myself to be a faithful lover, I should certainly accuse Love; but I now refrain from this for fear that it would double my shame and distress. But this much I can safely say: that deceit or faithlessness has never entered my mind since I have loved well; as a result of this I have suffered great evils: for thus does it befall the loyal!

II. And when the ear of corn bears no fruit, as the appearance of the flower led one to expect, do you imagine that this pleases the lord? Rather does he grow angry and vexed at it; and he seems to reflect on the coming year, when he knows and sees that his project is failing; for I have seen that a week-day was more profit to me than a Christmas day.

III. And I have seen the time, while I was prosperous in comparison with the present time, when I considered dishonourable many suits which I now accept to undertake. For a vanquished sufferer who pays court, still suffering, because he is not recreant—which would be most unseemly for him—receives according to how true love is to itself and the lover excellent.

IV. And who in such a case would feign rage to induce fear and trembling? When sheer desire does not assist, prayers and love-songs are little use to him. Therefore, a lover is laughable if he endures the torment of love and does not know how to rid himself of it, once he sees that it turns deceitful? Is then love like this?

V. Do you imagine, young and aged, since I rush into its tutelage, that I choose the lesser of two evils? King Louis would not do likewise! Ought one then to slay oneself with pleas? Well might I do so; for I know and believe, but speak this not for my own part, that for true, sincere lovers no progress can be made.

VI. From henceforth my song will seem a sermon, and, as I worship God, it has been a long time since you saw a troubadour less affected by shame and deceit. But, in order the better to seat my song, I seek out fine, tractable words which are all loaded and full of strange, natural meanings, and not everyone knows which they are.

VII. I care not; for I am angered by certain wretches, remote from renown and worth, who turn braggart in the hour that effort fails them. For lacking noble endurance because they are no one's equal, they are so harsh and pitiless that they will utter this clamour: 'Let us', they say, 'at least talk among ourselves!'

VIII. Beloved lady, I remember this much: that never since you made me the equal of a count, has such great suffering befallen me.

IX. And what are you and your song worth, Giraut, now that you are far from the people of Provence?

NOTES

1. Kolsen relates *amics* to *Amors:* 'Wenn ich mich für ihren wahren Freund hielte, würde ich die Minne sicherlich beschuldigen': 'Der Dichter fühlt sich nicht als wahren Freund der Minne, da er früher nicht immer *treu* geliebt hat. Daher bedeutet wohl in v. 7 *pos amei be* "seit ich aufrichtig liebte".' (ii. 58.) Giraut is probably expressing modesty about his worth as a lover. *Pos amei be* probably means 'since I have been loving this particular lady', as a compliment.

14-16. Lewent, 'Zum Text', p. 28, rejects Kolsen, 'er macht sich künftighin Sorgen', and translates: 'Und es ist klar, dass er (der in seinen Ernteaussichten Enttäuschte) sich über das Jahr (d. h. bis zur nächsten Ernte) im voraus Sorge machen muss.' Salverda de Grave, p. 58: 'mais il paraît que, quand il voit que (cette fois-ci) son affaire ne va pas à souhait, il pense à l'année qui suivra. (Ainsi, moi, je ne me décourage pas non plus et je ne renonce pas à mon amour malgré mes souffrances).' He interprets this to mean that the landowner, as the poet, resigns himself to present setbacks and places his hopes in the future (p. 106). These lines may be a reference to Matt. 13: 24-30: when the farmer discovers weeds in the corn, he plans to dispose of the weeds at the harvest. Giraut's theme in stanza II is that steady labour and eventual fruitfulness are better than fine appearance.

22. *plachs:* Kolsen: 'Wünsche'; Jeanroy, *AdM* xxi, 363-8: 'Il s'agit, sans doute, des reproches que la dame adresse au poète ou des difficultés qu'elle lui suscite, des ennuis, en somme, autrement désignés au v. 25.' Lewent, p. 29: 'Dinge'. *Plachs* may be 'suits' to the lady, or 'agreements' made with her (*PD* 295: 'querelle, différend; procès; objet d'un procès; question, affaire; convention, arrangement, accord . . .').

23 ff. Kolsen, Jeanroy, Lewent, Salverda de Grave, take 'So que plus li desconve' as the object of *blan*, but it may refer to the idea of the poet revoking his allegiance. vv. 26-7 Jeanroy punctuates and emends as follows: 'A, segon ques egals, L'amor e l'amic cabals': 'l'amant patient trouve, en proportion de l'égalité de son humeur, l'amour et son amie parfaits (tels qu'il les désire) . . . *Amic* n'est dans aucun ms., mais cette leçon me paraît exigée par le sens: G., comme bien d'autres troubadours, a souvent fait allusion aux services que peut rendre un véritable ami.' (*AdM* xxi, 363-8.) This confidant, arbitrarily introduced, is not mentioned elsewhere in the poem. Salverda de Grave, p. 97, translates the stanza: 'Et je me suis rendu compte que, au temps où, comparé au moment actuel, j'étais heureux, je considérais comme une honte bien des choses qu'aujourd'hui je supporte, comme (L. *com*, leçon de dix mss. sur 14) quelqu'un qui, vaincu, souffre et continue à servir sa dame, supportant — car il ne renonce pas à son amour — ce qui lui est le plus désagréable, car (L. *Que*, leçon de huit mss., entre autres *DIK* et *Sg*, tandis que trois lisent *Car*) dans la mesure où je lui étais fidèle (L. *l'era* (*l'er*), leçon de *IK* et de *Sg*) Amour était parfait pour moi (L. *era ab mi*).' Although this reading, 'Que segon que l'er' egals / L'Amors era ab mi chabals' is supported by several MSS., the reading of *CRa* (Kolsen) is

more compact and elegant, and fits better with Giraut's theme that it is in the nature of things that faithful lovers have no reward (see vv. 8–9, 44–5). To say that love was always perfect for him as long as he was faithful conflicts with this theme.

29. *l'os lor*. From the emphatic position of *lor* it probably means 'then' (cf. Kolsen, ii. 58) rather than 'leur'. Kolsen: 'um sie im Innersten zu erschrecken.' Jeanroy: 'Per espavantar los; lor Can . . . ', 'Et si quelqu'un affectait la colère (ou la rudesse) pour les effrayer (l'amour et l'ami), alors qu'il n'y a de leur part aucune bonne volonté, à celui-là serviraient de peu (à un autre moment) ses prières et ses chansons.' This depends on seeing *amic* in v. 27 as a confidant of the lover. The sense seems to be: the lover will have no success if he uses threats or complaints when inclination (on the lady's part) is absent.

31. Kolsen, *Cantics*: MSS.: chancics *c*, (originally), chanzics *a* and correction *c*, cançir originally *N*, iançics *Q*, castics *ABCIKMNRSg*, castic *D*, chas *V*. *Chastics* occurs in v. 64. Kolsen says *chantics* can mean a song of praise, but may also mean 'Schimpflied' as the Latic *canticum*, Jeanroy reads *chanzics* from *chanso*.

35. *venals*: 'deceitful' rather than 'venal'; see p. 23.

36. *lo*: either 'this' (Kolsen ii, 59, *SWB* iv. 414 ff.), or 'then', reinforcing *donc* (*PD* 228: 'là, alors').

37 ff. I follow Kolsen; Salverda de Grave, p. 90: 'La traduction ne peut être que: "Croyez-vous que jeune ou vieux, s'il est au pouvoir de l'amour, choisira le moins grand des maux?" ' But *cor* can be first person. In rushing into love's power, the poet makes his choice.

41–2. Salverda de Grave: 'On doit donc se tuer en priant et j'ai bien le droit (de le dire)' (p. 49). But Giraut means he has good cause to think he may die of love.

44–5. Salverda de Grave, p. 49: 'car le capital des amants sincères n'augmente pas.'

59. *Car ses bo sofrire*: I take *sofrire* as a noun. Kolsen: 'Denn ohne das Gute zu dulden.' Jeanroy: 'Car s'es bos sofrire per tan, car no van egal ab se': 'Car s'il y a un amant patient, ceux-là, parce qu'ils ne marchent pas du même pas que lui, sont si rudes et impitoyables qu'on les entend répéter à grand bruit: "Au moins parlons de lui (pour nous moquer de sa patience)".' Salverda de Grave: 'car sans jouir (L. *jauzire*, v. 59, leçon de *IK* et *Sg* . . .) de bonheur, pourtant — car ils ne se respectent pas (L. *ab se* . . .) — ils sont si méchants et si indignes . . . '. (See his Appendix, iii. 124 for his reasons for relying on readings common to *DIK* and *Sg*.)

69, 74. See Kolsen's notes, ii. 59–60.

The words themselves are not rare or difficult, and yet their meaning is not immediately clear. The reason for this seems to be that Giraut is trying to express a paradox about love: that love causes suffering, unjustly, and he has reason to complain; yet in accepting undeserved suffering he accepts the nature of love and improves in personal worth; and that he is trying to express this ambiguously, to bring out a sense of moral conflict by suggesting both the lover's instinctive reaction to ill treatment and his underlying welcome of the opportunity to test his moral strength. The first stanza expresses in an elaborate way[1] the poet's

---

[1] He combines a humility *topos* with *occultatio* (*Rhet. ad Her.* iv. xxvii. 37), a refusal to say what one actually is saying (because a direct reference 'aut longum est aut ignobile . . . ').

deference to love yet his inducement to complain: without being
certain of his faultless conduct as a lover, he is reticent in complaints, but at least he can safely say that he was never intentionally disloyal; his faithfulness has led to his being ill-treated, for
this is the nature of love.

The second stanza implies that labour and fruitfulness are
better than fine appearances. If the lord is not satisfied with the
harvest, he takes thought for the coming year: that is, he will
discard the useless corn or the weeds.[1] Giraut does not want to ·
be judged as fruitless, so he prefers week-days (work-days) to
holidays. The transition from stanza I is not explicit. Giraut
may be vague deliberately, for his comment on labour and fruitfulness could be applied both to himself and to love: either, the
lover may tire of waiting for love to bring him some reward, and
think of renouncing it in the future; or, since it is in the nature of
love that loyal lovers suffer unjustly (8–9), the lover must per-
severe and ripen morally, and not be distracted by 'holidays', for
such persistence tests his worth. Without perseverance he would
eventually be rejected by the *senhor*, Love.

Giraut says he now accepts certain suits to the lady, or agreements with her, that he formerly would have found shameful
(19–22). For a submissive, patient lover (23–5) is rewarded according to the nature of love ('according to how far Love is like
itself') and his own relative excellence (26–7). This seems to be
deliberately ambiguous, meaning both that the lover has only
himself to blame for his suffering, and that if he perseveres in
spite of suffering he will be rewarded. Giraut appears to be playing
with a paradox, that the lover must accept a certain kind of shame
as a test of his worth. On the one hand he speaks as the lover
who has reason for complaint; on the other, as one who accepts
humiliation, for it would be much more disgraceful to revoke his
allegiance.

Threats are useless in love, he continues (29–31); songs are
worthless if they are not inspired by love. Then he asks: is it
ridiculous for the lover to persist in the face of trickery, and is
this the nature of love? (32–6). No straightforward answer is given:
he admits that he has no intention of renouncing love, 'Pos en sa
bailia cor' (38), but rushing into its power is not something everyone would do, and is by no means the lesser of two evils. King

[1] See notes to vv. 14–16.

Louis had divorced Eleanor of Aquitaine, and exemplifies the haz-
ards of love. Again the second part of the stanza is ambiguous:
Giraut's claim that he may well die of love through his submissive
pleading, because he knows that sincere lovers are never the
successful ones, implies both complaint and acceptance.

The conflict between complaint and acceptance is resolved in
stanza VI, where he demonstrates that shame and deceit cannot
harm him: 'Trop a, no vitz trobador / Cui menhs noz' anta ni
trics.'

It appears that Giraut has followed the pattern of certain songs
of Marcabru and Peire d'Alverhne where the meaning is only
explicitly brought out towards the end of the song, after ambiguity or indirect expression of the theme in the first part. The
difficulties are increased in Giraut's song because of his vagueness
and circumlocutory style.

As soon as his stand is made clear, he explains that he has
filled his song with *estranhs sens naturals* (50–4). Those who do not
understand what these are, he reveals in stanza VII: they are
the churlish people who resort to empty boasting when they have
renounced perseverance. Such people cannot understand Giraut's
estranhs sens: firstly because they would not be able to accept
his moral theme, that a lover should accept unmerited suffering;
secondly, because his words have the double implication of
complaint against love and acceptance of the nature of love, and
the churlish people would see only the element of complaint.
These *estranhs sens naturals* are the ambiguous meanings or implications of his words, hard to grasp but *naturals* or inherent in
the theme.[1]

Unlike Marcabru Giraut does not play on the separate meanings of individual words, or the literal and figurative senses
of words and objects. He relies on ambiguity through vague
generalizations and unexplained metaphors, which in contrast to
Marcabru's colourful, detailed, and visual style, give an impression
of diffuseness. Again this may be inherent in the subject: the
conventional situation of love allows little scope for complex
thoughts.

[1] S. Santangelo, *Dante e i trovatori provenzali* (Catania, 1959), p. 180 n. 10, says
that *estranhs sens naturals* do not refer to the *trobar clus:* 'il poeta dice di non volere
troppo apertamente parlar male della donna che l'a bistrattato; il che è tutt'altra cosa.'
On the contrary, the *estranhs sens* refer to the acceptance of ill treatment as well as
the expression of discontent.

Dante quotes this song as an example of a composition on the subject of love.[1] He must have admired both the theme of humble and persevering love, and Giraut's command of ornate rhetoric.

4. *Composition in the 'trobar leu'*

Once having decided to turn to a lighter style, Giraut at first seeks clarity through plain and everyday language. In what may be his first *leu chanso*. 'A penas sai comensar' (IV), where he explains his reasons for the transition, his vocabulary and sentence structure are extremely simple, rarely passing beyond the barest statement. Whereas in his non-*leu* styles he finds rare and colourful ways of describing his literary skills: 'C'aixi l'escur e.l n'ebejn, / mon trobar ab saber prejn',[2] 'Vauc cerchan   Bos motz en fre / Que son tuch chargat e ple / D'us estranhs sens naturals',[3] 'Preir' eu ses glut / Un chantaret prim e menut',[4] the only image used in this song for his *trobar leu* emphasizes homeliness:

> Can auch dire per contens
> Mo sonet rauquet e clar
> E l'auch a la fon portar.   (IV. 12–14)

He makes the transition from the literary theme to the love theme so baldly that he can only be trying to make sure his listeners do not lose the thread:

> D'als m'aven a consirar;
> Qu'eu am tal que non enquer
> Per so car del consirer
> Sai be que fatz mesprezo.
> Que farai?   (22–6)

It occurs to me to consider something else; for I love such a one as I do not implore, because I well know that I do wrong in thinking of her. What shall I do?

The love theme proceeds in the plainest clichés: *ardimens* urges him to speak, *paor* holds him back (26–8); he would send a messenger if he could find one but his lady might blame him for it (29–32), since he ought to keep his love secret (*celar*, 33–5); her beauty renews his ardour and fear cools it (36–42), he cannot

---

[1] *DVE* I. xi. 2–3.   [2] See p. 119.   [3] See p. 126.
[4] See p. 138.

forget her and his thoughts are all with her (43–9). Only the brief-est image is admitted:

> Que gran batalha.n sofer,
> Car no.i vauc ad espero. (37–8)

For I endure great conflict from this (her beauty) which prevents me from spurring towards her.

Rhymes are commonplace, versification simple. Beneath the simplicity Giraut presents his ideas carefully: in the discussion of style in the opening stanzas, to which the rest is a technical illustration, notions of *vers*, *chanso*, *leuger* and *leu*, *cobert* and *clus* are carefully balanced, the arguments for *leu* presented circumspectly with both an appeal to general audiences and arguments to sup-porters of the *trobar clus*: he knows how to compose *plus cobert*, but reasons supported by knowledge of Rhetoric[1] demand that the style be made lighter. Even if the versification is simple Giraut does not seem to have sacrificed technical originality, for in Frank's *Répertoire métrique*[2] it is listed as unique. But the total impression of the song is one of barest simplicity.

This plain style proved controversial but not entirely successful. Peire d'Alvernhe,[3] taking up Giraut's phrase 'a la fon portar', laughed at Giraut in his satire on the troubadours:

> qe sembl' oire sec al soleill
> ab son chantar magre dolen,
> q'es chans de vieilla porta-seill; (XII. 14–16)

for he seems like a wine-skin dried up in the sun with his thin, doleful singing, which is the song of an old woman carrying a pail;

and it was probably the same song, certainly the same style, which provoked Raimbaut's many outbursts on the *leu chanso* with its 'rima vil' e plana'.[4] This plain style was too pedestrian for edu-cated poets such as Peire and Raimbaut, and on the other hand it failed to produce the light style of a Bernart de Ventadorn because, as Salverda de Grave said,[5] Giraut laboured with great effort to achieve clarity, and did not compose to express his own lyrical feelings.

---

[1] Educated contemporaries would probably have recognized that Giraut's argu-ments are drawn from Rhetoric. [2] See p. 224.
[3] Panvini, p. 18, rejects this idea, proposed by Kolsen (ii. 21), that Peire was referring to these lines, as 'una sottigliezza'; yet the images are too close to be acci-dental, especially in the context of singing.
[4] See pp. 169–78. [5] *Observations*, p. 86.

Giraut rarely, if ever,[1] repeats the style of 'A penas sai comensar'; he seeks a compromise between exaggerated simplicity and
the complexity of the *trobar clus*.[2] 'S'era no poia mos chans' (V), in
which Giraut comments on his *motz fatz e ses maestria*, is close to
'A penas' in simplicity of rhymes and vocabulary, but ostentatious
simplicity is tempered by the use of dialogue throughout the
whole composition. This enables Giraut to make an individual
impression both in style and perhaps in performance, for the
dialogue may have been sung by two people.

In 'Tot suavet' (XXVIII) Giraut emphasizes the clarity of his
style but embellishes it by concentrating on lightness, delicacy, and
musicality. 'A penas sai' and 'S'era no poia' had plain, commonplace rhymes; here they are not rare, but they are carefully
balanced in sound with two predominant vowels: *as, an, urs,
anha, ensa, uda*. The versification is more varied and complex,[3]
with frequent alliteration: *t*ot suave*t*, rie*n* joga*n*, Vau*c* un *ch*an-
*t*are*t* planan / De di*chs* es*c*urs, si s'era *p*las, / Poiri' entre.ls Chatalas
/ Passar en Proensa, *l*eu entenduda / Lai va*l* e *l*ai s'es*v*ertuda
(stanza I). Fineness and delicacy are produced by clipped sounds,
short words, diminutives, and short lines:

> Tot suavet e de pas
> Rien jogan
> Vauc un chantaret planan
> De dichs escurs . . .   (1–4)

---

[1] The language of Giraut's riddle song (LIII) is comparable, especially in vv. 1–6.
[2] The dating of Giraut's songs is uncertain; I suggest only as a hypothesis on
stylistic grounds that 'A penas sai' may be the first of Giraut's *leu* songs, since it
discusses the two styles in detail, seems to have caused strong reaction in Peire and
Raimbaut, and represents a new departure in its extreme plainness. According to
Kolsen's dating (ii. 284–6) it was composed about 1168, with other *leu* songs a little
earlier: 'Razon e loc' (XVII) 1167, 'Aital chansoneta' (XX) 1167–8, 'S'era no poia'
(V) before 1168. Panvini, op. cit., pp. 110–13, dates 'A penas' in 1188, after several *leu*
songs (V, 1170; XX, 1172; XXVIII, 1173; LVIII (the *tenso* with Linhaure), 1172). But
much of this dating by both Kolsen and Panvini rests on the doubtful basis of
Giraut's relationship with his lady or ladies (one, according to Kolsen, two according
to Panvini). In 'A penas' there is absolutely no indication of the identity of any lady
to whom it may have been addressed, and if it was meant for one particular lady, she
could have been at any of the many courts with which Giraut had relations (see A.
Kolsen, 'Der Trobador Giraut de Bornelh und seine Freunde', *Arch.* cxxvi (1911),
205). Panvini argues that 'A penas' must belong to the early stages of an affair since
the poet has not yet dared to confess his love, and it must belong to his second
affair since he addressed his first lady with songs in the *trobar clus*. Kolsen's date is
based on 'A penas' having been composed before Peire d'Alvernhe's satire.
[3] See p. 224.

Colour is added through proper names: *Chatalas*, *Proensa*, *Espanha*, *Espas*, *Milas*, *Argensa*, *Sanchs-Julias*.

In 'Leu chansonet' e vil' (XLVIII) Giraut seems to move even further away from plain statement, for although this is a song in the *trobar leu* and the theme is clearly enough stated in the introduction:

> Qu'eu dic qu'en l'escurzir
>   Non es l'afans,
> Mas en l'obr' esclarzir,   (7–9)

it is developed in a series of not particularly clear metaphors:

> E qui de fort fozil
> No vol coltel tochar,
> Ja no.l cut afilar
> En un mol sembeli;
> Car ges aiga de vi
> No fetz Deus al manjar,
> Ans se volc esalzar,
> E fetz esdevenir
>   D'aiga qu'er' ans
> Pois vi per melhs grazir.   (11–20)

And if a man is unwilling to sharpen his knife on a hard whetstone, let him not think he will whet it on a soft sable; for God did not make water from wine for the mere purpose of feeding, but wanted to exalt himself and turned what was formerly water into wine, for his greater glory.

This develops Giraut's theory that the *trobar leu* is a greater test of poetic skill than the *trobar clus*, not by logical argument but loosely connected analogies, which make the thought hard to follow. As God turned water into wine, not for mere utility but for the sake of his glory, Giraut appears to mean, so *leu* is more glorious than *clus*. These metaphors are closer to Giraut's *clus* techniques than to the style of the *trobar leu* in 'A penas sai', and indicate that he has moved away from stark simplicity to a compromise between this and his old style.[1]

Trobar leu therefore covers a fairly wide stylistic range, from plain statement, to clear styles with attempts to make an individual impression through dialogue or a special musical texture of

---

[1] The melody of this song appears to be fairly simple in comparison with, for instance, Peire d'Alvernhe's 'Dejosta.ls breus jorns', where the melody is ornately decorated. See F. Gennrich, *Der musikalische Nachlass der Troubadours* (Darmstadt, 1958), p. 63, no. 56 (Giraut) and p. 46, no. 36 (Peire).

the words, to a more elaborate metaphorical style where ambiguity is not intended, but where the sense is not clearly stated. This may account for the difficulty of distinguishing between Giraut's *clus* and *leu* songs: after the initial sharp contrast between the two, this contrast is subdued as Giraut attempts to reconcile clarity with his idea of a high style.

All of his *leu* songs, and his *chansos*, have smooth rhymes, while his *clus* songs and his *vers* often have rough ones, as shown in the following list.

Leu

IV	ar, er, o, ens
V	ans, ens, ers, ars, ia
XVII	oc, en, ais, ir, onge, ai, ar, os, alh
XXVIII	as, an, urs, anha, as, ensa, uda
XLVIII	il, ar, i, ir, ans
XLIX	ir, ai, en, ia, etz, aire
LI	ens, al, ans, er, ar, ars, ers, an
LXVIII	ais, ar, ans, ors, os, ers, as

Plan

XX	ana, es, es, ir, ais
XXV	ut, a, es, ira, an, aire
XXVI	an, es, atz, ona, e, en

(also XXVIII, LXVIII; see above)

Chansos

XXXI	er, en, aire, ida, ia, ai

(also IV, XVII, XX, XXVIII, XLVIII; see above)

Vers

IX	an, es, ors, atz, os
XVIII	ucha, anc, ir, itz, ans, ia
XXII	olh, an, ils, ors, ai, ans, ais, ers
XXIX	olh, or, ais, er, ans, os
XXXII	am, ors, atz, alh, etz, ems, atz
XXXIII	ams, es, ans, is, atz
XXXV	ol, er, ans, ais, ar, en, ai, or
LX	an, itz, ei, atz
LXII	utz, or, aire, aus

Clus

III	endres, aixe, as, ejn, ars, ojn
XXVII	ics, or, an, e, als

Smooth rhymes reflect the aim of the *trobar leu* to be pleasing, entertaining, and harmonious; rough rhymes recall the rough moralizing style of Marcabru and Peire d'Alvernhe.

5. 'Trobar prim'

From the time of Giraut and Raimbaut d'Aurenga the troubadours begin to use the term *prim* to describe their style. Arnaut Daniel particularly likes his style to be *plan e prim*.[1] The *trobar prim* emerges, not so much as a new style which is an alternative to *clus* or *leu*, but as a new approach which may coincide with either. Raimbaut combines *prim* with *lieu*:

> En aital rimeta prima
> M'agradon lieu mot e prim
> Bastit ses regl' e ses linha;　　　　　(II. 1–3)

[1] See p. 201.

In such a delicate little rhyme as this, light and delicate phrases delight
me, constructed without rule or line;[1]

Sordel composes in the *prim* style in his clear, *leu* song:

> Bel m'es ab motz leugiers a far
> Chanson plazen et ab guay so,
> Que.l melher que hom pot triar,
> A cuy m'autrey e.m ren e.m do,
> No vol ni.l plai chantar de maestria:
> E mas no.lh plai, farai hueymais mon chan
> Leu a chantar e d'auzir agradan,
> Clar d'entendre e prim, qui prim lo tria.[2]

It pleases me to compose an agreeable song with light words and
a gay melody, for the best lady that one could choose, to whom I
promise and yield and give myself, does not wish for learned singing,
nor does this please her; and since this does not please her, henceforth I shall make my song easy to sing and agreeable to hear, clear
to understand and exquisite to one who judges it with exquisite dis-
cernment.

Aimeric de Peguilhan links *prim* and *sotil* with *cara rima* and technical polish:

> Ses mon apleich   non vau ni ses ma lima,
> Ab que fabreich   motz et aplan e lim,
> Car ieu non veich   d'obra sotil e prima
> De nuilla leich   plus sotil ni plus prim,
> Ni plus adreich   obrier en cara rima
> Ni plus pesseich   sos digz ni miells los rim.[3]

I never go without my plane and my file, with which I fashion phrases
and plane and file them, for I see no subtle or delicate work of any
sort more subtle or more delicate (than mine), nor a more skilful
craftsman in precious rhyme, nor one who pieces his phrases together
more finely or rhymes them better.

In the eyes of Lanfranc Cigala, *escur*, *prim*, and *sotil* belong
together:

> Escur prim chantar e sotil
> Sabria far, si.m volia;
> Mas no.s taing c'om son chant afil
> Ab tan prima maestria,
> Que no sia clars com dia;

---

[1] See p. 182.
[2] Quoted by Levy, *SWB* v. 10; cf. C. de Lollis, XXII. 1–8. v. 3 de Lollis *Quar*
instead of *Que.l*.
[3] Shepard and Chambers, XLVII. 1–6.

Que sabers a pauc de valor,
     Si clardatz no.ill dona lugor;
         Qu'escur saber tota via
Ten hom per mort, mas per clardat reviu.
Per qu'eu chant clar e d'ivern e d'estiu.[1]

I should know how to compose a dark, clever and subtle song if I
wished; but it is unfitting for one to sharpen his song with such clever
artifice that it is not as clear as daylight; for wisdom has little value if
clarity does not give it light; for obscure wisdom is considered completely dead, but by clarity it comes to life. So I sing clearly in both
winter and summer.

For Giraut, *prim* describes a style which is finely polished, but
which is not clear enough for some people even in spite of his
efforts to make it plain:

         Era, si.m fos en grat tengut,
              Preir' eu ses glut
         Un chantaret prim e menut
              Qu'el mon non a
         Doctor que tan prim ni plus pla
                   Lo prezes
              Ni melhs l'afines;
              E qui.m crezes
              C'aissi chantes,
                   Polira,
                   Forbira
                   Mo chan
              Ses afan
                   Gran.
         Mas, a lor veiaire,
         Car no.n sabon gaire,
         Falh, car no l'esclaire
              D'aitan
Que l'entendesson neis l'enfan.[2]   (XXV. 1–19)

Since *prim* can describe clear and dark styles it is not primarily
concerned with degree of intelligibility or the way in which meaning is presented. It means 'fine, delicate, sharp, clever, subtle,
exquisite',[3] and may refer to the fineness and delicacy of form or

---

[1] Branciforti, XII. 1–10.   [2] See p. 109.
[3] Rayn. iv. 643, *SWB* vi. 547. Bernart Amoros says that one would have to be
very 'prims e sotils' to understand all of Giraut's poetry: 'que trop volgra esser
prims e sotils om qui o pogues tot entendre, specialmen de las chansos d'en Giraut
de Bornelh' (see E. Stengel, 'Le chansonnier de Bernart Amoros', *RLR* xli (1898),
350), but he does not refer specifically to the *trobar prim*.

the subtlety of skill or thought. Giraut's song, with its tight vowel sounds (*i*, *u*), short lines, and emphasis on the diminutive (*chantaret*, *menut*), is intended to be small and delicate, finely chiselled, miniature in its detail.

He describes his style in similar terms in 'Si.l cor no.m ministr' a drech' (XVI), which he calls *sotil*: 'fine, subtle, delicate',[1] *leuger*: 'light, agile',[2] and which has its expressions finely soldered together, *Sotils e menutz soudatz*.

> Si.l cor no.m ministr' a drech
> E mal so grat no l'afranh
> En un chantaret sotil,
> No m'es vis qu'era s'afranha,
>   Si no m'esfors' atz,
> En aitals motz peceiatz.
> Ja fo que.m n'entremetia
>   Plus qu'era no fatz,
>   Car melhs me lezia,
> C'a penas om conoissia
> Mos leugers dichs veziatz
> Sotils e menutz soudatz.[3]   (XVI. 1–12)

Like the song 'Era, si.m fos' (XXV), this is termed, diminutively, *chantaret*. *Motz peceiatz*, as *bels dichs menntz frais* (LXVIII. 1), appear to have no connection with *entier* and *frag* as they were used by Marcabru, Peire d'Alvernhe, or Bernart Marti,[4] but correspond with Aimeric de Peguilhan's boast that no one 'plus pesseich sos digz'.[5] Giraut probably wants to suggest the fineness of the individual words, the attention to individual detail, and the way they are skilfully and accurately pieced together.

6. *Giraut as 'Master of the troubadours'*

Giraut's prominence as a literary figure[6] is probably due not only to his learned knowledge of poetic craft and theoretical

[1] *SWB* vii. 849: 'dünn, fein, zart, schlank . . . scharfsinnig, geschickt, gewandt . . . scharf . . .'.
[2] See p. 104.   [3] See pp. 104–5.   [4] See pp. 10, 58–9.
[5] See p. 137. *peceiar* usually means 'to break to pieces, fragment': see *SWB* vi. 291, and Jaufré Rudel, VI. 46: 'Gart se no.i falha ni.l pessi.' But Mistral, ii. 512 gives the first meaning as 'rapiécer'.
[6] His biographer says he was 'meiller trobaire que negus d'aquels qu'eron estat denan ni foron apres lui; per que fo apellatz maestre dels trobadors' (Boutière and Schutz, p. 39). A large number of his songs, seventy-seven, have been preserved. He figures prominently in Peire d'Alvernhe's satire on the troubadours, being the second to be mentioned, after Peire Rogier.

formulations of *trobar clus* and *trobar leu*, but also to his wide range of interests and the diversity of his skills. His work covers a variety of subjects: love, courtly values, literary techniques, criticism of society, Christian values, and a wide range of genres: *vers* and *chansos*, political and moral *sirventes*, a *sirventes joglaresc*, *planh*, *alba*, riddle poem, *tensos*, and *pastorelas*, as well as the group of songs containing a mixture of lyrical and moral themes which Kolsen terms *Sirventes-Kanzonen*.[1] His styles, as we have seen, include *clus*, *leu*, and *prim* with a range of approaches within these catagories.

With each song he tries to make a new impression, with great technical diversity. His versification shows an extraordinary virtuosity, not so much in the use of difficult or grammatical rhymes such as we find in Raimbaut d'Aurenga, but in the originality of his rhyme schemes. Of his seventy-seven surviving songs no fewer than fifty have rhyme schemes which are unrepeated in the other troubadour lyrics which have been preserved.[2] Many of these also have a large number of short lines with *coblas unissonans* which require a large number of rhymes to be found.[3]

Although he employs rare or difficult rhymes in only a few songs,[4] Giraut frequently uses at least one unusual rhyme in each song to give a new musical impression. In nearly half of his poems he uses one or two rhymes which he does not repeat elsewhere,[5] and often such a rhyme occurs in the first line of the stanza where an immediate impression can be made on the listener: 'Razon e l*oc*' (XVII), 'Los apl*echs*' (XLII), 'Si.m sentis fizels am*ics*' (XXVII), 'Can creis la frescha folh' e.l r*ams*' (XXXIII).[6]

If the range of his vocabulary is smaller that Marcabru's or Raimbaut's, it is appreciably wider than that of Bernart de Ventadorn, with a higher proportion of unusual words.[7]

Giraut often tries to make a new impression by the emphatic use of a single stylistic device in one composition. In three songs

---

[1] See Kolsen, i. 494–5.

[2] See pp. 223–5.

[3] Giraut's ability to avoid repeating himself or other poets in so many songs suggests that he may possibly have had some system for recording rhyme schemes.

[4] III *endres, aixe*; XVIII *ucha, anc*; LXVI *agra, erc*; XXX *icha, ec*.

[5] See the Appendix, pp. 213–20. This happens in 33 out of 77 songs.

[6] The following begin with such a rhyme: III, XVI, XVII, XVIII, XX, XXVII, XXXII, XXXIII, XXXIX, XLII, LVI, LVII, LVIII, LXVI. Others begin with a rhyme occurring only once elsewhere: VI, XII, XLVIII, LV, LIX.

[7] See the appendix, p. 229.

dialogue occurs throughout (II, V, XXI): in 'Amars, onrars e charteners' (VI) abstract qualities are catalogued in every stanza:

> Amars, onrars e charteners,
> Umiliars et obezirs,
> Loncs merceiars e loncs grazirs,
> Long' atendens' e loncs espers . . .   (1–4)

In 'Leu chansonet' e vil' (XLVIII) the device is the repeated use of amplifying images, in 'Tot suavet' (XXVIII), of proper names.[1] 'Can la brun' aura s'eslucha' (XVIII) is based on images of the grotesque, conflict, disorder, and disease: his lady has led him out of the straight path: 'Car vos m'etz un pauc esducha' (9), she turns light to dark for him: 'Si que.m viratz en bru blanc' (10); *lucha, manc, clop, ranc* suggest conflict and disability both in imagery and sound (17–19), linked with emotional torment: 'Qu'en lech no posc eu dormir' (29), 'Que.l cor dins me crid' e m'ucha / Que no.l rompa ni l'esbranc' (33–4). Images of disease: 'No m'a laissat charn ni sanc' (41), 'Pustel' en son olh e cranc' (42) are mixed with images of failure and exclusion: 'de joy m'estanc' (3), '.s clucha / L'amors' (4–5), 'Per c'ai ma valor destrucha' (28), 'si.m falh mos chans' (7). In 'Er' auziretz   Enchabalir chantars' (XXX) he tries to make an immediate impact on the audience by pretending to shock:

> 'Er' auziretz   Enchabalir chantars:
> Qu'eu sui amics enchabalitz e pars!'
> Auiatz! e fon anc mais dicha
> Tan grans foli' en chantan?
> Greu n'eschaparai ses dan . . .   (1–5)

Now you will hear singing perfected; for I am a perfect lover and companion! Listen!—and was ever such great folly uttered in song? Hardly shall I escape unharmed . . .

Then the theme of folly is repeatedly emphasized: 'nescis parlars' (9), 'Tenia.l drech per envers' (15), 'Mou mas chansos e mos vers / Com fols de saber esters' (23–4), 'Fols trascudatz' (39), 'Fola res' (43), 'Saber d'enfan!' (45), 'Fols, c'as dich?' (61), 'fols es mers!' (66). With a great variety of such technical devices Giraut tries to make a new impact with each new song.

Dante will have appreciated Giraut's knowledge of literary

[1] See p. 135.

theory and his considerable craftsmanship. But he also praised him as *poeta rectitudinis*.[1] Of the four songs of his which Dante mentions in the *De Vulgari Eloquentia*,[2] two are moralizing works (LXV, LXXIII), of which 'Per solatz revelhar' (LXV) is quoted as the example of poetry on the subject of *virtus*. In it Giraut complains of the decline of the world and points to the particular hypocrisies of courtly society which professes civilized values while condoning looting and theft:

> Vos vitz torneis mandar
> E segre.ls gen garnitz
> E pois dels melhs feritz
> Una sazo parlar;
> Er' es pretz de raubar
> E d'ebranchar berbitz.
> Chavalers si' aunitz
> Que.s met en domneiar,
> Pos que tocha dels mas moltos belans
> Ni que rauba gleizas ni viandans!   (21–30)

You used to see tourneys ordered, with people well equipped in armour following them, and hear tell for a season of those the most skilfully felled; now to be noble means to rob and divide sheep from the flock. Shame on the knight who starts to court a lady after he has touched bleating sheep with his hands, and robbed churches and travellers!

Of Giraut's seventy-seven songs, twenty-seven[3] are either moralizing works or include a large section of moralizing content, and one of Giraut's main interests was in giving instruction on how to behave according to Christian principles.

His didactic approach affects his love songs as well as his *sirventes*, and as Salverda de Grave remarked, lyrical themes are for Giraut 'en grande partie matière de moralisation'.[4] Whereas Bernart de Ventadorn tries to create emotion directly in the listener, or analyses feelings from a psychological point of view, Giraut enlarges on them didactically and sees them in the light of moral behaviour. So both poets treat the theme of folly in

---

[1] *DVE* ii. ii. 9; cf. Kolsen, 'Der Trobador Giraut de Bornelh als poeta rectitudinis', *Arch.* cxxxvii (1918), 79–80.

[2] 'Si.m sentis' (XXVII), i. ix. 2–3; 'Per solatz reveillar', ii. ii. 9; 'Ar' auziretz', ii. v. 3; 'Si per mon Sobretotz', ii. vi. 5–6.

[3] 15 *sirventes*, 12 *Sirventes-Kanzonen*, according to Kolsen (i. 494–5).

[4] *Observations*, p. 6.

love; but whereas Bernart uses it to give the impression of
a turbulent state of mind:

> Amors, aissi.m faitz trassalhir
> del joi qu'eu ai, no vei ni au
> ni no sai que.m dic ni que.m fau.
> cen vetz trobi, can m'o cossir,
> qu'eu degr' aver sen e mezura
> (si m'ai adoncs; mas pauc me dura,)
> c'al reduire.m torna.l jois en error.
> pero be sai c'uzatges es d'amor
> c'om c'ama be, non a gaire de sen,   (XIII. 19–27)

Love, you make me tremble so much with the joy I feel, I neither
see nor hear nor know what I am saying or doing. A hundred times I
find when I think about it that I ought to have sense and moderation
(at once I have it; but it does not last long), for as it diminishes my
joy turns to distress. Yet well I know that it is customary in love that
one who loves well has little sense,

Giraut reasons over folly in a didactic way, weighing up the
correct balance of wisdom and folly in the true courtly lover from
an objective point of view:

> Car qui.l drech enten
> D'amor ni.n sospira,
> No.i pot aver gran sen
> De gran jauzimen,
> S'ab foldat no.i vai;
> C'anc drut savi gai
> No vi, c'ans esmera
> Lo sen la foldatz;   (XLIII. 61–8)

For one who understands what is correct about love and sighs for it
cannot have great wisdom from great joy if he does not enter into it
with folly; for I have never seen a wise lover gay, for rather does folly
perfect the wisdom;

or he presents himself, not directly as a poet of feeling, but as an
example of what the lover should be:

> C'al comensar
> En cuder' eu plus leu passar;
> Mas pois, per la fe que dei vos,
> M'es si chamjat — que del laissar
> No sui ni serai poderos!
>   Per qu'eu egalh,
>   Si noca.us par,
> Los fols e.ls savis amoros.   (XVII. 68–75)

For at the beginning I should have imagined I could more easily extract myself from this (love), but since then, by the faith I owe you, things have so changed for me—that I am not and shall not be capable of leaving! Therefore I am similar, even if this is not apparent to you, to the foolish and the wise lovers.

Giraut's importance in the formulation of the *trobar leu*, his knowledge of literary theory, the weight of his moralizing themes, and his ability to make a new impression with each song through a wide range of technical skills, his learning and varied interests, must have been appreciated by his own audience, and must also have helped to earn him his prominent place among Dante's 'eloquentes doctores' and his title of 'master of the troubadours'. But is it really surprising that Dante finally judged him to have been overrated?[1] It may be, as Hoepffner suggests,[2] that, in indicating his considerable preference for Arnaut Daniel, Dante is primarily concerned not with the two troubadours themselves but with using them as an artifice for comparing Guittone unfavourably with Guinizelli. Yet Giraut's virtues are of the pedestrian kind: a fact which his friend, patron, and rival Raimbaut d'Aurenga does not fail to exploit.

[1] *Purgatorio*, XXVI. 119.
[2] E. Hoepffner, 'Dante et les troubadours', *Études italiennes*, iv (1922), 193–210 (esp. 201–2).

4

RAIMBAUT D'AURENGA[1]

At the time of Peire d'Alvernhe's satire on the troubadours at Puivert, which Pattison dates to 1170,[2] Giraut was in the company of several leading troubadours including Bernart de Ventadorn and Raimbaut d'Aurenga. The three have quite different attitudes to the controversy over *trobar clus* and *trobar leu*. Bernart composes from choice in his light, lyrical style without ever mentioning *trobar leu*; Giraut gives in to public pressure for a light style but creates his own learned version of it; Raimbaut, an amateur poet who can largely please himself, defends the *trobar clus* and makes fun of the *trobar leu*.

1. 'Trobar clus'

It is now generally recognized that Raimbaut is the Linhaure of the *tenso* with Giraut on the *trobar clus*.[3] Raimbaut, like Giraut, discusses the *trobar clus* only when it has become controversial. He mentions it only once by name, in the *tenso*; and even then, while defending it, he does not describe its technique. His arguments are not very specific. They do not, as some scholars have thought,[4] prove that he set out to defend the values of the aristocracy against the intrusion of the lower classes, or to exclude the *vilan* from his audience. Raimbaut simply recognizes that some of his listeners are stupid or uneducated, and that to please everyone he would have to lower his standards:

> Ara.m platz, Giraut de Borneill,
> Que sapcha per c'anatz blasman

---

[1] Except where otherwise stated, I use Pattison's edition. He dates Raimbaut's career from about 1162 to 73 (see Pattison, pp. 36–45).   [2] p. 41.

[3] See p. 110.

[4] Köhler, pp. 142–3, 149. Pollmann, 'Trobar clus', p. 36 n. 116, however, sees Raimbaut's arguments as literary and not social, and considers that the question for Raimbaut is the artistic worth of composing hermetically or not (p. 35). Raimbaut is not necessarily going so far as to defend hermetic poetry.

> Trobar clus, ni per cal semblan.
> Aiso.m digaz,
> Si tan prezatz
> So que es a toz comunal;
> Car adonc tut seran egual.[1]   (XXXI. 1-7)

Now I should like to know, Giraut de Bornelh, why you keep finding fault with the closed style and for what reason. Tell me this: if you really esteem so highly what is common to everyone; for then all will be equal.

'So que es a toz comunal' probably does not mean 'what everyone can understand', but 'what everyone can *compose*'; as he says in 'Pos trobar plans' (XVI), listeners want to hear 'tals motz . . . c'om tot jorn ditz e brai' (5-7): 'such words as those which people say and shout out every day'. To Giraut's objection that only a light and even menial song is popular, he retorts that the praise of fools is worthless:

> Giraut, non voill qu'en tal trepeil
> Torn mos trobars que ja ogan
> Lo lauzo.l bon e.l pauc e.l gran.
> Ja per los faz
> Non er lauzatz,
> Car non conoisson ni lor cal
> So que plus car es ni mais val.[2]   (15-21)

Giraut, I don't want my composition to result in such an uproar that from now on the noble and the few and the great would never praise it. It will never be praised by the fools, for they do not recognize or care about what is most valuable or precious.

He seeks the praise of the discriminating few who would despise him if he wrote for fools. But he does not say he has any intention of systematically excluding them from his audience by writing hermetic songs. He simply pays them no attention. Giraut replies

---

[1] Pattison translates *trobar clus* as 'obscure style'; but see my comments on pp. 90 ff.

[2] *trepeil*: Jeanroy, *AdM* xxi (1909), 363-8: 'action de piétiner' (Mistral, *trepé*): 'Je ne veux pas que mes poésies soient foulées aux pieds (par une foule ignorante).' But see *SWB* viii. 446: 'Unruhe, Verwirrung', Appel, *Arch.* xcvii (1896), 187, and Pattison: 'confusion'. Pattison places a semicolon after *trobars* (v. 16): 'may the good and the small and the great never praise them henceforth' ('them'='my composi-tions'). *Pauc* must mean 'few' or 'select few' rather than 'small'. 'Small' would then be opposed to *gran*, and Raimbaut does not want the praise of 'small' or 'foolish' people. Appel, *Raimbaut von Orange*, p. 31, follows *ER*: 'Torn mos trobars que hom am tan / L'avol co.l bo, e.l pauc co.l gran': 'Giraut, nicht will ich, dass mein Dichten in solche Verwirrung hineingerate, dass man das Schlechte ebenso liebe wie das Gute, das Kleine wie das Grosse.'

that it is pointless to compose a song which is not popular; Raimbaut answers that he sings for his own satisfaction, and that there must always be a scale of values by which a song is to be judged:

> Giraut, sol que.l miels appareil
> E.l dig' ades e.l trag' enan,
> Mi non cal sitot non s'espan.
>   C'anc granz viutatz
>   Non fon denhtatz:
> Per so prez' om mais aur que sal,
> E de tot chant es atretal.   (29–35)

Giraut, provided that I fashion the best and continually sing it and bring it forward, I do not care if it is not spread abroad. For great abundance was never something precious: for this reason gold is valued more highly than salt, and it is the same with all singing.

By 'great abundance' he means either that his song would be like all the other commonplace songs, or else that it would be too well known. What is commonplace cannot, he says, by definition have special value. Without 'systematic obscurity' Raimbaut writes to please himself and the discerning few, and is contemptuous of popular opinion. He makes no mention of deliberate hermeticism.

Raimbaut's style and intentions are so varied and capricious, his statements so often loaded with humour, that his comments on style can only be examined within the context of his individual works. In this section four songs are discussed which appear for different reasons to be connected with the *trobar clus*. All four have different intentions and only one, 'Cars douz', appears to be a fully serious *clus* composition, in which Raimbaut interweaves 'Cars, bruns e tenz motz'. In discussing this particular song I basically follow the edition of J. H. Marshall.[1]

I
> Cars, douz e feinz   del bederesc
> M'es sos bas chanz,   vas cui m'azerc;
>   C'ap joi s'espan,   viu e noire,
>   El temps qe grill   prob del siure
>   Chanton el mur   jos lo caire,   5
> Qe.s compassa e s'esqaira;
> Sa vos cha plus leu qe siura,
> E ja nuls non s'i aserga
> Mas grils e la bederesca.

---

[1] 'On the text and interpretation of a poem by Raimbaut d'Orange (*Cars douz*; ed. Pattison, I)', *MA*, vol. xxxvii, no. i (1968), pp. 12–36.

II   Cars jois e gens,   ses fuec grezesc,   10
    Els paucs enfanz   pasc e conderc,
      Qe no.ls enjan   ni ten loire,
      Mas en brezill   no m'aus pliure.
      Don mi rancur?   Qe.il blanc-vaire
      Fan amistat pig' e vaira;   15
      Savis er fols qi s'i pliura:
      Qe grieu er q'el eis conderga
      Fis jois, ses flama grezesca.

III   Cars, bruns e tenz   motz entrebesc:
    Pensius, pensanz,   enqier e serc —   20
      Com si liman   pogues roire
      L'estrain roïll   ni.l fer tiure —
      Don mon escur   cor esclaire.
      Tot cant Jois genseis esclaira
      Malvestatz roïll' e tiura,   25
      E enclau Joven en serca,
      Per q'Ira Joi entrebresca.

IV   Car naus ni leinz   ni flums on pesc
    No m'es enanz,   c'ar vei Joi berc,
      Anz vau troban,   com vis d'oire   30
      Qe mont' el cill   al fol iure.
      Tant vei Pretz dur   per qe laire
      Lauzengiers conten e laira;
      E sos amars digz eniura
      Prez, per qe Jois fraing e berca: 35
      Qi.s vol, critz qe.l pren e pesca.

V   Car s'es empeinz,   c'anc no m'espresc,
    Vidal Costanz,   Marti Domerc:
      No.m puesc ses bran   d'els escoire,
      Per qe.m corrill,   c'ab un guiure   40
      De mal aür   nafro.l paire,
      Don lo fils sofris e paira
      Malvestat, qe.l nafr' e.l guiura.
      E jai Costanz a Domerga:
      De domnei q'enois l'espresca!   45

VI   Car penti.m meinz   qe no paresc
    Als paucs emblanz   del menor derc
      Qe van duptan   aur per coire;
      Car al perill   on ie.m liure

Venc un tafur   qi n'er fraire,   50
Qe.l nesis malvatz fatz fraira
Lai on lo francs fis se liura.
E non cre jois plus aut derga,
Qe.l crims nais anz q'el paresca.

VII   Cars con argens,   esmer e cresc: 55
Ab durs colps, tanz   con hom fai clerc,
Vau chastian   pres lo roire.
Mas per un fill   pot reviure
So cui m'atur,   de bon aire:
Si co.l venz vai sus en l'aira   60
Lo sieus noms viu, e reviura
Pretz e Joi. Qe.l morgu' e.ill clerga
Dieu prec c'aital baron cresca.

VIII   Cel qi fa.l vers si compaira
Ab leis qe ja non esquiura,   65
Qe non tem correg ni verga
Lo fuecs q'escompren ses esca.

IX   Raembautz torn' e repaira
Lai on Pretz viu e reviura,
Al comte, cui Dieus azergua,   70
Barselones, honor cresca.

I. Precious, sweet and inventive to me is the wren's low song, towards which I raise up my spirit; for with joy it unfolds, comes to life and grows, at the time when crickets near the cork-oak are chirping by the wall beneath the corner-stone, and aligns and squares itself; his song falls lighter than cork; and let no other add his voice to these but a cricket and the wren's mate.

II. Precious and gracious joys I nourish and uphold without deceitfulness in the little children, without deceiving them or setting a trap for them, for I dare not place my trust in shifting sands. Why then do I complain? Because the whited sepulchres make friendship turn speckled and pied. The wise man will be a fool if he trusts in them, for it will be difficult even for him to uphold pure joys without cunning stratagems.

III. Rare, dark and tinted words I twine together! With deep meditation I seek out—as if by filing I could rub away the unseemly rust and the loathsome dross—how I may brighten my gloomy heart. All that Joy most graciously brightens, Evil encrusts with rust and dross; and it encircles Youth in a moat, so that Sorrow entangles Joy.

IV. For ship or boat or river where I fish is of no avail to me, since I now see Joy shattered: rather I am tossed from side to side (or: I am

composing) like wine from a wine-skin which goes to the foolish
drunkard's head. I see Worth so hard that some evil-tongued thief
disputes and yaps, and his bitter words make Worth drunk, so that
Joy is broken and shattered. Let any who will cry out that he is
catching it like a fish on a hook!

v. For without my ever awakening, Vidal Costanz and Martin
Domerc have pushed themselves forward: without a sword I cannot
save myself from them, and I complain for that reason; for with a
viper which bodes ill they wound the father, as a result of which the
son suffers and puts up with evil tongues, which wound and sting
him. And Costanz sleeps with Domerga: may misfortune wake him
from amorous dalliance!

vi. For I am not abandoning the struggle so much as I seem to be in
the eyes of the insignificant pilferers of the lowest rank, who always
suspect that gold is mere copper. For in the danger into which I
deliver myself, I have defeated a scoundrel who will be exactly like
them, for this stupid fellow smells out evil doings where the noble
and courtly man gives himself completely. But I do not believe he
(the courtly man) will raise up joys any higher, for ugly rumour is
born even before he appears.

vii. Precious as silver, I become purified and grow in value. With
hard blows, as many as they give schoolboys, I give moral instruction
by the evergreen oak. But through one son of a noble family, there
may revive that to which I hold fast. As the wind rises on the threshing-
floor, so his name lives, and will bring back to life Worth and Joy.
Let monk and nun pray God to exalt such a noble youth.

viii. May he who composes this *vers* be judged in the company of her
whom he will never abandon; for the fire which is kindled without
tinder fears neither strap nor rod.

ix. Raimbaut makes his way to the place where Worth lives and will
live again: to the Count of Barcelona—may God exalt him and increase his honour!

NOTES

Except where indicated, I have followed Marshall's translation.

1. *e feinz*: Marshall emends this to *ensenhz*, 'sign'. MSS.: *a* e fis, *M* e fi, *D* efenz, *IK*
efeinz, N² e feing. Appel, *Raimbaut von Orange*, p. 86: *feinz* (?), 'troubled' (?)
from *se fenher* 'to bestir oneself, take pains' (p. 89); Pattison: 'fictitious', arguing
that the poet was not actually listening to the wren's song as he was composing.
Marshall rightly discards these translations. He also points out that the syntax is
unparalleled, as far as he knows, in troubadour usage. He suggests that *e
fenhz* may be an error for *ensenhz* or *esenhz*, 'mark, outward sign', which is
however a rare and perhaps doubtful word: 'not so far as I know, otherwise
attested in OPr. But OFr. has *enseing* (Godefroy, iii. 233; *TL* iii. 520); and, in
view of the pairs *senh–senha* and *entresenh–entresenha*, the existence of *ensenh* (*insigne*)
beside *ensenha* (*insignia*) would be perfectly normal. The rarity of the word
would sufficiently explain the scribal error.' (p. 18.)

Fenhz could have other meanings: (a) 'striving, aspiring', cf. *fenhedor*:

> Qatre escalos ha en amor:
> Lo premiers es de *fenhedor*
> El segon es de preiador,
> E lo tertz es d'entendedor,
> E al qart es drutz apelatz.

(O. Dammann, *Die allegorische Canzone des Guiraut de Calanso: 'A leis cui am de cor e de saber' und ihre Deutung* (Breslau, 1891), p. 74), where *fenhedor* means 'aspirant, suitor', and Peire d'Alvernhe, I. 40: 'per qu'el lai se'n fenha', 'why he should be a suitor to that lady'; this would link with the next line, 'vas cui m'azerc': the wren's song would seem to be 'aspiring' as it unfolds in joy, and in turn inspires the poet to raise up his spirits. (b) 'feigned' (*SWB* iii. 439: 'ersinnen, erdichten, heucheln...' *fench, fenh* 'falsch, heuchlerisch') perhaps in the sense of 'mysterious' or 'devious', like the poet's 'bruns e tenz motz'. (c) 'inventive', because the wren's song represents imagination and creativity. (Cf. *fictio*, L & S 744, I. 'A making, fashioning, forming, formation'; II. In partic. A. 'A feigning, counterfeiting, disguising'; and Lausberg, 1115, A 2, p. 535 where *fictio* means the creation of poetic fictions).

This would not solve the problem of the unusual syntax, but this should not perhaps be an overriding objection in view of the extraordinarily complex verse form, in which, Marshall points out, 22 out of 72 syllables are tied by rhyme.

7. *Qe.s compassa*: Marshall takes this to refer to *caire*, 'squarely placed there in its position'. It has more point if it refers to *sos bas chanz*: the wren's song combines joy and precision or discipline. By contrast, Raimbaut's song 'En aital rimeta prima' (II) is 'Bastit ses regl' e ses linha' (3), being more light-hearted and relaxed.

10. *Ses fuec grezesc*: Greek fire was regarded as a treacherous means of war in the twelfth century: see Pattison, p. 68.

19. *tenz*: Marshall: 'obscure'. It means 'tinted, dyed' (*SWB* viii. 168: *tenher*, 'färben') and suggests colour. Giraut regards something 'tinted' as rich or valuable, for he says that the churlish suitor is made pale and faded by his excesses: 'c'aixi desfil' e *destejn* / desaffrenatz domneihars. / qui.l pretz no.i garda ni.l sojn' (see pp. 161, 169). Quintilian IV. ii. 117, mentions 'verba *sensu tincta*', words 'tinted with meaning'. Raimbaut may have had in mind Rhetorical colours, or Marcabru's *cent colors* (see pp. 21 ff). Appel translates 'farbige Worte' (p. 93).

30. *troban* may be from *trobar* 'to compose'; Marshall takes it as equivalent to *torbar*, 'to trouble, confuse, be disturbed' (*PD* 366), cf. *torban*, 'battu (des vagues, de la tempête)?' (ibid.)

32. *dur*: Marshall 'firm', but it may mean 'hardened'.

38. i.e. slanderers or, more probably, seducers: the 'son' suffers because his legitimacy is questioned, either because of gossip or because his 'father' has been wounded by the mother's adultery. And seducers sleep with each other's wives [v. 44]. Cf. Marcabru, V. 19–24 and pp. 50–1.

49. *venc*: Marshall present tense, but cf. Anglade, *Grammaire*, p. 297.

D. Scheludko, 'Anlässlich des Liedes von Raimbaut d'Aurenga *Cars douz*', *Arch. Rom.* xxi (1937), 285–97, sees this poem as 'a particularly crass example of this poet's efforts to renew conventional themes and material by stylistic means and thus to inject new life into them' (p. 291).

The theme is the struggle for creative joy to overcome contaminating evil. The poet defends his joy by preserving a generous, creative spirit, by keeping vigilant watch over the young, and by the act of composing poetry. The conflict follows a movement in progressive stanzas from the evocation of joy to the poet's awareness of its susceptibility to contamination, his struggle to remove it, his pessimism that joy is utterly broken, followed by a determination to sever himself completely from its enemies and a renewal of the struggle in which he sees himself as victor.

The wren's song, rare, sweet, low, suggesting a precious mystery, is a symbol of the poet's joy. He lifts up his spirits in aspiration as the song unfurls full of life and growth: 'C'ap joi s'espan,   viu e noire.' The crickets sing beside the cork-oak: an image which, while bound by the rhyme, emphasizes the mood of rarity. The wren's song is not only full of joy; it is 'aligned and squared', exact and disciplined. This sets the tone for the poet's mood: joy in poetry and music, creativity and idealism, and a sense of discipline in the need to purify his heart of 'L'estrain roïll ni.l fer tiure' which threaten to cloud and confuse it. Raimbaut invokes the voices of the wren and the crickets alone, excluding, in anticipation, those of *Malvestatz*, *Ira*, and the *laire Lauzengiers*.

Like other troubadours[1] he encourages only the noblest aspirations in the young: 'Cars jois e gens, ses fuec grezesc' (10), and seeks strenuously to preserve his own moral integrity: 'Mas en brezill   no m'aus pliure' (13). But the *blanc-vaire*, the hypocritical and corrupt, undermine true friendship; the wise man must shun them because it is hard enough for him to uphold joy in its integrity even by himself, without their influence. From the precious joy of the opening stanza the poet's mood has turned cloudy with pessimism.

The wren's song, precious both for its joy and its rarity, was an image both of a joyful heart and of poetic artistry. The fusion of these elements continues and develops as Raimbaut seeks, by intertwining 'Rare, dark and tinted words' in poetic creation, the means of freeing himself from contamination. The images in stanza III intentionally suggest both the poet's mood and his technique in composition. His words are 'Cars, bruns e tenz' because his mood is rare, sombre, and mysterious, subtly coloured; simultaneously the words in his poetry are rare: *bederesc*, *grill*,

[1] Peire d'Alvernhe, XI, 31–2: 'Quar er m'abelis e m'es bel / qu'el mieu joi s'enans la jovens'; Giraut de Bornelh, LXVI. 41–3: 'S'om agramen no m'acolhis, / Si.m ponh ni manei ni m'esterc / Los jovensels ni.ls enantis.'

siure, fuec grezesc, brezill, dark and tinted with an allusive, meta-phorical style. He is shrouded in thought, 'Pensius, pensanz' (20), partly in mental conflict, but partly because he follows his model Marcabru[1] in feeling that arduous thought is needed to clarify one's mind and words. *Liman,* which describes the filing away of impurity from the heart, is commonly used as an image of the polishing of poetic style,[2] while *roïll* can also be an image for stylistic faults: sometimes, as in Marcabru's case, with the emphasis on impurity or inaccuracy of thinking,[3] but sometimes referring to technical imperfection.[4] The two elements are present in Raimbaut's mind. The technical mastery of the whole work is the formal expression of his aspiration to perfect joy. The phrase 'Don mon escur cor esclaire' (23), besides describing the poet's state of mind, recalls Marcabru's attempts 'D'esclarzir paraul' escura':[5] to clarify difficult ideas by the precise and truthful use of words. In certain respects Raimbaut is very close to Marcabru: he sees poetic eloquence as a means of unfolding truth from darkness. 'Don mon escur cor esclaire', together with *enclau* and *entrebesca,* suggests that Raimbaut is referring to the *trobar clus.* By its form and structure the song demonstrates the interweaving of *Joi* and *Ira,* and the confining of *Joven.* From the confinement of evil influences *Jois* strives towards brightness and clarity.

Gradually the poet becomes aware of the rust and dross corrupt-ing joy; in stanza IV joy seems to be utterly broken and worth is drunk or confused by the spite of the slanderers. The conflict between *Joi, Pretz,* and the *Lauzengiers* seems to be less of a personification of virtues and vices in society, as Marcabru might have portrayed them,[6] than a representation of the poet's own state of mind, as his idealism succumbs to the onslaughts of mean, spiteful people and as this makes him 'drunk' with confu-

[1] Marcabru's influence on this song has been examined by Appel, *Raimbaut von Orange,* p. 86, Scheludko, *Arch. Rom.* xxi (1937), 285–97, and Pattison, pp. 67 ff.

[2] Cf. Arnaut Daniel, ed. Toja, II. 12–14: 'obre e lim / motz de valor / ab art d'amor', X. 4: 'qan n'aurai passat la lima'; Aimeric de Peguilhan, ed. Shepard and Chambers, XLVII. 1–2: 'Ses mon apleich non vau ni ses ma lima, / Ab que fabreich motz et aplan e lim'; *limae labor,* Horace, *Ars,* 291 (Lausberg, *Registerband,* p. 738).

[3] 'Lo vers comens', 51–2: 'que no.i pot hom trobar a frau / mot de roïll'. Marcabru had opened his song by blaming the *trobador . . . entrebesquill* and praising his own *trobar naturau*: see p. 28.

[4] Cf. Peire d'Alvernhe, XV. 63: 'e no.i a motz fals que rovelh'; see p. 76.

[5] See pp. 16 ff.

[6] Scheludko, *Arch. Rom.* xxi (1937), 285–97, however, sees Raimbaut as imitating Marcabru closely in the struggle between vices and virtues.

sion. By *troban* (30), which Marshall gives as equivalent to *torban*, 'tossed from side to side', expressing the poet's drunkenness, Raimbaut may also mean to remind us of his poetic activity, for this is part of his joy. This might possibly explain why the images of vv. 28–9, 'Car naus ni leinz ni flums on pesc / No m'es enanz', in contrast with the rest of the poem, seem either trite or illogical.[1] Raimbaut may be deliberately making his *trobar* sound garbled or drunk.

From his state of drunken confusion he moves on in stanza V to anticipate an abrupt severance with the corrupters of joy: 'No.m puesc ses bran d'els escoire' (39), whom he depicts in Marcabrunian terms. Although he appears to be yielding to their influence in his drunken state, this state is transitory. In stanza VI he says that the 'paucs emblanz   del menor derc' cynically (because they demean everything, even gold) underestimate him. In fact, he has defeated[2] someone who represents them all, 'un tafur qi n'er fraire' (50). Whether this person is a political figure, perhaps Raimbaut's enemy Bertrand des Baux, as Pattison suggests,[3] or some other personal foe, or even the *tafur* within his own heart, is uncertain. The way in which he gains victory is by a generous spirit which overcomes cynicism or meanness: the ignorant man smells out evil where the noble man 'se liura', 'gives himself completely'. Yet *Jois* is always in danger of being forestalled by *crims*: either 'crime' or 'evil slander', and the victory is never complete.

As his joy triumphs the poet improves and grows inwardly, 'Cars con argens'. Recalling his obligation to instruct the young, to which he referred in stanza II, he chides and teaches 'pres lo roire', which, if this is the correct reading,[4] perhaps represents lasting growth. Raimbaut puts his hope in a new young baron (*un fill*, v. 58), who, although very unlikely to mean Christ as Pattison suggested,[5] is perhaps seen as a kind of Messiah, whose name lives 'Si co.l venz vai sus en l'aira'.[6]

[1] For various attempts to interpret this, see Appel, *Raimbaut von Orange*, p. 90; Pattison, p. 70; Marshall, p. 23. If *serca* means 'moat' (v. 26) as Marshall suggested, perhaps Raimbaut means he is unable to cross it to rescue *Joven*, but *on pesc* would not seem to have any sense in such a context. 'To go fishing like a fool' means to achieve nothing: cf. J. Morawski, *Proverbes*, no. 1947: 'Qui fol envoie a la mer n'i a ne pois(s)on ne el', and Raimbaut, XX. 24: 'c'als q'en fol pesc!'

[2] For *venc*, from *venser*, cf. p. 151 and Marshall's notes on p. 27. This offers much better sense than 'came' or 'see' (Veig *a*, Veg *IKN*[2], in which Marshall sees a *lectio facilior*).   [3] p. 71.   [4] Marshall's emendation, p. 29 (lais coire *DIKMN*[2], lo goire *a*.)   [5] p. 71: he sees *leis* (65) as the Virgin Mary, and 'Lo fuecs que compren ses esca'

[Note 5 cont. and note 6 on next page]

The song ends with compliments to the poet's lady: the composer wishes to be judged, probably both morally and artistically, in the light of his pure love for her; and with compliments to the Count of Barcelona whom Raimbaut is on his way to visit.

The *trobar clus* here[1] is much more than the interweaving of complex rhymes,[2] or even of these combined with rare words and images used for their own sake. It is the binding together of meanings and form where the form itself is an image of the meaning. Rare words, rhymes, and images are the formal result of a feeling of rare *Jois*. The troubadour's technical activity in creating his work is a theme threading through the main theme of joy seeking to overcome evil, and artistic achievement establishes through the form the victory of joy. Raimbaut's *trobar clus* involves the interlacing of meanings such as we found in Marcabru: not so much the distinct layers of meaning as in the *gap*, but suggested meanings weaving through each other, as in Marcabru's 'Contra l'ivern'.[3]

Besides binding meanings and form together, Raimbaut also unfolds the theme gradually through the form. The theme develops from stanza to stanza as his mood moves from the evocation of joy through pessimism to victory. Marcabru had previously sought to bring out truth from mystery or confusion, 'D'esclarzir paraul' escura', and in certain songs unfolded his meaning gradually through images or interwoven ideas. Giraut described in theoretical terms how the poet's *razo* reveals itself in the *trobar clus*. However, from the point of view of the listener or reader Raimbaut's words and theme do not become more explicit towards the end of the song, as Marcabru's did. The

(his text) as 'the fire kindled without a spark', the Immaculate Conception; the interpretation of *fill* as the Christ (as a second meaning in addition to the reference to the son of the Count of Barcelona) is an extension of this. Marshall rejects this as arbitrary: *esca* means 'tinder' not 'spark', and the syntax requires the intransitive verb *escomprendre*. 'The fire which burns without tinder is surely the poet's love, which grows without encouragement from the lady or, possibly, without her presence' (p. 30).

    [6] Cf. Osea 13: 3 (Marshall, p. 29).

    [1] Raimbaut does not say this song is *clus*; but since he defends the *trobar clus*, and since this is one of the most complicated songs of the troubadours, these seems little doubt that it is.

    [2] See, however, Mölk pp. 89 and 125. But complex rhymes were not essential to the *trobar clus*, as one of the earliest known *clus* poems, 'Be m'es plazen' of Peire d'Alvernhe (Del Monte, VIII) has easy rhymes and unoriginal versification (I. Frank, 193, 9).   [3] See pp. 43–9.

'illumination' comes within the poet's heart, it 'brightens' as joy defeats evil.

This song, which Pattison considered an imitative 'early production',[1] marks a culmination of the *trobar clus* where the choice of medium corresponds intimately with the poet's intention and state of mind. Whereas Bernart de Ventadorn's joy rises and falls with the impulse of mood and needs the apparent freedom and artlessness of a 'natural' style, Raimbaut's joy is like a rare work of art which can only be fixed and assured by thought and discipline. Raimbaut creates poetically in a style which Giraut de Bornelh only describes in theory and imitates with a merely technical application of rhetoric.

In the song 'Ar vei bru, escur, trebol cel' (X). Raimbaut speaks of *digz escurs* (13), and this, coupled with the difficulty of the poem, its rare rhymes and language, suggest that Raimbaut is composing in the *trobar clus*. The intention behind the song proves to be very different from the one behind 'Cars douz'.

The text is Pattison's, with modifications as indicated in the notes.

I   Ar vei bru, escur, trebol cel
        Don per l'air vent' e giscl' e plou,
        E chai neus e gels e gibres,
        E.l sol qu'era cautz, ferms e durs
        Es sa calors teun' e flaca,   5
        E fuelh e flors chai jos dels rams
        Si que en plais ni en blaca
        Non aug chans, ni critz mas dins murs;
        Per qu'ieu chantarai alques grams.

II   Mas aura ni plueja ni gel   10
        No.m tengr' ieu plus que.l gen temps nou
        S'auzes desplejar mos libres
        De fag d'amor ab digz escurs;
        So don plus Temers m'essaca
        Qu'ira.m fes dir midons e clams;   15
        Que mais d'amor don m'estaca
        No chantari' ab nulhs agurs
        Tro plais vengues entre nos ams.

---

[1] 'The style of the poem is in keeping with an early production. The young poet imitated Marcabru, and imitation is much more apt to appear in early works of poets of original genius than in their later compositions' (p. 72). M. de Riquer questions Pattison's dating of this song in *ZRP* lxxii (1956), 453–6.

III Mas d'aisso que.m sap pro a fel
     Puesc chantar, don grans mals mi mou: 20
     Dels fals, plus ponhens que gibres,
     Envejos, parliers, mals tafurs,
     Q'us quex ponha, et ataca
     Com als fis drutz sia Joys lams;
     Et on qu'aia porc ni vaca   25
     Ilh n'auran pro, e.l vis er purs;
     E pueys fan grans critz, rotz e brams.

IV   Qu'ieu sai un trachor mal fizel
     Que par qu'aia sen meins q'un bou
     Et es ben dels regoïbres   30
     Quar ponha cum traia segurs
     Son senhor que.l cor l'ensaca;
     E s'er' entoisseguatz els cams
     No.s cug que.l quezes tiriaca,
     Ans li querri' ab totz aturs   35
     Com lo pendes ab fortz lïams.

V   Quar anc Caïm, qu'acis Abel,
     No saup de tracïon un ou
     Contra lieis, — mas ieu par ibres,
     Quar li dic so don sui madurs,   40
     Si.m carga lo col e.m maca;
     Mas tan me destrenh plus que fams
     Quan me soven de la raca,
     Que non aus parlar neis per iurs
     De lieis, quan me membra.l satams!   45

VI   E si.m saubra.l chantars a mel
     Ab mon vers qu'ai fait pres d'an nou,
     Quan guarengals e gingibres
     An lur sazo ab mains gasurs,
     E Mos Estreups qu'es part Jaca   50
     No faria tal per dos dams,
     En aquesta rima braca,
     Ab qu'en fos sieus Acres e Surs,
     E de sai Peitaus e Roams.

VII Qu'er si be.s fer de l'esclaca   55
     S'il no men ab sos diz escurs
     Si sui cel que i serai lams.

VIII Mos vers, qu'enaici s'estaca,
     Volgra que.m fos portaz segurs
     A Demoniad' e que.l fos grams.   60

I. Now I see sombre, dark, stormy skies, which cause it to blow and whistle and rain throughout the atmosphere, and snow and ice and frost descend, and the sun, which was hot, strong and harsh, its heat is feeble and sickly; and leaves and flower fall down from the branches so that in hedges and grove I hear no songs nor cries but those indoors; wherefore I shall sing somewhat gloomily.

II. But for my part I should not pay any more attention to wind or rain or ice than to the gentle new season if I dared to unfold my books of deeds of love in dark language—from doing which Fear drags me back all the more because my lady made me speak of anger and complaints; so that never again should I sing of the love with which she transfixes me, under no circumstances whatever, until some pact should be made between us.

III. But I am allowed to sing of that which indeed is bitter to me and causes me great evil: of the false, envious, gossiping, evil scoundrels, more biting than vipers: for each one strives and vies to make Joy into filth for true lovers; and wherever there may be pork or cow they will have plenty of it, and the wine will be undiluted; and then they will utter great cries, rumbles and roars.

IV. For I know one untrustworthy traitor (archer) who seems to have less sense than an ox and certainly belongs to the second harvest, for he strives to betray his master in safety and put his heart in a sack; and if he were poisoned in the fields let him not imagine that I would look for an antidote for him: instead I should try my utmost to have him hanged with strong ropes.

V. For Cain who killed Abel never knew a jot about treachery in comparison with her—but I seem drunk for I tell her what is bursting out of me, she so burdens my neck and bludgeons me—but it torments me more than hunger when I remember the jade, that I daren't speak even in curses about her when I recall the devil that she is!

VI. And yet singing *will* be honey-sweet to me with my *vers* which I have made at the New Year, when galingale and ginger have their season with many a glutton; and My Stirrup-Ring who is beyond Jaca would not do the same as I do in this miry rhyme for two deer, even if Acre and Tyre might be his, and here Poitou and Rouen.

VII. For now, whatever the fracas, if she isn't lying with her black words, I shall be the one to be thunderstruck.

VIII. My *vers*, which is thus fastened up, I wish to be safely carried to Demoniac and to bring her gloom.

NOTES

4–5. *E.l sol qu'era cautz . . . Es sa calors*: the syntax is odd but the variants suggest no alternative (except for colors, *C*; valors *NN²*; uala *R*).

11. *No.m tengran*, Pattison's text, appears in none of the 5 MSS. and he does not comment in the notes. According to his edition the MSS. read: *CE* tengrieu (*E* tengreu), *NN²* tengro, *R* tengra. There is no reason not to take *C* since this is

Pattison's base, especially as he keeps the accusative *gen* rather than *gens* of *NN*[2] (*E* gen missing, *R* gay). *Gel* in v. 10 is also accusative.

14. *R* mestaca, *E* mi seca, *N* me siaca, *N*[2] niesiaca, *C* messaca. Pattison: *m'es jaca*, 'protects me', following *NN*[2] (supported by *R* in v. 16), from *jaca*, 'jaque de mailles', *PD* 216, 'an unusual word forced by the rare rhyme' (p. 103). This seems far-fetched. *Eisagar* (*eisegar*, *esagar*), *PD* 135, 'arranger, mettre en état; exécuter, décider; partager, faire le partage du bétail (ou de l'argent gagné par la vente des bêtes) entre propriétaire et métayer; repartir (la taille)', or *esagar* (*asagar*, *asajar*), *PD* 29, 'essayer, éprouver, tenter; aborder, attaquer' are possibilities, but offer no satisfactory sense that I can see. I tentatively suggest following *C* with *m'essaca* or *m'ensaca*, meaning 'draws me away', 'tears me back'. This second meaning is not given in Rayn. or *SWB* but appears in Godefroy, *Lex.* 176 *ensachier* 1. 'mettre dans un sac / emporter / couvrir d'un sac', 2. 'tirer / attirer / arracher'. This meaning, which fits the sense here, differs from the meaning of *ensaca* in v. 32, and so need not be rejected on grounds of repetition. The use of *ensaca* in v. 14 could be humorous and fairly concrete: Fear keeps the poet away from the 'sack' or 'trap', keeps him out of trouble.

15. *ira* and *clams* belong together and *midons* must be the subject. Pattison: 'although desperation (formerly) caused me to speak of my lady and to complain'.

24. *lams*: Pattison, 'lightning' *SWB* iv. 312, 'how joy may be brief as a lightning-flash for true lovers'. This seems unlikely. *Lams* occurs also in v. 57 and probably means 'lightning' in only one of the two lines, and it seems more appropriate to v. 57 (see below). Meyer-Lübke, 4861, gives *lam* as 'schwach, gebrechlich'; *lama* 'Sumpf', südfrz. *lamo* 'Schmutz'. *Lams* im v. 24 may therefore be an adjective meaning either 'debilitated' (linking with the image in stanza I of the enfeebled sunlight which symbolizes the weakening of courtly virtues), or more strongly, 'filthy, base'.

30. *regoïbres* Pattison links with *voïbre*, *revoïbre*, *reboïbre* (*SWB* vii. 76, viii. 812), meaning 'second growth (of hay or pasturage)' (p. 103). He thinks this means, figuratively, 'from the country' and therefore 'churlish', quoting in support of this XXXIX. 18 where Raimbaut says that the *lauzengiers* 'seem to have been brought up among the hills', 'that is, far from the influence of civilization'. *Regoïbres* is clearly abusive. The image of second growth could suggest something stunted or second-rate. This image may well be linked with *cams* (v. 33), which in turn may be connected with the reference to Cain and Abel in v. 37; Cain having killed Abel *in agro* (Gen. 4:8). The *trachor* is perhaps harvesting hearts 'in the fields' and gathering them up in his 'sack'.

36. *pendes*: Pattison 'bind' (*pendre* for *prendre*). But Raimbaut has said he would like to see this traitor dead, for he would seek no antidote to his poison.

39. *lieis*: Pattison mistakes feminine for masculine ('him') and misses the point: the poet 'accidentally' reveals that he is accusing his lady.

40. *madurs*: Pattison 'aged'. It seems to me that Raimbaut is 'ripe' or 'bursting' with the recriminations he has been keeping to himself but which threaten to break out at any moment.

42. Pattison: *Mas tan me dol la pen' e la fams*: this gives the line one extra syllable. MSS.: *NN*[2] Em dol tant la pen' e la fams, *C* mas tan me destrenh plus que fams, *R* Mas tan me dol la penel fastic. Pattison does not comment on his version; there seems no reason not to follow his base, *C*. (*E* is missing.)

43. *raca*: Pattison, 'unworthy woman'; the word is much stronger: Rayn. v. 29 'rosse'.

44. Pattison: *Non aus parlar neis dels perjurs / De lieis*, 'I do not dare speak even of his (Love's) false statements about her', 'It is impossible to decide whether *perjurs de lieis* means "her false statements" or "his (Love's) false statements about

her".' (p. 103.) The sense of either of these, in this context, is unclear: why should the poet not dare to speak 'even of false statements'? I am inclined to follow *NN²* here (*NN²* per iurs, *R* pels iurs, *C* peiurs, *E* missing). The poet is so brimming over with abusive recrimination that he dare not speak of his lady even with curses—because these would not do justice to his feelings. *CR* parlar, *NN²* chantar: *parlars* or *chantars* appears in v. 46 (*C* chantar, *N* parlars, *N²* parlas, *R* palays, *E* chantars); Pattison's order, v. 44 *parlar*, v. 46 *chantars* is appropriate to the context.

51. *dams*: Pattison: 'injustices' (=*dans*, see *PD* 104). As Raimbaut has mentioned gluttony and New Year feating he may mean *dams* as 'deer': a reward for which *Mos Estreups* would not dare to be outspoken as Raimbaut has been. The *senhal* suggests contempt.

52. *braca*: Pattison: 'lowly'. *PD* 52; 'vil, abject'. *Brac* means 'mud' or 'slime' and *brac* as an adjective can mean 'filthy, muddy' (Meyer-Lübke, 1264: 'schmutzig').

55–7. Pattison: 'For now—however well one strikes with the . . . —if she (?) does not lie with her ambiguous speech, I am indeed the one who will suffer in this affair.' He hesitates between seeing *esclaca* as a sort of weapon or as a man's name (*Esclaca*). L. Pollmann, '*Trobar clus*', p. 40, sees the passage as to be understood in a literary sense, translating as Pattison but filling in *esclaca* (a weapon) and substituting 'he' for 'she'. He links *esclaca* with Marcabru's *estoc breto* (see pp. 21 ff. of my chapter on Marcabru), both of which he sees as a 'Deckname für das "trobar clus" ' (p. 41). Raimbaut says, he thinks, that it is not enough to compose in the *trobar clus*: one must also 'tell lies'. 'Lies', he considers, is a *motz escurs*, an 'ideological *senhal*' behind which is hidden the school of Ventadorn seen from the perspective of 'amor segura'. He claims that Bernart Marti had attacked its 'bel mentir' (Hoepffner, IV) and that Marcabru also does so in rejecting 'sentensa folatina' and the confusion of 'hoc e no' of the 'troba n'Eblo'. He concludes that Raimbaut here finds it necessary to include in the programme of *trobar clus* this 'bel mentir' of courtly love, which consists in writing of joy even when one is not answered by the *dompna* (p. 41). This rests on the following hypotheses: that a weapon, even if referring to verbal conflict, is necessarily an image of the *trobar clus*; that *diz escurs*, even if linked with the *trobar clus*, necessarily implies hidden meaning: *diz escurs* may here mean 'black, angry word'; that the unattested weapon *esclaca* exists; that *il* is nominative masculine singular. (J. Anglade, *Grammaire*, p. 245, gives *il* as nom. masc. plural and *ilh* as fem. sing. nom., emphatic form, with *il* as masc. nom. sing. 'très rare'.)

Esclaca seems to be linked with *esglai*, *esglag*, *esclai*, meaning 'terror, pain, noise, tumult' (*PD* 167), *esglaiar*, *esclaiar*, 'to kill with a weapon; terrify; fear'; or with Old French *esclace* 'éclat, bouillon' (Godefroy, *Lex.* iii. 398: 'Encuntre terre en chient les esclaces (de sang)', *Rol.* 1981 Müller), *esclachier* 'briser' (ibid.: 'Qui contre lui se met en place / Cel est bien atains de la mace / Ou qu'il nel confonde et esclache / C'il n'est tieus qui trop d'armes sache', *Rose*, Vat. Chr. 1858, fo. 132b). A weapon may be intended in Raimbaut's song, but v. 55 may simply mean that a fearsome mêlée is taking place. Both would refer to the poet's grim battle with his lady. *Si be.s fer de l'esclaca* could mean either 'whatever mêlée is raging', or 'whatever blows are being struck with the *esclaca*', or perhaps 'even if she is rushing from the fray'.

57. *Lams* means 'lightning' or 'thunderbolt' (*SWB* iv. 312; see note to v. 24). Raimbaut seems to mean that he would be thunderstruck to learn that his lady was telling the truth. *Que i* is an emandation of *quel* (*NN²*) (Pattison).

58. *s'estaca*: Pattison: 'restrains itself'. *Estacar* means 'attach, bind, fix' (see above, v. 23); the *vers* is 'bound up' or 'firmly fixed', in other words, at an end.

Raimbaut 'outdoes' and makes fun of the opening, by now conventional, in which images of sombre winter announce a grim mood. Wind, rain, snow, ice, frost, leaves, and flowers rush pell-mell through the air. Courtly life, symbolized by the sun, turns weak and flaccid, and the cries to be heard are no longer the twittering of birds but the complaints and quarrels of stay-at-home, stagnating people. This serious moral theme is lightened when it is realized later in the poem that *critz* here anticipates the *critz* of rowdy gluttons who are in fact people enjoying a New Year feast, and are probably Raimbaut's audience. The poet sings 'alques grams' (9): a half-hearted gloom, after the intensity of his wintry beginning.

In fact, Raimbaut confesses that the season makes no difference to him either way. But timidity holds him back from 'unfolding his books of love in dark words': he dares not reveal all the dark secrets about his love, for his lady has already caused him to speak out angrily, with the result that he is not allowed to speak of love at all until a truce has been reached. It is not clear whether the lady has forbidden him to sing, or whether he dares not speak of love for fear of expressing his views on it too violently.

If he cannot sing of love he is allowed to sing of the slanderers who undermine joy, the gluttons who have their fill of 'pork and cow' and utter loud groans and rumbles, not only from backbiting but from over-eating. There is little doubt that this ostensible attack on the *lauzengiers* is humorous, since Raimbaut sings at the New Year 'Quan guarengals e gingibres / An lur sazo ab mains gasurs' (48-9), and is probably enjoying them himself.

He singles out the worst among them: 'un trachor mal fizel', whom he depicts with humorous abuse: 'Que par qu'aia sen meins q'un bou' (29), and who turns out to be none other than Love, for even if he is not named he is the one who tries to trap people's hearts. *Trachor* is a pun on 'traitor' and 'marksman',[1] doubly characterizing Love. Raimbaut turns inside out the conventional attitude to Love: usually it is the lover who seeks an antidote to love, but the poet declares that if the *trachor* Love were

---

[1] *SWB* viii. 348 quotes A. Jeanroy, *R* xliii (1914), 441 on Peire Vidal, 'E trobera ses falhensa / Dous frug d'onrada semensa / E cort de valen senhor / An un avinen trachor': 'Non "traître", mais "archer"; cf. str. III et IV; ou peut-être le poète joue-t-il sur le double sens du mot.' Cf. A. S. Avalle, *Peire Vidal*, p. 111, note to v. 56. Cf. *SWB* viii. 342: *trach* (4) 'Wurfgeschoss, Pfeil'; (8) *ome de trach* 'Bogenschütze'.

poisoned, rather than help him with an antidote he would seek the most effective way of dispatching him.

Yet the greatest traitor of all, worse then Cain, is *lieis*—a reference to the lady which Raimbaut lets slip as if by accident. He seems to be drunk for saying such a thing: yet he is bursting to speak his mind, she bludgeons him so fiercely (41). His feelings are out: she is a *raca*, a 'jade'—and even oaths are inadequate to describe such a demon! By 'not daring' to speak 'even in oaths' he humorously retains the convention of the lover's 'timidity'.

Frankly, he admits, he is very much enjoying his song at the festive season (46–7). *Mos Estreups* would shrink from following his example in such a *rima braca*, however. This person is probably an 'amant martyr' type of poet who would never dream of using such scandalous language to a lady.

Raimbaut takes a final tilt at his lady: whatever the uproar of battle between them, or the blows being delivered, she is the one who is lying; and now that the song is bound up, he hopes it will annoy her intensely.

This poem is so full of humorous twists that it is difficult to draw conclusions from it about the *trobar clus*. It is not to be taken as concerned with literary theory,[1] nor is it a means of attacking uncourtly people secretly or of fooling them by pretending to mean one thing and in fact meaning another, as Pollmann has argued.[2] Like Guilhem IX, Raimbaut begins in an apparently serious vein which turns into burlesque,[3] the point of which the *gasurs* at his table are unoubtedly meant to enjoy. The elements which link this song with what we have already seen in the *trobar clus*, are the gradual unfolding of the *razo* (only in stanza V does Raimbaut reveal that he has been referring all along to his lady's treachery), and the use of words in double senses: *estaca*, 'transfixes' (16), 'fastens up' (58), *lams*, 'weak' or 'despicable' (24), 'thunderstruck' (57), *trachor*, 'traitor' and 'archer' (28), *ensaca*, 'drags back' (14) (?), 'captures' or 'puts in a sack' (32), *digz escurs*, 'dark words', 'angry words' (13), 'black, slanderous words' (56).

In the first stanza of the poem 'Una chansoneta fera' (III) Raimbaut seems to mix references to *trobar clus* and *trobar leu*, saying that his song 'conceals meaning' or 'conceals sense', but

---

[1] Pollmann, '*Trobar clus*', p. 40; see my note to vv. 55–7.

[2] Ibid., pp. 39–40.

[3] See L. Topsfield, *NMi*, vol. lxix, no. 2 (1968), pp. 280–302.

will be easily understood by one who 'expounds' it reasonably. Pattison is puzzled that Raimbaut should apparently declare that the song is obscure, since it is no more difficult than others in which he says the meaning will be clear, and concludes that the poem 'belongs to the series in which Raimbaut was shifting from the style of Marcabru to the *chanson leu*'.[1] U. Mölk quotes this first stanza to show that Raimbaut was trying to combine clarity of meaning with difficulty of rhyme, in a modification of the *trobar clus*, to produce the *trobar prim*.[2] The sense of this passage is not, however, brought out by Pattison's translation, which Mölk follows, and depends in particular on understanding the word *laner*.

> Una chansoneta fera,
>   Voluntiers laner' a dir;
>   Don tem que m'er a murir,
>   E far l'ai tal que sen sela.
> Ben la poira leu entendre
>   Si tot s'es en aital rima;
>   Li mot seran descubert,
>   Al quec de razon deviza.　　　　　(III. 1–8)

Laner is taken by Pattison as synonymous with *levet*, the reading of *a* as against *CR*. But the sense is 'low, common, base'.[3] His

---

[1] p. 77.　　　　　　　　　　　　　　　　　　　　[2] pp. 127–8.

[3] *SWB* iv. 318: 'E'n Perdigos ditz cum joglars laniers, / Qu'en penr' aver a tota s'esperansa' (Appel, *Chrest.* 2, 98, 37), where Rayn. iv. 16 translates 'avide', Appel 'habgierig', and Levy: 'Ist nicht vielmehr "gemein" zu deuten?' Other examples in Rayn. support Levy's translation: 'Totz temps me laisson derrier, / Quan m'an mes en la mesclada, / Li gentil e li lanier' (B. de Born, 'Rassa mes'). Meyer-Lübke, 4876, *lanarius*, discusses OF *lanier*, ' "Wollweber", in der Merowinger Zeit ein verächtlicher Ausdruck, daher afrz. *lanier* "träge" . . . prov. *lanier*'. Cf. Giraut de Bornelh, LXXV. 56, who calls the *joglar* Cardalhac a 'Joglars laniers', playing on the sense of 'woolly' because of Cardalhac's name, but also implying abuse (see Kolsen's glossary, *Giraut de Bornelh*, ii. 206); and *TL* v. i. 151 'von niedriger Gesinnung; feige, träge, faul'; 154: 'Bezeichnung einer (niederwertigen) Falkenart'.

v. 2 *a* levet is probably a *lectio facilior* which the scribe assumed from *leu* (v. 5).

v. 6 *en aital rima*: Pattison sees this phrase as a link with songs II and IV which use the same phrase: 'En aital rimeta prima / M'agradon lieu mot e prim' (II. 1–2), 'Apres mon vers vueilh sempr' ordre / Una chanson leu per bordre / En aital rima sotil' (IV. 1–3). In IV it seems clear that *aital* links the song with the *vers* just sung or composed, to which Rambaut refers. But it is not certain that the same applies to II, where he could simply mean: 'In such a clever little rhyme as this I like light and clever words.' Similarly in III, 'Si tot s'es en aital rima' probably means 'Even if it is in such a rhyme as this (in which meaning is concealed)'. *rima*: Mölk (p. 127) takes this to refer specifically to *rhymes*. It can mean both 'rhyme word ending' (e.g. A. Daniel, XII. 8: 'que no.i aia mot fals ni rim' estrampa'), and 'poem', as Raimbaut

little song will be of a 'low sort', and for fear of the disapproval it will provoke, he will have to conceal the meaning—but anyone with any sense will soon be able to see through it.

I should like to compose a ditty to be sung in a low way: but I'm afraid it will be the death of me and so I shall make it such that it hides meaning. It will easily be understood even if it is in such a rhyme; the words will be unveiled to anyone who expounds it reasonably.

In this deliberate jumble of phrases suggesting both *trobar clus* and *trobar leu*, Raimbaut slyly tilts at both: firstly by making a song 'to be sung in a low way' he makes fun once more of Giraut's defence of a style that is *vil* or *venarsal*: his song will be 'low', but not in the sense meant by defenders of the *trobar leu*: and secondly he makes fun of the pedants who pride themselves on knowing how to understand the hidden meanings of words. And so he merrily brushes aside the whole *clus–leu* argument.

These literary allusions are merely the prelude, in the style of Guilhem IX, to a sexual *gap*. Though clothed in more courtly apparel than Guilhem's 'Ben vuelh',[1] Raimbaut's song is no less intended as an account of his erotic adventures. He boasts of his 'conquest' (16); God has 'rewarded him to his liking': 'Dieus m'a pagat a ma guiza' (24); when he lies down at night he reflects on how best to serve his lady according to hers:

> Domna, can mi colc al sera,
>   La nueyt (e tot iorn) cossir
>   Co.us pogues en grat servir;   (33–5)

his appeal for her favours, while clad in the vague periphrasis of courtly language, leaves no doubt as to his goal:

> Domna, si no.us alezera
>   Mos cors, lay on yeu dezir,
>   Res plus tost no.m pot aucir,   (41–3)

which is more explicit in the *tornada:*

> Deu prec tan de mort m'escrima
>   Donna, e m'aia suffert
>   Tro qu'ie.us embraz ses chamiza.   (57–9)

uses it in *rima braca* (X. 52). See also Rayn. v. 96, and G. Mari, *SFR* viii (1901), 35–88, especially 39, 47, 68.

v. 8 *deviza:* Pattison 'divides', but what does this mean? See *PD* 124: 'séparer; exposer, raconter; dépeindre; enseigner?; discuter; déterminer; détailler'. *Devizar de razon* might mean 'to determine the nature of the theme'.

[1] Jeanroy, VI.

No great perception is needed, Raimbaut declares, to see the
sexual undertones of this piece of apparently courtly gallantry.

This is obviously not serious *trobar clus*. But the combination
of learned literary allusions and sexual comedy is not new; it
seems to belong to a genre. Besides Guilhem's 'Ben vuelh', a
further song of Raimbaut's may be mentioned: 'Lonc temps ai
estat cubertz' (XXVIII), where *cubertz* hints at *trobar clus* while
the song proves to be a joke about the poet's avowed castration.
Marcabru combined sexual and literary themes in 'D'aisso lau
Dieu'. In a *sirventes* attributed to Marcoat,[1] 'Mentre m'obri eis
huisel', the author praises his *bos moz clus* (v. 26), while his theme
is the disability of a cripple and probably has sexual undertones,
and he calls his song a *sirventes escubel*, a 'trashy *sirventes*'.[2] These
songs seem to mark a line of development of the *trobar clus*
distinct from the more serious tradition which includes Marcabru's 'Contra l'ivern', Peire's 'Be m'es plazen', and Raimbaut's
'Cars douz'.

'Assatz m'es belh' (XVII) has been seen as a discussion of the
trobar clus and *trobar leu*, mainly from the first three stanzas. But
the sense of the work as a whole has not been examined.

I   Assatz m'es belh
           Que de novelh
           Fassa parer
           De mon saber
           Tot plan als prims sobresabens   5
           Que van comdan
           Qu'ab sen d'enfan
           Dic e fatz mos captenemens;
           E sec mon cor
           E.n mostri for   10
           Tot aisso don ilh m'es cossens.

II   Qui qu'en favelh,
           Lo m'es pro belh
           De mon saber:
           Qu'en sai mielhs ver   15
           (Sitot no suy mout conoyssens)
           Que.l trop parlan
           Que van comdan

<hr>

[1] Dejeanne, *AdM* xv (1903), 362; see p. 63.
[2] See p. 167.

'Folhs es. — Non es. — Si es sos sens.'
Qu'ar tost salh for   20
Ab belh demor
Gen motz leugiers, cortes talens.

III   Ab sen novelh
          Dic e favelh
          Mon saber ver   25
          E.l fas parer
          Lay on tanh que sia parvens;
          Que son enfan
          Li mielhs parlan
          Vas me; e sai qui.m n'es guirens,   30
          Ab que.m demor
          Gen dins mon cor
          Si que.l dir no.m passa las dens.

I. It is very pleasing to me once again to demonstrate my wisdom
quite plainly to the refined, extra-clever people who keep saying that
I speak and conduct myself with childish folly. And I follow my heart
and outwardly show only as much of it as my lady (*or*: my heart)
permits me.

II. Whoever argues about it I am quite pleased with my wisdom; for
I know more truth about it (even if I'm not very discerning) than
the talkative people who say: 'He is mad.' 'No he isn't.' 'That's his
wisdom.' For now there spring forth quickly gracious, airy words,
courtly desire, with seemly pleasure.

III. With new wisdom I speak and pronounce my true knowledge
(secret knowledge, *CDM*), and make it apparent there where it is
fitting for it to be seen; for the best speakers among them are children
in comparison with me; and I know who is guarantor of this for me,
provided that it remains well within my heart so that no word of it
should pass my lips.

NOTES

11. *ilh*: IKN² read el, *CDM* ilh (*D* ill, *M* il), *R* De tot so don mes pus cozens. Appel,
    Raimbaut von Orange, p. 25 : el.   •
19. Pattison: 'He is crazy'; 'No, he isn't'; 'Indeed what he says is'. Appel, p. 24:
    'folhs es? non es? sí es sos sens!' 'ist er ein Tor? ist er's nicht? ja, sein Sinn
    ist töricht!' Raimbaut's words recall Giraut de Bornelh, V. 16–19: 'E donc non
    entens / C'us motz fatz fass' apprendens / E ses maestria? — / Si fatz be, mas tot
    es sens! —' Perhaps Raimbaut's words should be punctuated: 'Folhs es. — Non
    es: si es sos sens.' ' "He is mad." "No he isn't: this is his wisdom!" '
22. Pattison: *Gen motz leugiers, cortes, valens*, an eclectic reading. IKN² are missing;
    C Gen mout leu les forses talens, *D* Gen motz liuier cortes talen, *M* Gen motz
    leugier cortes talen, *R* Gen mos laus letz cortes uales. Appel, *Raimbaut von
    Orange*, p. 25 : gens m.l., cortes talens.

25–6. Pattison's text is only in *R*; *IKN*² are missing; *CDM*: E fatz parer / Mon cubert uer (*DM*: faz). Appel, p. 25 : 'dic e favelh / mon cubert ver / e fatz parer'.

Pattison (p. 124) says that vv. 5–8 show that 'Raimbaut will write clearly, abandoning the obscure style under pressure of criticism. The opponents of the *trobar clus* accuse him of being childish or insane (19). Yet in the end he produces a not too simple specimen of the *trobar car* (71).' Köhler (pp. 143–4) sees in the reference to *cubert ver* (25–6, *CDM*) evidence that Raimbaut is concealing from foolish people a 'precious, concealed truth'. Mölk (p. 129) sees the song as an especially fine example of the *trobar prim*, in which Raimbaut mixes easy (stanzas I–III) and rarer (IV–VI) rhymes (*ic*, *eg*), and mentions *motz leugiers* in *a vers ab diz car* (v. 71). *Leugier* and *car* he considers equivalent to *leu e prim*. Pollmann ('*Trobar clus*', p. 34) quotes v. 22 in Pattison's version: 'Gen motz leugiers, cortes, valens' to argue that the *trobar leu* claims to be the courtly means of expression; that *leugiers*, *cortes*, and *valens* belong together, whereas a *clus* poet would have juxtaposed *clus* and *cortes*.

Raimbaut scoffs at the 'wisdom' of 'clever' people who say he acts and talks like a fool (6–8). He intends to ignore them, following the dictates of his heart and revealing his true feelings only to the extent that his lady (or his inclination) indicates that he should (9–11). He makes fun of the so-called wise people who try to analyse what he says and does to see if there is any sense behind it (17–19). Even if he seems undiscerning to them, he is pleased with his own version of wisdom, as he now proposes to demonstrate with 'Gen motz leugiers, cortes talens'. This reading, supported by the majority of manuscripts,[1] takes up the double theme of the poet's words and behaviour: 'Dic e fatz mos captenemens' (8).

If *motz leugiers* are meant to refer to the *trobar leu*, then Raimbaut's promise to produce this is contradicted immediately in the following stanza where he seems to speak in *clus* terms: he speaks with new *sen*, 'meaning' or 'wisdom', which he reveals only to the right person (26–7), namely his lady. Provided that he keeps her identity secret (31–3), she can guarantee that he surpasses all 'Li mielhs parlan'. He implies that he surpasses them not only in words but in deeds also: he is a more eloquent poet and a better lover.

Now in the fourth stanza his 'wisdom' is revealed:

Don d'amar dic:
Qu'am si ses tric
Lieys qu'amar deg,
Que.l miels adreg
(S'eron sert cum l'am finamens)

[1] See note to v. 22 on p. 166.

M'irion sai
Preguar hueymai
Que.ls essenhes cum aprendens
De ben amar;
E neus preguar
M'en venrion dompnas cinc cens.   (34–44)

So I say of loving: that I love so guilelessly the lady whom I ought to love, that the most adept (if they knew how truly I love her) would come here to beg me from now on to teach them as students about how to love well; and similarly five hundred ladies would even come to beg me about it.

His wisdom, which outweighs all the talk of the clever people, consists in his amorous accomplishment. This can be taken on a flippant level, and also on the level that Raimbaut *does* know how to love his lady well and this is a matter entirely between themselves, other people's opinions being superfluous and unsolicited. If he speaks with 'folly', as he does in his *rima braca* (X), or in 'Una chansoneta fera' (III), he and his lady have their own understanding with one another.

In the rest of the song Raimbaut demonstrates his flippant disrespect for everyone who criticizes him: his heart is so 'ric' that it makes him the equal of kings and dukes, whom he treats contemptuously if they are discourteous to him (45–55).

Raimbaut must have had the *trobar clus* and *trobar leu* in mind here; he is clearly concerned with 'ways of speaking' (8, 29), and he mentions both *motz leugiers* and concealed meaning.[1] But his flippancy in making fun of conventional attitudes precludes the possibility of drawing conclusions about the two styles from this poem. What is clear is that he associates *motz leugiers* and *cortes talens* with stuffiness. Raimbaut promises to give the pedants what they want; but instead of light, graceful words in the *trobar leu*, expressing courtly platitudes, he gives them *motz leugiers* in the sense of 'flippant' or 'frivolous' words,[2] and *talens* which may be less *cortes* than they seem. As for his *saber ver* or *cubert ver*, the sense which he reveals 'where it is fitting', this is not a secret meaning: it is the true state of his feelings about his lady, which he intends to keep private. Allusions to *clus* and *leu* are brought in more for

---

[1] *cubert ver*, *CDM*; in any case he makes his sense only apparent 'Lay on tanh que sia parvens'. *Leugier* itself only appears in one MS., *M*: cf. note on line 22, p. 166, but makes the best sense.

[2] Rayn. iv. 59–60; *SWB* iv. 376.

the sake of tilting against conventional attitudes and giving his flippancy an edge by the serious, literary mode of expression, than because he sets out to compose in the *trobar clus*, *leu*, or *prim*, or to make any statement about style as such. When he mentions his *diz car* (71),[1] he probably uses *car* as a general term of praise, related particularly to the complex rhyme scheme,[2] or to the content: namely that he has spoken of his love for his lady.

'Cars douz' is Raimbaut's only serious attempt to compose in the *trobar clus*. In all other songs where elements of it occur, the intention and the effects of using a *clus* framework are humorous. Raimbaut's *clus* techniques in 'Cars douz' are modelled on those of Marcabru: the *razo* is gradually unfolded and moves towards a sense of clarity within the poet's mind; literary and moral themes are interwoven, and words are richly coloured and tinted with meanings. Traditional, Marcabrunian elements are combined with a personal view of *jois*. 'Ar vei' uses similar technical elements to those of 'Cars douz': the gradual unfolding of the *razo*, the rare rhymes, words, and images, the ambiguity of meaning; but the literary framework is used for burlesque purposes. In 'Una chansoneta fera' Raimbaut makes fun of *clus* and *leu*, probably composing in neither: the song is 'low, scurrilous', a joke in the tradition of Guilhem IX or the *sirventes escubel* attributed to Marcoat. 'Assatz m'es belh' mixes literary ideas with a personal theme, a discussion of the poet's *foudat*, in a highly individual way, and indicates that Raimbaut probably thought of *leu* as the style of conventional, banal ideas, and *clus* as the style of individual poetry. None of these songs shows 'systematic obscurity' or an intention to exclude the *vilan*. The complex style of 'Cars douz' expresses a personal struggle, not intentional esoterism. Raimbaut's jokes are not intended to be esoteric. If in 'Assatz' he keeps his 'truth' to himself, this 'truth' is not the meaning of the poem, but the true state of the relationship between himself and his lady.

2. '*Trobar leu*'

Although Raimbaut composes in a light style for his own purposes, he never accepts the *trobar leu* as it is put forward by Giraut

---

[1] 'E.t voill pregar, / Vers, ab diz car / Que lai en Urgel te presenz' (70–2). All MSS. (*DIKN²*) have *clar* for *car*, but the versification demands *car*: see Pattison's explanation, p. 125, n. to v. 64.

[2] Frank, 182, 1; see p. 226.

de Bornelh. The new-fangled *trobar leu* he dignifies anomalously
with *clus* terms:

> Aissi mou
> Un sonet nou
> On ferm e latz
> Chansson leu,
> Pos vers plus greu
> Fan sorz dels fatz.
> Qu'er er vist,
> Pos tan m'es quist,
> Cum sui senatz;
> Si cum sol,
> Fora mos cors vesatz,
> Mas chamjar l'ai pos quex o vol.   (XVIII. 1–12)

Thus I begin a new melody in which I fasten and bind up a light *chanso*,
since the heavier *vers* make the witless deaf. So now it will be seen,
since so much is demanded of me, how wise I am; I would be gay
in my former fashion, but I shall change since this is what everyone
wants.

After 'ferm e latz', terms leading one to expect the *trobar clus*,[1] the
effect of 'Chansson leu' is one of bathos. By the antithesis *leu/greu*
Raimbaut suggests that the *trobar leu* is 'easy' rather than 'difficult'
and thereby slyly pokes fun at those who claim that the *trobar leu*
is just as difficult to compose as the *trobar clus*.[2] He also implies
that the subject-matter of his *chanso* will be 'light, insubstantial,
frivolous', rather than 'serious, weighty'; and, of course, that the
fools will find it easy to understand. In all cases he condescends
to sing for those who find *vers plus greu* beyond them.[3]

In the song 'A mon vers' (XXX) he descends, this time angrily,
to the level of the *fatz* to refute them in their own language.

> A mon vers dirai chansso
> Ab leus motz ez ab leu so
> Ez en rima vil' e plana
> (Puois aissi son encolpatz
> Qan fatz avols motz als fatz),

---

[1] Pollmann, '*Trobar clus*', pp. 41 ff., notes this, and thinks the elements of parody
in this song are *clus*, since the meaning is expressed indirectly. But not all parody
or irony is necessarily *clus*.

[2] Cf. Giraut de Bornelh, XLVIII. 1–10 (see p. 104).

[3] Köhler, p. 144, thinks that vv. 5–6 show that the *trobar clus* intentionally ex-
cludes fools from hearing a valuable truth which is unsuitable for their ears. But
Raimbaut simply makes fun of dim-witted listeners. He does not *set out* to make them
'deaf'.

E dirai so q'en cossir —
Qui qe.m n'am mais o.m n'azir!   (XXX. 1–7)

With my vers I shall sing a *chanso*, with easy words and an easy tune
and in plain and common rhyme (since I am blamed so much for
fashioning expressions which are worthless to simpletons), and I
shall say what I really think about them—whoever may love me more
or hate me for it!

In his opinion fools have been arguing ignorantly about love,
saying that a lady ought not to love a nobleman. His description
of their style of singing is entirely pejorative. Where for Giraut
leu meant 'light', for Raimbaut it means 'easy', 'facile'; where
plana for Giraut meant 'smooth', for Raimbaut it means 'plain';
vil means not 'humble' but 'menial'.[1] Ironically he refers to his
usual style as *avols*—from the point of view of the *fatz*: either
because they cannot understand what he says, or because they
dislike it, for its style or content. The purpose of using their
language is to leave no doubt as to his meaning, as he indicates
in stanza VII:

E dirai en mais? — ieu no!
Ar en aquesta sazo!
Mas si negus hom si vana
C'ab me se.n contrast' iratz
Adoncs m'auziretz viätz
Tals motz per me ses mentir
C'om non poiria cobrir.   (43–9)

And shall I say more about it? Not I! not now at present! But if any
man presumes to dispute angrily with me on the subject, then you
will soon hear such words from me that certainly could not be concealed.[2]

Cobrir is doubtless an allusion to the *trobar clus*. Raimbaut says
there will be nothing 'veiled' about his meaning.

In the song 'Apres mon vers' (IV) he wants to compose 'Una
chanson leu per bordre';

Apres mon vers vueilh sempr' ordre
Una chanson leu per bordre
En aital rima sotil;
Mas ges non ai' us de tordre
Si.m pert ma par ni.m ten vil
Q'ieu vas mon miels no.m apil.   (IV. 1–6)

---

[1] Giraut's use of pejorative terms such as *vil* represented false modesty, to forestall objections from critics. See pp. 105 ff.

[2] *m'auziretz* (47) should perhaps be *n'auziretz*, to avoid redundancy in v. 48.

After my *vers* I want to weave at once a light *chanso* for jousting, in similar subtle rhyme; but never let me be like the turtledove, if my mate abandons or scorns me, so that I do not take comfort in what is to my advantage.[1]

Keeping the *rima sotil* of the *vers* he has just composed or sung,[2] he composes a *chanso* which is 'light for jousting', meaning that Raimbaut intends to attack certain ideas in a light-hearted way. *Leu* here refers not to the style but the tone, and the content, in which he parodies and turns upside-down conventional attitudes to love and treatments of the love theme.

In 'Una chansoneta fera' (III) he promises that his song will be easily understood: 'Ben la poiria leu entendre' (5); here once more he is joking about different styles to give a mock-learned introduction to a light-hearted theme.[3]

Motz leugiers (XVII. 22),[4] as we have seen, he thinks of disparagingly as the style desired by the *prims sobresabens*, the accompaniment of conventional platitudes and *cortes talens*.

Trobar plan, which for Giraut meant a smooth, polished, and sometimes clear style, Raimbaut regards as the commonplace mode of expression used by undistinguished people every day; yet since this appears, he says, to be what is wanted, he will outdo everyone in being commonplace:

> Pos trobars plans
> Es volguz tan
> Fort m'er greu s'i non son sobrans:
> Car ben pareis
> Qi tals motz fai
> C'anc mais non foron dig cantan,
> Qe cels c'om tot jorn ditz e brai
> Sapcha, si.s vol, autra vez dir.   (XVI. 1–8)

Since the plain style is so much in demand I shall be very displeased if I am not supreme in it: for it is obvious that someone who composes such words as have never been heard before in song, will know how

---

[1] *per bordre*: Pattison: 'playful'. Rayn. ii. 212: *bordir*, etc., 'behourder, joûter, folâtrer, s'amuser, bondir'; *beordar* 'behourder, joûter, faire des tournois, des joûtes'. Raimbaut may mean, that he is playfully tilting at accepted conventions. Pattison, p. 53, thinks Raimbaut distorted the language to form *bordre* from *bordir*, but D. R. Sutherland says that the language allows for such flexibility ('Flexions and categories in Old Provençal', *Transactions of the Philological Society* (1959), p. 69).

[2] Pattison thinks Raimbaut refers to 'En aital rimeta' (II); see his p. 81, notes to vv. 1–3.

[3] See p. 162.   [4] See p. 168.

to speak those which are spoken and shouted every day, if he so desires, on another occasion.

While this has been taken as evidence that Raimbaut felt it necessary to express himself well in all styles according to the occasion,[1] his point is humorous: if he can create original works, he can certainly do well at being commonplace.

Whenever Raimbaut refers to the *trobar leu* or *trobar plan*, his remarks are disparaging or satirical.

Leu can, however, mean 'light' or 'graceful' outside the context of the *trobar leu*. In 'Cars douz' the wren's song, *cars* and symbolic of the poet's *trobar clus*, 'cha plus leu de siura' (7), 'falls more lightly than cork'. It has the same sense in the song 'En aital rimeta prima' (II), in which Raimbaut chooses 'lieu mot e prim'; 'light and delicate words' (2).

Raimbaut, like Giraut, seems to distinguish between *vers* and *chanso* according to whether a composition belongs to the *trobar leu* or not. After his *vers* he composes 'Una chanson leu per bordre' (IV. 1–2); he weaves a 'chansson leu' since 'vers plus greu / Fan sorz dels fatz' (XVIII. 1–6). When forced to use an easy style to communicate with the *fatz*, he 'sings a *chanso* with his *vers*', 'A mon vers dirai chansso' (XXX. 1): this seems to imply that his song is a *vers* from the point of view of its serious subject-matter, but a *chanso* in its easy style.

Of the eleven songs called *vers*, none belongs to the *trobar leu* or *plan* except for 'A mon vers dirai chansso', whose case is special.[2] Six songs are called *chanso*: one is a joke at the expense of the *trobar plan* (XVI); in three, *vers* and *chanso* are opposed to one another (IV, XVIII, XXX); one parodies the style of Bernart de Ventadorn (XIX).[3] The remaining one, 'Ben s'eschai' (XXI) is not *leu* for it has rare rhymes: *ort, ap, aug, esc, out, aut*, but Raimbaut pretends to be competing in it with the *joglars*. It seems then that Raimbaut thought of *chanso* as a light or frivolous song usually in the *trobar leu*.[4]

When Raimbaut declares his intention to compose in the *trobar*

---

[1] Köhler, p. 143.

[2] I, V, X, XI, XVII, XX, XXXV–XXXIX.

[3] See p. 177.

[4] Pattison, pp. 38–9, rejects the possibility of a chronological division in Raimbaut's use of *vers* and *chanso*, and accepts Gennrich's musical distinction between the two genres (F. Gennrich, *Grundriss einer Formenlehre des mittelalterlichen Liedes* . . . (Halle, 1932), pp. 237–45).

leu or *plan*, this intention is almost invariably humorous. One exception is the song 'A mon vers' (XXX) in which he uses the plain language of the *fatz* for the sake of clear exposition and argument:

> Qecs a dreig que se.n razo,
> Mas vers venz qui be.l despo,
> Ez ieu dic paraula sana:
> Que mieills deu esser amatz
> Rics hom francs ez enseignatz
> Qu'il pot pro e bel chausir
> Per dompna q'aus precs soffrir.   (XXX. 22–7)

Each man has a right to argue about it, but the one who expounds it well conquers the truth, and I speak sound words: for a sincere and cultivated nobleman should be loved by preference, since he can discern advantageously and well for the lady who dares to listen to his prayers.[1]

Otherwise, he makes fun of the *trobar leu* in many ways: of its stylistic techniques, and the conventional attitudes which he associates with it.

In 'Pos trobars plans' (XVI) plain language serves to indicate his real opinions:

> Per tal joi soi coindes e vans,
>   Qe mais val neis
>   Desirs q'ieu n'ai
> D'una qe anc no.m ac semblan
> (Pels sainz c'om qer en Verzelai!)
> D'autre joi c'om puesca jauzir.
>
>   Son ben aurans!
>   C'ar, per talan
> Solamen, so francs et humans,
>   De dir ves leis
>   Ben, ni.m fas gai.
> Qe.m val si per lieis trag mal gran?
> Si lo mal q'en trac no sap lai,
> Mi eis voil d'aitan escarnir.   (XVI. 11–24)

For such a joy as this, I am both charming and so light-headed that the mere desire for it, from a lady who never showed me favour, is worth more (by the saints one seeks at Vézelay!) than any other joy which one might enjoy to the full! I must be mad! For now mere

---

[1] See p. 171. Appel, *Raimbaut von Orange*, pp. 16–17, Pattison, p. 172, think this song replies to the *tenso* between Giraut de Bornelh and Alfonso II of Aragon (Kolsen, LIX).

desire makes me kind and gentle in speaking well to her and makes me act gaily. What is the point of suffering for *her* sake? If *she* fails to recognize the hardships that I suffer, then *I* am making a fool of myself.

Elsewhere smooth, courtly language is punctuated with uncourtly bluntness:

> Mas no say anctos
> Vas vos, qu'ades recaliva
> Mos leus cors on piegz m'en vay.
>
> Mas vos avetz — don morrai,
> Amors — l'us de Barabas;   (XIX. 19-23)

But I do not know how to act shamefully towards you, for my fickle heart is continually re-kindled where things go worst for me. But you act—and this, Love, will be my death—like Barrabas!

> Per que, si.m peza, dirai,
> Amors, tan ves vos que cas;   (XIX. 29-30)

Wherefore, even if this grieves me, I shall speak to you, Love, as if I were a dog.

Conventional *topoi* are twisted or turned upside-down: Raimbaut poses as the suppliant lover, playing on the theme of the lover's uncertainty and of *amor de lonh*, with a sardonic aside on his new-found method of paying court:

> Pauc soi certans!
> (Ves qe.us reblan,
> Domna.) De vos so molt londans!
>
>   (XVI. 49-51)

I am very unsure of myself! (You see how I court you, lady.) I am very far away from you!

The same *amor de lonh* theme receives summary treatment in 'Aissi mou':

> Amors, rim
> Co.s vuoilla prim;
> Pos m'etz de latz
> En que poing?
> C'ab colp de loing
> Son pres nafratz!   (XVIII. 37-42)

Love, I rhyme (or 'burn') as excellently as may be wished. Since you are at my side, why do I strive? For with a distant blow I am closely wounded.

He discards the conventional virtue of patience and 'Respeitz loncs' (XVI. 40):

> Qe jai
> Me posca, de so qe.il deman,
> Et atretan tost, Dieus, si.l plai,
> Co fes vin d'aiga, devenir.   (XVI. 45–8)

May God, if he will, bring me joy in that which I ask of him, and as quickly as he made wine from water!

He overturns the conventional notion of boorishness: *he* is churlish for loving against his own interests:

> Ades mi datz plus d'esmay
> On mielhs suy ves vos sertas.
> E fauc hi ben que vilas,
> Quar per mal suy amoros.   (XIX. 15–18)

You always bring me the most distress where I am the most faithful to you. And in this I certainly act like a boor, since I am in love to my disadvantage.

He parodies the *topos* of the lover's fidelity:

> Mas ges non ai' us de tordre
> Si.m pert ma par ni.m ten vil
> Q'ieu vas mon miels no.m apil.   (IV. 4–6)

But may I never act like the turtledove, if my mate abandons or scorns me, so that I do not take comfort in what is to my advantage.

The *trobar leu* is a pretext for Raimbaut to make fun of courtly *topoi* and social conformity.

He mimics or twists stylistic devices commonly used by poets of light style. Ratiocination serves not to discuss the lover's state of mind, but to come to the logical conclusion that self-denial is not to be recommended:

> Tan aut mespreis
> Mon cor, car sai
> Q'enfol. M'aurei donc faz l'efan?
> — Tot voll cant vei. — Respeit segrai.
> — Respeitz loncs fai omen perir.[1]   (XVI. 36–40)

I despise myself so much because I know I am going mad. Shall I then have made a fool of myself?—I want everything I can see.—I shall wait in patience.—A long wait makes one perish!

---

[1] Raimbaut may be punning on the *senhal* Bon-Respeit (Appel, *Raimbaut von Orange*, p. 44).

He makes fun of the rhetorical device (*praecisio*) often used by poets who claim they are afraid to speak their mind about love and break off in mid sentence:

> E tem a dir . . . Quals? — C'om pliva
> So que.us cofon e.us dechay.
>
> Mas ieu o dic; e si.n bray
> Ni m'en desmen hom vilas,
> Vengua armatz en us plas;
> E sia orbs o gelos,
> S'ieu no volri' esser jos,
> Vencutz; qui.s vol, so escriva;
> Sol vers no fos si.m n'esglay.   (XIX. 34–42)

And I fear to say . . . What? — Let one speak out about the cause of your destruction and ruin! And I *do* say it and if I shout it aloud, and any boorish man contradicts me, let him come armed into the lists and, provided that I didn't choose to lose, let him be vanquished, blind or jealous; anyone may put that in writing if he wishes—except that this would not be true if I were afraid of him.

Rhetorical questions are unexpectedly and truthfully answered:

> Amors, cum er? Que faray?
> Morrai frescx, joves e sas,
> Enaissi dins vostras mas?
> Oc! Murir, si.m pliu per vos![1]   (XIX. 1–4)

Love, what will happen? What shall I do? Shall I die thus, fresh, young and healthy, in your hands? Yes! Die I shall, if I trust you!

Raimbaut makes fun of the learned use of authorities:

> Cil qi m'a vout trist-alegre
> Sap mais qu'i vol sos ditz segre
> Qe Salamos ni Marcols
> De fatz ric ab ditz entegre:
> E cai leu d'aut en la pols
> Qi.s pliu en aitals bretols.   (IV. 19–24)

The one who has made me sorrowful-gay knows that I wish to follow her dictates more than Solomon and Marcol of the noble deeds and upright sayings: and he who puts his trust in such stupid fellows easily falls from high up down into the dust.

His playful treatment of rhetorical devices parodies the *trobar leu*;

---

[1] This song may parody or reply to Bernart de Ventadorn: 'Amors, e que.us es vejaire? / Trobatz mais fol mas can me? / Cuidatz vos qu'eu si' amaire / e que ja no trop merce? / Que que.m comandatz a faire, / farai o, c' aissi.s cove; / mas vos non estai ges be / que.m fassatz tostems mal traire.' (IV. 1–8) Bernart sent this song to Tristan, whom Pattison identifies with Raimbaut (p. 24).

but it extends to other styles, too, for in two songs he builds a whole composition out of the single device of repetition. In 'Ar non sui jes' (XXXVI) he repeats *malastrucs* in some form in every line; 'Ab nou cor' (XXXV) has a different key word for each stanza which is repeated in each line. Raimbaut thereby outstrips his competitors in dexterity and at the same time laughs at the futility of such exercises.

Raimbaut shies away from clichés, and if he says he will compose in the *trobar leu* or *plan* this almost invariably means he will make fun of *leu* attitudes and style, as a 'fols cantayre cortes' (XXIV. 33).

A few of Raimbaut's thirty-nine songs are composed in a clear, straightforward style, without especially rare words or complex versification, and are not termed *leu* or *plan*. These include a conversational reply to Peire Rogier (VI), a *carta* (XXIII), and a few love lyrics. One of these, 'Dona, si m'auzes rancurar' (XXVI), contains the kind of clichés which he usually ridicules: 'ploran mi clamera' (2), 'no vos deg encolpar' (3), 'tot qan faitz e dizetz / M'es bon' (5–6). This may be the result of composing in a set genre, the petition.[1] In his other love songs Raimbaut always gives an individual impression: in 'Ara.m so del tot conquis' (XXIX) the rhyme in *el* introduces unusual, if not strikingly rare words: *gragel, sembel, revel, espel, sagel, cervel*; in the song 'Un vers farai de tal mena' (V) rhymes are again unusual (*ena, esca, ensa, aug, iva, onh*), with key words repeated to give an impression of joy and life: *gaug* in the fifth line of each stanza, *viva* in the main body of the song and twice in the *tornadas*. Raimbaut uses lighter styles when he so chooses, but he refuses to classify them as *leu*.

3. 'Trobar ric', 'trobar prim'

Trobar ric has been seen as a 'solution' to the conflict between *clus* and *leu*, combining clarity of meaning with richness of form, especially rare rhymes and vocabulary.[2] L. Pollmann[3] considers that Raimbaut, followed by Arnaut Daniel, separates the technical side of the *trobar clus*: in his view, artistic rhymes and stanzaic

---

[1] The song lists arguments why the lady should take the poet as her lover (35).

[2] Both Pollmann ('*Trobar clus*', p. 44) and Mölk, p. 130, see it as a 'Lösung'.

[3] Loc. cit.

structure, from its function of concealing meaning and playing on it, and gives it a new function: of making artistic form the adequate expression of an exalted love.

U. Mölk[1] prefers to call the compromise between *clus* and *leu* the *trobar prim*, since *prim* is common to Giraut de Bornelh, Raimbaut, and Arnaut, who never use the term *ric*. He defines this style as a combination of clear meaning with subdued *clus* technique: the retention of rare rhyme but the removal of internal rhyme, with the rhymes themselves somewhat simpler than those of 'Cars douz'.

He sees songs II, III, IV, and XVII of Raimbaut as examples and discussions of the *trobar prim*, and follows Pattison in thinking that II, III, and IV are linked together.[2] Each of these mentions *aital rima:* 'en aital rimeta prima' (II. 1), 'en aital rima' (III. 6), 'en aital rima' (IV. 3), and the poet's 'will' to sing: 'Pos mos volers s'i apila' (II. 4), 'Voluntiers laner' a dir' (III. 2), 'Apres mon vers vueilh sempr' ordre' (IV. 1). Each song also mentions *leu*: 'M'agradon lieu mot e prim' (II. 2), 'Ben la poira leu entendre' (III. 5), 'Una chanson leu per bordre' (IV. 2). He thinks that II. 1, 'En aital rimeta prima', refers back to 'Cars douz', drawing attention to their similarity in rhyme while differentiating between their clarity: 'M'agradon lieu mot e prim' (2). The three poems, Mölk concludes, are similar in rhyme, all being somewhat simpler than 'Cars douz', and all are *leu*.[3] At the same time, he claims, the songs of the *trobar prim* should not be 'without worth',[4] and hence Raimbaut mentions his *sen* in III: 'E far l'ai tal que sen sela' (4), and calls his rhyme *prim* or *sotil* (II. 1; IV. 3). In 'Assatz m'es belh' (XVII), he observes, Raimbaut also stresses his *saber* (4, 14) and combines *motz leugiers* (22) with *diz car* (71), thus uniting clarity with worth.

But the repetition of such phrases as 'aital rima' and 'volers' are slight evidence to show that Raimbaut must have been linking these songs stylistically. In III, 'aital rima' probably refers to the

---

[1] Op. cit., pp. 126–30.

[2] *Raimbaut d'Orange*, pp. 73–4, 77, 81.

[3] He argues that Raimbaut abandons internal rhymes in the *trobar prim*; but XVIII, which he classes as *prim* (p. 131), could be arranged to show internal rhyme:

'Aissi mou   un sonet nou   on ferm e latz

Chansson leu,   pos vers plus greu   fan sorz dels fatz' . . .

(See Appel, *Raimbaut von Orange*, p. 80).

[4] p. 128.

song itself being composed.[1] In this song the mention of *sen* is humorous.[2] In XVII *motz leugiers* is meant satirically and does not refer to a serious literary intention.[3] *Lieu* in II may not refer to the *trobar leu* at all but may simply mean 'light, graceful', as it does in 'Cars douz'.[4] 'Leu per bordre' (IV. 2) indicates the subject-matter of the poem which will make fun of conventional attitudes to love.[5] Once these songs are analysed individually it becomes very doubtful that there is one unifying stylistic theory behind them; they indicate rather the variety and playfulness of Raimbaut's moods.

So the problem remains: what are *trobar ric* and *trobar prim*? Are they the same style, do they provide a 'solution' to the conflict between *clus* and *leu*, do they refer to a particular, well-defined style?

The term *ric* is used by Peire Vidal:

> Ajostar   e lassar
> Sai tan gent motz e so,
> Car del car   ric trobar
> No.m ven hom al talo,
> Quant n'ai bona razo.[6]

I know how to couple and lace words and music together so graciously that no one can compete with me in the precious, noble style, when I have a good theme for it.

Peire does not use particularly rare words or rhymes in this song so *ric* does not necessarily imply these.[7] *Ric* and *car* suggest, simply, 'splendid', 'valuable'. Similarly Raimon de Miraval uses *ric* in a vague, perhaps not even literary sense:

> Dreg a mon belh Mai d'Amic
> T'en vai, chansos, qu'ilh t'entenda,
> E si tan fai que t'aprenda,
> Ben tenh mon chantar per ric;
> Qe re qu'ilh pretz no.s bayssa ni.s gavanha,
> Que.l sieus lauzars daur' e.l blasmars estanha.[8]

---

[1] See p. 163, n. to v. 2.   [2] See p. 164.   [3] See pp. 167 ff.
[4] See p. 173 ff.   [5] See pp. 171 ff.
[6] ed. Avalle, III. 1–5. See p. 96.
[7] Cf. Avalle's note: 'a differenza dei corifei del *trobar ric* non ha però abusato di forme rare.'
[8] Ed. Topsfield, XIII. 41–6.

Go directly, song, to my fair Mai d'Amic, that she may hear you; and
if she does so much as to learn you, I certainly consider my singing
rich; for nothing which she prizes declines or deteriorates in worth,
since her praise gilds and her censure turns to lead.[1]

Possibly Giraut de Bornelh hints at *trobar ric* when he says
he has uttered a *rics motz* in claiming to follow the style of
Linhaure:

> E pero veiatz en l'escolh
> Linhaure vers de trobador
> E no.m n'aiatz per gabador,
> Si tan rics motz me passa.l cais;   (XXIX. 55–8)[2]

but if so it is only a slight hint. Raimbaut may also hint at *trobar
ric* in the song 'Un vers farai de tal mena' (V):

> Un vers farai de tal mena
> On vuelh que mos sens paresca,
> Mas tant ai *ric' entendensa*
> Que tostz n'estauc en bistensa
> Que no posca complir mon gaug . . .   (V. 1–5)

I shall compose a *vers* in such a way that I intend my meaning to be
apparent in it; but I have such a lofty aspiration that I soon become
doubtful whether I can bring my joy to completion . . .

Primarily his *ric' entendensa* means his aspiration to the love of a
high-born lady (*nomenativa*, v. 48), and the *sen* which he wants
to make apparent is his petition for joy. Possibly a secondary,
literary sense is suggested in passing, but again if so, this is only
a slight hint. From these references it seems doubtful that the
troubadours thought of a special style as *trobar ric*: *ric* means
simply 'noble' or 'splendid', it is a vague term of praise indicating
that the poet thinks his style is a high style.[3]

The same is probably true of *car,* which Peire Vidal uses
synonymously with *ric*. It does not denote a style distinct from
clus since Raimbaut describes his *clus* style in 'Cars douz' as *cars*.
Raimbaut's biographer uses *car* and *clus* synonymously: 'mas
mout s'entendeit en far caras rimas e clusas',[4] where *car* means

---

[1] *estanha,* literally 'turns to tin'.   [2] See p. 97.

[3] Other uses of *ric* in a literary context are no more specific: 'De motz ricos no
tem Peire Vidal' (Uc de l'Escure, quoted by Rayn. v. 95) merely takes up Peire's own
words; cf. Peire, XXXV. 1–2: 'Pus ubert ai mon ric thesaur / Trairai.n un gai sonet
novell'; Bartsch, *Chrest.*, Berlin, 1892, 239. 36: ' . . . en Barral, lo senhor de Mar-
selha, lo quals volia melhs a Peire Vidal qu'az ome del mon per lo ric trobar e las
ricas folias que Peire Vidals dizia e fazia. . . .'

[4] Pattison, *Raimbaut d'Orange,* p. 200.

'rare'.[1] But Peire Raimon de Tolosa[2] combines a *leu* style with *car* music:

> Ab son gai, plan e car
> Faz descort leu e bon,
> Avinen per chantar
> E de bella razon.   (I. 1–4)

With a gay, smooth, precious melody I compose a light, fine *descort*, pleasing to sing and on a fine theme.

Raimon de Miraval uses *car* as a vague term of praise:

> Per donas desconoisens,
> Que per un' autra.n son ditz,
> S'es d'alques camiatz mos sens,
> Car las pluzors
> No sabon entendre lauzors;
> Per q'ieu no vuelh mos bels ditz plazens cars
> Pauzar davan a lurs nessis cuiars,
> Pus plazers non es cabalos;
> Ans me vir vas autras razos.   (IX. 10–18)

Because of ill-bred ladies, for these are named here on account of one particular one, my intention has somewhat changed, for most of them do not know how to accept praise; so I do not intend to set forth my fine, pleasing, precious words before their ignorant presumptions, now that delight is tarnished; but I turn to other themes.

So while *car* can have a special connotation in *caras rimas*, 'precious, rare rhymes', usually it means 'valuable' in a general sense.

The characteristics of Giraut's *prim* song 'Era, si.m fos en grat tengut' (XXV), were the poet's happy mood: 'si.m fos en grat tengut' (1), the ease with which he claimed he would compose: 'Ses afan / Gran' (13–14), and the delicate, fine, and polished words employed (*prim, menut, pla*). The same elements appear in Raimbaut's song 'En aital rimeta prima' (II): he chooses light and delicate words, and composes without apparent difficulty, as the result of inclination rather than constraint:

> En aital rimeta prima
>   M'agradon lieu mot e prim
> Bastit ses regl' e ses linha,
> Pos mos volers s'i apila;   (II. 1–4)

In such a delicate little rhyme, light and delicate words please me, built without rule or line, since my inclination is fixed upon it.

---

[1] Cf. Aimeric de Peguilhan: 'obrier en cara rima' (XLVII. 5): see p. 137.
[2] Ed. A. Cavaliere.

The most striking feature of the style is not the use of rare and grammatical rhyme, which Raimbaut also uses in the *trobar clus* ('Cars douz'), but the finely detailed texture of sounds and images, and the combination of rare expressions with smooth sounds. Like Giraut, Raimbaut uses diminutives: *rimeta, auzelletz*, to suggest smallness; and tight, small, smooth sounds: all rhymes contain the vowel *i* (*ima, im, inha, ila, inh, il, ilha, ilh*). Images reinforce the impression of lightness, smallness, and whimsicality: 'Per q'ieu sec e pols e guinh' (13), 'Mas ha sos cors no frezilha / Q'a mi.l sors promes frezilh' (39–40), 'Don mos cors sailh fort e grima / Si q'en trep e saut e grim (41–2), 'Maldic lo jorn mil vetz cilha / Q'aduis mon cor pres de cilh' (50–1).

In his 'chansoneta leu per bordre' (IV) composed 'En aital rima sotil' (3) he again uses finely textured rhymes with tight or delicately rounded-off sounds: *il, ols, om, ist, ics*, here set off by contrasting rhymes of longer vowel sounds: *ordre, iure, erga, egre, eire, olvre, eda, erma, auja, aiga*.

Prim and *sotil* seem above all to suggest a texture. *Trobar prim* may be a compromise between *clus* and *leu* in that it combines rarity and richness of rhymes and vocabulary from the Marcabrunian tradition with the light touch and smooth polish sought in the *trobar leu*; but it may simply represent a search for new forms.

The textural elements of the *trobar prim* are repeated in other works, but in new combinations with different sound effects. In the song 'Er quant s'embla' (XIII), tight, clipped sounds: *cisclar, mut, freit, remut, fait de drut*, and monosyllables: *ram, som*, are combined with the harsh, biting sounds of the *trobar braus*: *fraisse, s'entressecon, rusca, cisclar*, in a Marcabrunian nature opening:

> Er quant s'embla.l foill del fraisse
> E.l ram s'entressecon pel som
> (Que per la rusca no.i poja
> La dolz' umors de la saba)
> E.ill aucel son de cisclar mut
> Pel freit que par que.ls destrenga —
> Mas ges per aitant no.m remut
> Que.l cor no.m traia fait de drut.   (XIII. 1–8)

Now when the leaf is stolen from the ash and the branches wither up at the tree-top (for the sweet humour of the sap no longer mounts to it through the bark), and the birds are dumb from their whistling because of the cold which seems to oppress them—for all this I never cease to let my heart draw out from me actions suited to a lover.

In 'Ar resplan' (XXXIX) the texture is completely harsh and jagged:

> Ar resplan la flors enversa
> Pels trencans rancx e pels tertres,
> Cals flors? Neus, gels e conglapis
> Que cotz e destrenh e trenca;
> Don vey morz quils, critz, brays, siscles
> En fuelhs, en rams e en giscles . . . (XXXIX. 1–6)

Now shines the inverse flower among the cutting rocks and the hills. What flower? Snow, ice and frost which sting and torment and cut; from which I find cheeps, cries, calls, whistles dead among leaves, branches and twigs . . .

In 'Entre gel' (XV) rough and anti-lyrical sounds, meant to suggest the poet's *braus pensars*, are offset in each stanza by the word rhyme *genta*, which brings out the joyful side of his mood:

> Entre gel e vent e fanc
> E giscl' e gibr' e tempesta
> E.l braus pensars que.m turmenta
> De ma bella dompna genta
> M'an si mon cor vout en pantais
> C'ar vauc dretz e sempre biäis;
> Cen ves sui lo jorn trist e gais.   (XV. 1–7)

Ice and wind and mud and squall and frost and tempest and the stormy thoughts about my fair, gentle lady which torment me, have so agitated my heart that I walk now straight, now crooked; a hundred times a day I am sad and gay.

Raimbaut experiments with a variety of textures which include *prim* and *braus*, in many combinations. Texture is one way in which he tries to make a unique impression with each new song.[1]

It may be convenient to call these experiments, and the search for new and rare forms without the *clus* elements of intertwined meanings and gradual unfolding of the *razo*, *trobar ric*; but it is doubtful whether the troubadours themselves ever did so. They appear not to have thought of separate, well-defined styles until some conflict arose between obviously different attitudes to

---

[1] Cf. also his rare rhymes and complex versification with a large number of word rhymes, grammatical rhymes, internal rhymes (Pattison, pp. 49–50; see also my Appendices, pp. 213–20, 226–7). 22 out of 39 of his rhyme schemes are unique (pp. 226–7).

style. In any case, Raimbaut is not the first to compose in a rich but clear style; Peire d'Alvernhe does so in 'Deiosta.ls breus iorns',[1] and so does Marcabru in moralizing songs. So *trobar ric* cannot really be seen as a 'solution' to the conflict between *clus* and *leu*. Neither is it necessarily devised as the suitable expression of a noble love. Raimbaut often experiments with language for its own sake; his delight in stylistic acrobatics, more than his feelings of love, often provokes his mood of *foudat gaia*.[2]

Raimbaut defends *clus* and *car* styles as the most valuable and the most calculated to satisfy a personal ambition to compose the most worthwhile poetry, whatever the general public may think. But he takes a great many different approaches to style, always looking for a new and often whimsical way of expressing and guarding his individuality.

---

[1] See pp. 86 ff.

[2] Cf. especially 'Ar resplan' (XXXIX), the complex forerunner of the *sestina*.

5

ARNAUT DANIEL: 'MIGLIOR FABBRO DEL PARLAR MATERNO'[1]

DANTE honoured Arnaut Daniel above all other vernacular poets before himself. In Arnaut's work the eloquence of the troubadours reaches its culmination. Dante calls Arnaut a *fabbro*, a 'craftsman'; in this he praises Arnaut not simply as a technician, but as a complete poet, 'a consummate artist, the poet-craftsman who is master in his *ars* and his language'.[2] In this

[1] I follow the edition of Toja. He dates Arnaut's career from about 1180 (pp.7–11).

[2] Ibid., p. 89. For a full account and discussion of criticism of Arnaut, see the section 'Arnaut e la critica' in Toja's edition. Early critics of this century saw Arnaut as a skilful but uninspired technician, artificial and obscure (J. Anglade, *Les Troubadours*, pp. 135–8), 'cramped and affected' (A. G. Ferrers Howell, 'Dante and the Troubadours' in *Dante, Essays in Commemoration* (London, 1921), p. 211), a 'ciseleur' treating 'des pensées fort banales et des sentiments à fleur de peau' (A. Jeanroy, *Poésie lyrique*, ii. 47–51). Dante's praise of Arnaut in the *De Vulgari Eloquentia* (ii. ii. 9; ii. vi. 5–6; ii. x. 2) and *Purgatorio* (XXVI. 117) (see Toja, pp. 65 ff.) was explained on grounds of technique by these and other scholars (see Toja, pp. 81 ff.; Chaytor, *The Troubadours* (Cambridge, 1912), pp. 55–6; H. Hauvette, *La France et la Provence dans l'œuvre de Dante* (Paris, 1929), pp. 121–3. U. A. Canello, however, found Arnaut able to 'far vibrare la corda del sentimento' (p. 13), and R. Lavaud suggested that obscurity and artificiality might result from our incomplete understanding of the text (*AdM* xxii (1910), 19). K. Vossler felt that Dante shared with Arnaut a special 'Seelenzustand', combining a sense of constrained passion, sensuality, and irony (*Die göttliche Komödie*, ii. 448–52). A. Berry saw Arnaut as a 'mystique de la rime' (*Florilège des troubadours* (Paris, 1930), p. 187). A. Viscardi stressed Arnaut's individual artistic qualities: 'un parlare strano ed avvolto, intessuto di contrasti bruschi ed aspri, con chiaroscuri crudi e linee nude a recise e taglienti' (*Storia*, pp. 161–71). S. Battaglia emphasizes the unity in Arnaut of form and inspiration: 'La disciplina che s'è imposta nell'esercizio della tecnica e dello stile corrisponde al chiuso travaglio della sua umanità. Per esprimere la sofferenza solitaria e raffinata che i trovatori hanno scelto a loro unica realtà spirituale, diventavano necessari i modi ermetici di cui si vale Arnaldo Daniello . . .' (*Le rime 'petrose'*, p. 35.) A similar view is held by A. Del Monte, whom Toja praises for 'Il saggio più completo sulla poesia di Arnaut' (p. 141), who considers that Arnaut's style was hermetic, not because he followed the *trobar clus*, but as the 'conseguenza della singolarità del suo stile, filiazione del suo individualissimo sentire e del modo in cui egli spera di poterlo trasmettere' (*Studi*, pp. 73–96 and 89). For Dante's praise of Arnaut and the possible reasons for it, see especially Toja's section 'Dante e Arnaut', pp. 65–99 of his edition, and his bibliography on pp. 389–90.

chapter I consider, not so much the reasons for Dante's praise, since this has been widely discussed by many scholars, but how his eloquence develops, supersedes, or differs from the eloquence of earlier troubadours, and how it is related to the different troubadour styles of *trobar clus*, *prim*, or others.

1. *Art and love*

Arnaut takes no part in literary controversy; active discussions of different styles are over.[1] His comments on style are all variations of a single theme: the unity of love and art. Love inspires him and directs his craftsmanship:

> obre e lim
> motz de valor
> ab art d'Amor,   (II. 12–14)

I fashion and file words of worth with art of love;

> En cest sonet coind' e leri
> fauc motz e capuig e doli,
> que serant verai e cert
> qan n'aurai passat la lima;
> q'Amors marves plan' e daura
> mon chantar, que de liei mou
> qui pretz manten e governa.   (X. 1–7)

In this gracious, gay little melody I fashion words, carpenter and plane, so that they will be true and certain when I have passed the file over them; for Love swiftly smoothes and gilds my singing, for it proceeds from her who maintains and upholds reputation.

Love is also the fruit of art:

> So.m met en cor q'ieu colore mon chan
> d'un aital flor don lo fruitz si' amors,
> e iois lo grans, e l'olors d'enoi gandres.   (XIII. 5–7)

I take thought to colour my song with such a flower that its fruit will be love, and joy the seed, and the perfume flight from sorrow.

Love commands and teaches him:

> farai, c'Amors m'o comanda,
> breu chansson de razon loigna,
> que gen m'a duoich de las artz de s'escola, (XVI. 3–5)

I shall compose, for Love thus commands me, a brief song on a long theme, for graciously it has trained me in the arts of its school;

---

[1] Later poets do take sides, however. L. Cigala rejects *trobar escur, prim*, or *sotil* (see p. 137). Raimon Vidal blames those who pretend to understand obscure poetry (E. Stengel, pp. 68–9).

the joy of nature may inspire him to sing, but Love alone guarantees artistic perfection:

> Autet e bas entre.ls prims fuoills,
> son nou de flors e rams li renc,
> e no.i ten mut bec ni gola
> nuills auzels, anz brai' e chanta
> cadahus
> en son us;
> pel ioi q'ai d'els e del tems
> chant, mas amors mi asauta,
> qui.ls motz ab lo son acorda.　　　(VIII. 1–9)

High and low among the first foliage the lands are new with flowers and boughs, and no bird holds dumb beak or throat, but calls and sings each in his fashion. I sing for the joy I have in them and in the season, but it is Love that delights me and harmonizes words and music.

Love demands the highest standard of workmanship;

> e doncas ieu q'en la genssor entendi
> dei far chansson sobre totz de bell'obra
> que no.i aia mot fals ni rim' estrampa;　(XII. 6–8)

and therefore I who aspire to the most gracious of ladies ought to make a song of beautiful craft, surpassing all other men, so that there is no false word in it nor faulty rhyme.

Grief at the lady's coldness dulls inspiration:

> e no.us cugetz que de mon dol
> esper a far bona chanson,　　　　(VI. 3–4)

and do not imagine that in my grief I hope to compose a fine song,[1]

but sometimes art enables the poet to perpetuate love in spite of his suffering:

> Ges per maltraich q'ieu soferi
> de ben amar no.m destoli,
> si tot me ten en desert,
> c'aissi.n fatz los motz en rima.　　(X. 36–9)

Not for abuse which I endure do I desist from loving nobly, although she holds me exiled, for thus I fashion words in rhyme about her.

Together with love and art is fused the poet's *valor:* 'obre e lim / motz de valor' (II. 12–13),[2] 'q'ieu chant e vaill / pel ioi qe.ns fim' (II. 39–40).

---

[1] Cf. VII. 56–8, XIV. 41–4.

[2] *motz de valor*: Toja, p. 202: 'preziose parole'. Arnaut probably wants to suggest both artistic and moral worth, cf. vv. 39–41. The theme of moral worth also appears in XIII. 20–1 and X. 8–10.

It is a troubadour *topos* that love inspires the poet both to improve his moral worth and to compose fine songs; a *chanso* had to be believed to be so inspired. The biographer of Daude de Pradas said that he 'fez cansos per sen de trobar, mas no movian d'amor, per que non avian sabor entre la gen, ni non foron cantadas.'[1] Bernart de Ventadorn repeats continuously that love is his inspiration. But Bernart's mention of craft and artistry is slight: love fills him with joy so that he must sing to express his feelings. For Arnaut, love is not only the cause of singing; the feelings he has in love and the feelings he has for artistic perfection are inseparable. Other troubadours before Arnaut: Peire d'Alvernhe, Giraut de Bornelh,[2] said that the joy of love, moral worth, and artistic perfection were bound together; but no poet repeats this as single-mindedly as Arnaut. This single-mindedness must have helped to establish his reputation with Dante.

G. Toja[3] observed that in no earlier troubadour are there to be found as many references to technical craftsmanship as in Arnaut Daniel. Although Arnaut takes no part in stylistic controversy he describes the polishing, shaping, ornamenting of his style, the harmonizing of its various elements, in a fine work of art (*bell'obra*, XII. 7): 'obre e lim' (II. 12), 'plan' e daura' (X. 5), 'fauc motz e capuig e doli' (X. 2), 'qan n'aurai passat la lima' (X. 4), 'q'ieu colore mon chan' (XIII. 5), 'fatz los motz en rima' (X. 39), 'qui.ls motz ab lo son acorda' (VIII. 9).

Such images of the poet-artisan are found in medieval works on Rhetoric, but are also troubadour *topoi*.[4] Although Arnaut's

---

[1] Boutière and Schutz, p. 233.

[2] See pp. 69 ff. and 123.

[3] p. 74.

[4] Polishing: Giraut de Bornelh, XXV. 10–12: 'polira, / forbira / mo chan', XXVIII. 3–4: 'Vauc un chantaret planan / De dichs escurs'; Cercamon, III. 34: 'motz politz'; Cigala (ed. Branciforti), XII. 14: 'obra polia', cf. Toja, p. 277; Scheludko, *Arch.Rom.* xv (1931), 142; *Rhet. ad Her.* III. 8: 'inventione perpolita'; M. de Vendôme (Faral), 167: 'verba polita'. Filing: Raimbaut d'Aurenga, 'Cars douz' 21–3: 'Com si liman pogues roire / L'estrain roïll'; Aimeric de Peguilhan (ed. Shepard and Chambers), XLVII. 1–2; cf. Toja, p. 277; *DVE* II. vii. 5 'vocabula pexa, dolata'; Scheludko, loc. cit.; Lausberg, *Registerband*, 738: 'limae labor'. Sculpting: Peire d'Alvernhe, 'Sobre.l vieill trobar' v. 39: 'Ab joi pic e gaug'; Marcabru's lady sculpts false appearances with her words ('Ans que l'ivern' 16) and Giraut's love sculpts and carves his lady's face for him in his imagination, XLIV. 78–80: 'Si.m desbois' e m'entalha... Sas avinens faissos'. Gilding: see Toja, p. 277; P. Vidal (ed. Avalle), VII. 82: 'de vos dauri mon chantar'; IV. 14: 'Motz ab us sonetz dauratz'; Marcabru, XXV. 24: 'La falsa razos daurada'. Colouring: Guilhem IX, VI. 2; and see my remarks on p. 26.

biographer says that he 'amparet ben letras',[1] and Raimon de Durfort calls him 'Arnautz l'escoliers',[2] Arnaut acknowledges only the school of love:

> farai, c'Amors m'o comanda,
> breu chansson de razon loigna,
> que gen m'a duoich de las artz de s'escola   (XVI. 3–5)

By mentioning his *breu chansson* Arnaut may conceivably refer in passing to Rhetorical *brevitas*,[3] but by indicating his *razo loigna* he follows the troubadour *topos*: 'the more my song is heard, the more it is worth',[4] and uses a modesty formula: he can only hope to treat the theme of love briefly. In comparison with Peire d'Alvernhe and Giraut de Bornelh, Arnaut minimizes his display of learning. At this time a troubadour, even if he were learned, was not encouraged to appear too much so: Peire Rogier reminded Raimbaut d'Aurenga,

> No.us fassatz de sen trop temer,
> per qu'om digua: 'trop es senatz'.[5]

Do not make yourself too feared for your learning so that people say, 'He is too clever'.

Arnaut says that one can discriminate between true and false love without the art of writing:

> Ben conosc ses art d'escriure
> que es plan o que es comba,   (IV. 41–2)

I know well enough without the art of writing what is plain and what is rough.[6]

Whatever his knowledge of Rhetoric, it is not a knowledge which Arnaut wants to display too ostentatiously, since he wants above all to stress that he is inspired by love.

2. *Arnaut and the different troubadour styles*

Scholars disagree over the style to which Arnaut's work belongs. Anglade called him 'le représentant le plus illustre du *trobar clus*';[7]

---

[1] Boutière and Schutz, p. 59: 'Et amparet ben letras e delectet se en trobar. E abandonet las letras, e fetz se joglars . . .'.   [2] Toja, p. 90, vv. 29 and 37.

[3] See Geoffrey of Vinsauf, *Poetria Nova*, 700–3 (ed. Faral).

[4] See Jaufré Rudel, VI. 1–6, Marcabru, 'Aujatz de chan', 1.

[5] C. Appel, *Das Leben und die Lieder des Trobadors Peire Rogier* (Berlin, 1883), VIII. 29–30.

[6] Lavaud, *AdM* xxii (1910), 40 'Qui plan o qui es de tomba', 'qui est d'aplomb ou qui penche vers sa perte'.   [7] Anglade, *Hist. somm.*, p. 63.

Jeanroy, while admitting that Arnaut's style 'n'est pas un modèle de limpidité',[1] considered that Arnaut lacked the complexity of thought characteristic of the *trobar clus* and so classed his style as *trobar ric*.[2] More recently, M. Bowra thought Arnaut deliberately chose a middle way between *clus* and *leu* in *trobar ric*;[3] but S. Battaglia[4] and A. Del Monte[5] considered his style hermetic, *clus*, but as the result of a highly individual inspiration rather than an intention to follow earlier models of the *trobar clus*.[6] In recent works on *trobar clus* and *trobar leu* by L. Pollmann and U. Mölk, Arnaut receives only brief mention: Pollmann sees him as the discoverer of *trobar ric*,[7] Mölk prefers to call his style *trobar prim*.[8]

The only one of these ideas based on any statement made by the poet is that of M. Bowra, who suggests that Arnaut, while evidently composing in a rich and difficult style, defends himself against possible accusations of obscurity in the following lines:

> Maint bon chantar levet e pla
> n'agr' ieu plus fait, si.m fes socors
> cella qe.m da ioi e.l mi tol.   (VII. 56–8)

He translates *levet e pla* as 'light and easy', and is followed by Toja: 'leggieri e facili', 'leggieri, agili nel ritmo e facili ad intendersi'.[9] Bowra links this text with the song 'Chansson *do.ill* mot son plan e prim' (II. 1), translating *plan e prim* as 'simple and fine'.[10] However, we have seen that the *trobar prim* in Giraut and Raimbaut was characterized by smoothness and polish. Since Arnaut himself stresses the polish, the filed and smooth-planed quality of his style, these two passages probably refer to this: *plan* meaning 'smooth', and *levet*, 'light, graceful'.

Arnaut does not mention the *trobar clus*. He makes no comment

---

[1] *Poésie lyrique*, ii. 50, n. 4.   [2] Ibid., pp. 41 ff.
[3] 'Dante and Arnaut Daniel', *S* xxvii (1952), 473–4.
[4] *Le rime 'petrose'*, p. 63: 'Il suo "ermetismo" è rivelazione d'assoluta sincerità, e gelosa confessione della propria segretezza.'
[5] *Studi*, p. 89.
[6] Del Monte does, however, see in Arnaut's 'hermeticism' 'una parte programmatica. Egli non si smarrisce nell'illusione di volgarizzare il proprio stato ed è troppo ligio alla tradizione per non vantarsene e custodirlo da indegne curiosità: egli vuole comunicarlo solo a chi è "pross e de ric pretz manenta" (IV. 65)', (p. 89.)
[7] 'Trobar clus', p. 44.   [8] p. 136.
[9] *S* xxvii (1952), 473–4. Toja, p. 242 and note p. 241. Canello, p. 126: 'facili e piani'; Lavaud, *AdM* xxii (1910), 55: 'légère et aisée'; note: 'je prends *levet* comme convenant plutôt au rythme, et *pla* aux paroles.'
[10] Loc. cit.; Canello, p. 121: 'piane e peregrine'; Lavaud, *AdM* xxii (1910), 26: 'à la fois simples et fines'.

on meanings strange or concealed, on closed or locked expressions, on the unfolding of the *razo*. He 'colours' his song: but his use of the term differs from Marcabru's: the early troubadour was full of *cent colors*, meanings or appearances changing and shifting, while Arnaut uses 'colour' in the sense of 'decorate', 'embellish'. But he does bring ideas of the *trobar clus* into his songs in a new way. *Clus* terms and images suggesting the *clus* style are transferred to a different subject. The poet says he will be *clus*, or 'silent', about the *lauzengiers*:

> mas pels us
> estauc clus
> qe d'autrui ioi fant greus gems,   (VIII. 23–5)

but concerning those who utter grievous groans over another's joy, I remain closed;

and he is also 'closed' (*prems*) and 'sombre' (*brus*) towards everyone but his lady, to guard secrecy:

> anz sui brus
> et estrus
> ad autras e.l cor teing prems,
> mas pel sieu ioi trep' e sauta:
> no vuoill c'autra m'o comorda.
>
> Arnautz am' e no di nems,
> c'Amors l'afrena la gauta
> que fols gabs no la.ill comorda.   (VIII. 50–7)

but I am sombre and brusque towards other ladies and keep my heart fastened shut, but it leaps and frisks for the joy that she bestows; I do not want another lady to seize it (my heart) from me. Arnaut loves and speaks not too much, for Love reins in his throat so that foolish boasting does not steal it from him.[1]

Lack of encouragement from his lady makes him conceal many truths, and only her favour could make him reveal clearly his locked-up thoughts:

> q'ieu soi fis drutz,
> cars
> e non vars,
> ma.l cors ferms fortz
> mi fai cobrir
> mains vers;   (IX. 42–7)

for I am a true lover, dear and not fickle, but my firmness and strength make me conceal many truths;

[1] Lavaud, *AdM* xxii (1910), 167, v. 54: *o* 'ce bien'.

dels qetz
precs
c'ai dedinz a rencs
l'er fors rendutz
clars
mos pensars;   (IX. 56–61)

my thoughts about the silent pleas I have in ranks within me will be rendered forth clearly to her.

The words *clus*, *brus*, and the images of closing and concealing thoughts, and of those thoughts eventually being made clear, recall the *trobar clus* of earlier troubadours, especially Raimbaut: 'Cars, bruns e tenz motz',[1] 'Mon cubert ver',[2] 'Pensius, pensanz enquer e serc . . . Don mon escur cor esclaire'.[1] Arnaut uses these literary words and images evocatively, not to describe a style, but to suggest a mood of mystery, of restrained and concentrated thoughts and feelings.

Even if Arnaut takes no part in literary controversy, and mentions no style individually except the *trobar prim*, this does not preclude him from developing particular stylistic methods of earlier troubadours.

3. *'Trobar clus'*

From the discussion of earlier songs we have suggested that the *trobar clus* is flexible and treated differently by different poets, but that it may be characterized by the gradual unfolding of the *razo*, as the poet clarifies his state of mind or some difficult thought, and the binding together of meanings through the figurative use of words. Arnaut may have followed this tradition in his *sestina*. Although the individual words of this work are not difficult, Arnaut's intention is very uncertain; but if my interpretation is correct, his *razo* appears to move from the plane of physical love towards *fin'Amors*, possibly even beyond that to purely spiritual love; and the movement in the *razo* is guided by the shifting emphasis given to literal and figurative implications in the refrain words.

I   Lo ferm voler q'el cor m'intra
         no.m pot ies becs escoissendre ni ongla
         de lausengier, qui pert per mal dir s'arma;
         e car non l'aus batr' ab ram ni ab verga,

[1] See pp. 149 ff.   [2] See pp. 166 ff.

sivals a frau, lai on non aurai oncle,   5
iauzirai ioi, en vergier o dinz cambra.

II   Qan mi soven de la cambra
      on a mon dan sai que nuills hom non intra
      anz me son tuich plus que fraire ni oncle,
      non ai membre no.m fremisca, neis l'ongla,   10
      aissi cum fai l'enfas denant la verga :
      tal paor ai que.ill sia trop de l'arma.

III   Del cors li fos, non de l'arma,
      e cossentis m'a celat dinz sa cambra !
      Que plus mi nafra.l cor que colps de verga   15
      car lo sieus sers lai on ill es non intra;
      totz temps serai ab lieis cum carns et ongla,
      e non creirai chastic d'amic ni d'oncle.

IV   Anc la seror de mon oncle
      non amei plus ni tant, per aqest' arma !   20
      C'aitan vezis cum es lo detz de l'ongla,
      s'a liei plagues, volgr' esser de sa cambra ;
      de mi pot far l'amors q'inz el cor m'intra
      mieills a son vol c'om fortz de frevol verga.

V   Pois flori la seca verga   25
      ni d'en Adam mogron nebot ni oncle,
      tant fin' Amors cum cella q'el cor m'intra
      non cuig fos anc en cors, ni es en arma ;
      on q'ill estei, fors en plaz', o dins cambra,
      mos cors no.is part de lieis tan cum ten l'ongla. 30

VI   C'aissi s'enpren e s'enongla
      mos cors en lei cum l'escorss' en la verga ;
      q'ill m'es de ioi tors e palaitz e cambra,
      e non am tant fraire, paren ni oncle :
      q'en paradis n'aura doble ioi m'arma,   35
      si ia nuills hom per ben amar lai intra.

VII   Arnautz tramet sa chansson d'ongl' e d'oncle,
      a grat de lieis que de sa verg' a l'arma,
      son Desirat, cui pretz en cambra intra.

1. The firm desire which enters in my heart no scandalmonger, who
damns his soul for slander, can ever lacerate with beak or nail; and
since I dare not strike him with switch or rod, secretly at least, where
I shall have no uncle, I shall delight in joy, in orchard or in chamber.

II. When I recall the chamber where to my loss I know that no man enters, but that all are more [impeding] to me than brother or uncle, not one part of me does not tremble, even to the nail, as the child before the rod: I so fear that I may be hers too much in soul.

III. Would I were hers in body, not in soul, and she allowed me secretly within her chamber! For more than blow of rod it pains my heart that her own slave cannot enter where she is; always I shall be with her as flesh and nail, and not believe rebuke from friend or uncle.

IV. Never did I love the sister of my uncle more or as much, by this soul! For close as finger is to nail would I be, if it pleased her, to her chamber; with me the love which enters my heart can do more, at its whim, than strong man with brittle rod.

V. Since the dry rod blossomed and nephew and uncle issued from Sir Adam, such noble love as that which now enters my heart never was, as I think, in body, or is in soul; wherever she may be, out in the open square or within her chamber, I do not leave her while nail [life] yet holds.

VI. For my self thus grafts and inserts its scions into her as the bark into the rod; for she is my tower and palace and chamber of joy, and I love not brother, parent or uncle so much, for from this my soul's joy in Paradise shall be doubled, if ever any man enters therein from loving well.

VII. Arnaut dispatches his song of nail and uncle for the pleasure of her who holds the soul of his rod: to his *Desirat*, whose chamber reputation enters.

NOTES

12. The MSS are divided between 'que.ill sia' (*ABDEH*) and 'no.l sia' (*CMMcSSgU-cg'g''*). Canello and Bartsch are to be rejected: see Toja, p. 380. The reading of *IK*, 'que sia prop de s'arma' (not included in variants by Toja), does not link well with v. 13. Lavaud follows *ABDEH*; 'telle peur j'ai qu'à elle soit trop de mon âme' (*AdM* xxii (1910), 462). Toja discards this (p. 380): 'È illogico che il poeta tema che la sua donna appartenga troppo alla sua anima.' (But Lavaud's translation does not mean this.) In his view the only reading that makes sense is *no.l sia*: 'tal paura ho di non essere abbastanza suo con tutta l'anima.' It seems to me that either reading is plausible: (i) *no.l sia*: the poet is afraid his love for the lady is not spiritual enough, so she will reject him, and he goes on (st. III) to wish he could be rid of the spiritual side of love which impedes physical satisfaction; (ii) *que.ill sia*: he is afraid his love for her is *too* spiritual, or else too much in the mind, and hence not physical enough. In either case, the poet seems to be faced with the spiritual side of love impeding physical intimacy. If *ABDEH* are followed, it is not clear whether *arma* at this point in the poem refers to the spiritual and hence the nobler side of *fin'Amors*, or whether it merely refers to the poet's fantasy or dream world. If the former is true, the poem shows the poet struggling to resist, then eventually accepting, the rigours of *fin'Amors*; if the latter, it represents a progression from physical desire frustrated by the fact that fulfilment comes only in fantasy, towards a nobler love where the spiritual and physical are fused.

39. *cui pretz en cambra intra*: Toja: 'la cui virtù in camera entra' (note, p. 384: '. . . la sua camera, dove per ora entra solo Madonna'). Canello, p. 138: 'nella cui stanza il Pregio ripara.' I prefer Canello's version: the *cambra* is identified throughout the song with the lady herself, and in wanting to enter it, the poet wants to be united with her, either physically or spiritually. It seems startling, from the point of view of the imagery, to separate the lady from the *cambra*. *Pretz* enters her *cambra*, that is, she and *Pretz* are one. Lavaud's version, 'dont la réputation en (toute) chambre entre' (*AdM* xxii (1910), 465), even further weakens the continuity of imagery in *cambra*.

The first stanza creates the conventional setting of erotic joy; 'iauzirai ioi, en vergier o dinz cambra'. The poet circumvents the spies and guardians; his *ferm voler* directs itself secretly to the place of joy.

His confidence gives way to fear, in stanza II, as he becomes aware of obstacles and pain which stand in the way of satisfying his desire. The key to this change of mood is v. 12: 'I so fear that I may be hers too much in soul.' Purely erotic desire is now mixed with an awareness of spiritual love, which the poet wants to reject for fear that it may interfere with or replace physical love.[1]

He longs for physical love alone: 'Del cors li fos, non de l'arma' (13); and he expresses the intensity of physical desire in images of pain (15) and flesh (17). He wants to close his ears to 'chastic d'amic ni d'oncle' (18). Since he has said he wishes he were his lady's in body and not in soul, he probably means that the *chastic*, the rebukes of friends or relatives, would disapprove of his desire for a purely erotic love.

The first lines of stanza IV seem to be ironic in their preciosity: the poet never loved his own mother as much as this lady! His love is so powerful that he now recognizes his frailty in the face of it, and submits to its control. A subtle change has taken place, for now Arnaut no longer struggles with the conflict of physical and spiritual love, but accepts that love must do its own will with him, for he is no more than a *frevol verga*.

In stanza V the real turning-point of the *razo* occurs. *Fin' Amors* is mentioned for the first time, and there is no longer any conflict between *cors* and *arma*. The *fin' Amors* which now enters the poet's heart is unequalled elsewhere, either in body or in soul: 'non cuig fos anc en cors, ni es en arma'.[1] He now desires to be with his lady, not merely in the setting of erotic love, *dins cambra*, but wherever she is: 'on q'ill estei, *fors en plaz'*, o dins

[1] See above, note to v. 12.

cambra'. This antithesis brings together physical and spiritual love; they now exist together in harmony, in *fin'Amors*.

Now union between the poet and his lady can take place (31–32). This union is expressed in acutely physical, almost carnal terms; at the same time it looks forward to spiritual joy: 'q'en paradis n'aura doble ioi m'arma' (35).

It is possible that a religious thread of meaning is also present. At least, much of the imagery is Christian, though it is hard to tell whether Arnaut intended to suggest a mystical meaning, or whether he used mystical imagery simply to express the aspirations of *fin'Amors*. Firstly, the word *arma* is extremely rare in Provençal love poetry; it usually appears only in a religious or moralizing context.[1] Secondly, *la seca verga* in v. 25 introduces an image of the Virgin Mary.[2] This in itself might be insignificant because the poet is bound by the demands of his rhyme scheme and needs a variety of ways in which to use the word *verga*. But other images suggest that this one was not arbitrary: 'tors e palaitz e cambra' are also images used for the Virgin;[3] the key image of the whole song, of the lover's desire to enter the lady's *cambra*, is reminiscent of the *hortus conclusus*;[4] Arnaut specifically mentions the entry of his soul into Paradise (35–6), thus making the same parallel between the lover's physical union with his beloved and the soul's entry into heaven, as Christians did for the *Song of Songs*;[5] and he uses the *senhal* 'Desirat', also used by Marcabru following an image of the *hortus conclusus*:

> L'amors don ieu sui mostraire
> Nasquet en un gentil aire,
> E.l luoc(s) on ill es creguda

---

[1] See L. Pollmann, 'Arnaut Daniel und die Entdeckung des Raumes', *GRM*, N.F. xv (1965), 2–14 (especially 9–10), and Rayn. ii. 89.

[2] Toja, p. 380.

[3] She is called *turris salutis* (PL *Indices*, ii. 520) and *palatium regis aeterni* (PL *Indices*, ii. 514). Cf. Petrus Cellensis, *Sermo* VI, PL ccii. 654: 'Ecce Virgo sapiens, quae habet oleum effusum in ventre suo cum lampade mirabilium operum, quae introivit cum sponso; imo, inquam, introivit sponsus, et filius ejus Jesus; tanquam . . . a coeli palatio, potius horto venustiore, vel paradiso delicatiore. Ecce Virgo: . . . turris ad pavidos . . .' Cf. D. Scheludko, *ZFSL* lx (1935–7), 23–5.

[4] See above; also Peter Damian, *In Cantica Canticorum*, PL cxlv. 1145: 'Anima quippe sancta jure Christi amica et sponsa vocatur; quia illi per fidem dilectionemque conjungitur.' Cf. Alanus de Insulis, *Elucidatio in Cantica Cantic.* PL ccx. 82.

[5] S. Bernard, *Serm. in Cant.*, PL clxxxiv. 837: 'Uterus Mariae Virginis Paradisus'; cf. Bernard's comments on the passage 'Introduxit me rex in cellaria (cubiculum) sua', PL clxxxiii. 81; Alanus de Insulis, PL ccx. 56.

> Es claus de rama branchuda
> E de chaut e de gelada,
> Qu'estrains no l'en puosca traire.

> Desirat per desirada
> A nom qui.n vol Amor traire.   (V. 49–56)[1]

The Latin equivalent *Desideratus* was a name for Christ.[2] It seems
that in stanza VI Arnaut means to suggest that once *fin'Amors*
has entered into his heart and been accepted by him, he senses an
immediate and intense union with his lady:

> C'aissi s'enpren e s'enongla
> mos cors en lei cum l'escorss' en la verga,   (31–2)

and an immediate bliss:

> q'ill m'es de ioi tors e palaitz e cambra;   (33)

but that he also looks forward to another, future joy, a 'double
joy', of the spirit alone, which is won by force of love:

> q'en paradis n'aura doble ioi m'arma,
> si ia nuills hom per ben amar lai intra.   (35–6)

Perhaps he reaches beyond *fin'Amors* to mystical, Christian love,
anticipating Dante; perhaps Christian imagery is a way of evoking
undefined but always developing aspirations of *fin'Amors*.[3]

The movement of the *razo*, from erotic desire to a disturbed
sense of conflict in the poet's mind, leading to the growth of
fin'Amors and idealistic hopes for the future, follows a similar
structure of the *razo* in Raimbaut's 'Cars douz', where serene joy
gives way to moral anxiety and struggle, eventually surmounted
by a growing optimism, as the heart of the poet 'brightens', he
maintains a personal integrity, and looks forward to the growth

---

[1] See pp. 52.

[2] Ibid.; it is possible that *Desirat* may be a *senhal* for Bertran de Born, but the
evidence for this is very slight. Barbieri found a Latin gloss in a manuscript indicating that Bertran and Arnaut were such close friends that they called each other
Desirat (see Toja's note, pp. 382–3). Lavaud (*AdM* xxii (1910), 116) is inclined to
accept this because he finds links between the two poets. Toja, however, follows
Kolsen (*DDJ* viii (1924), 55–8), who observes that the gloss and Barbieri's account
have no more certainty than the *Vidas*, and that Bertran never uses *Desirat* in
his surviving works. According to J. Anglade, *Onomastique des troubadours* (Mont-
pellier, 1916), p. 97, and F. Bergert, *Die von den Trobadors genannten oder gefeierten
Damen* (Halle, 1913), p. 116, Arnaut is the only troubadour to use this name.

[3] Perhaps *amor de lonh:* cf. Jaufré Rudel, V, stanza VI: 'Dieus . . . Mi don poder
que cor ieu n'ai, / Qu'ieu veya sest' amor de lonh, / Verayamen, en tals aizis, / Si que
la cambra e.l jardis / Mi resembles tos temps palatz!'

of joy in society through a new young nobleman.[1] The content
of Arnaut's *razo*, concerning exclusively aspects of love and almost
entirely ignoring moralizing and social elements such as are
present in Raimbaut's song, most closely parallel the song 'Quan
lo rossinhols el folhos' of Jaufré Rudel.[2] In this song the poet
moves from erotic joy: 'Mi ven al cor grans joys jazer' (7), to
unsatisfied desire: 'D'un amistat suy enveyos' (8), which in-
creases to anxiety, 'D'aquest' amor suy cossiros' (15) and heated
frustration:

> D'aquest' amor suy tan cochos
> Que quant ieu vau ves lieys corren
> Vejaire m'es q'a reüsos
> M'en torn e qu'ela.s n'an fugen;   (22–5)

until he turns away from this kind of love and seeks a better:

> Amors, alegre.m part de vos
> Per so quar vau mo mielhs queren,   (29–30)

which moves him to seek God in Bethlehem (stanza VI).

Arnaut's rhyme words are the key to the development of the
razo, and bind up the strands of thought. *Cambra* at first is the
conventional setting for erotic love (6), and an image of the lady's
physical love (7, 14, 22); in stanza V it takes its place beside
platonic love as one part only of *fin'Amors* (29), then turns into
a symbol of complete bliss, the Paradise found in physical and
spiritual union (33). *Ongla* expresses harm (2) and fear (10), then
a desire for intimacy unobtainable (17, 21), then life itself (30) and
the growing union between the lover and his lady (31); *verga* is
at first an image of pain and punishment (4, 11, 15), then of the
poet's admission of weakness and his surrender to the need for
spiritual as well as physical love (24), then of growth and life
(25, 32). *Intra* marks the changes in the poet's mind: at first the
initial impulse to love enters his heart (1), 'Lo ferm voler' which
leads to the eventual blossoming of *fin'Amors*; in the next two
stanzas the poet's aspirations are blocked, 'on a mon dan sai que
nuills hom non intra' (8), 'car lo sieus sers lai on ill es non intra'
(16), the love again enters his heart (23) and becomes *fin'Amors*
(27), and the poet anticipates the entry of his soul into Paradise
(36). *Arma* belongs at first to a conventional curse on the slanderers (3), then reflects the poet's fear and rejection of the spiritual

---

[1] See pp. 147–56.   [2] Ed. Jeanroy, I.

side of love (12, 13); it becomes ironic in self-mockery (20) as he
realizes the force of love and the need to accept this side of it;
soul and body are united in *fin' Amors* (28), and finally the soul is
seen in the context of Paradise (35). The choice of the last word
rhyme, *oncle*, is enigmatic. S. Battaglia finds that it makes the
lyrical thought banal; that each time it appears at the end of a
line it seems merely an expedient, and spoils the effect of the rest.[1]
Del Monte sees it in a subtler way: '*oncle* dissolves the knot
of sentiment with a prosaic intrusion',[2] it introduces an ironic
realism in which the tormented state of the poet is resolved
in the smile of a play on sounds which is difficult and risky.[3]
Even if it is our impression, however, that *oncle* is banal, we
cannot be sure that Arnaut's audience would have reacted to it
in the same way. In any case, in the poem it represents 'friends,
relatives, protectors'[4] or simply 'other people'. It marks, as
the other rhyme words do, the development of the *razo*. At
first it stands for the lady's guardian (5), then more vaguely for
impediments to the poet's love (9); in stanza III it stands for moral
advisers, not now those who protect the lady, but those who
counsel the poet for his own good but whom he wants to ignore
(18); the next mention of *oncle* brings irony and self-mockery
(19); in stanza V the structure of antithesis and chiasmus links
la seca verga with *arma* and *nebot ni oncle* with *cors*,

> Pois flori la seca verga
> ni d'en Adam mogron nebot ni oncle,
> tant fin' amors cum cella q'el cor m'intra
> non cuig fos anc en cors, ni es en arma;   (25–8)

suggesting that *oncle* stands for the old, physical life which is mov-
ing on to the new, spiritual one; and in stanza VI it stands for the
earthly loves which give precedence to the poet's love for his
lady, the only love which will lead him to heaven.[5]

---

[1] *Le rime 'petrose'*, pp. 48–9.   [2] *Studi*, p. 86.
[3] Ibid., p. 87: 'In questo stile composito son fusi l'impeto lirico e la pausa ironica,
l'allusione umbratile e il dato crudamente realistico, la delicatezza e la trivialità, il
malinconico e il grottesco, l'etereo e il cavilloso.'
[4] Cf. Jean Bodel's *Congé* (in P. Ruelle, *Les Congés d'Arras* (Liége, 1965), p. 86,
vv. 25 ff.): 'Quers, se tu trop vilains nen iés, / Ja ne li oncles ne li niés / N'erent de
mon escrit plané.'
[5] There may possibly be a Christian meaning in *oncle*. The New Testament often
refers to relatives as earthly attachments or impediments: Mat. 10: 21 ff.; Marc. 3:
31 ff.; Luc. 8: 19–21; 14: 26; 21: 16; 18: 29–30: 'Qui dixit eis: Amen dico vobis,

So the rhyme words by their change in meaning or association are the means of unfolding the *razo*, reflecting the movement in the poet's state of mind, and binding together the elements of physical and spiritual love. Arnaut does not play on the double, distinct meanings of words as Marcabru and to some extent Raimbaut did, but he uses words to carry different associations or figurative implications, following the tradition of *trobar clus*, while at the same time developing it in a unique way through the form of the *sestina*, the language, and the theme, which concentrates exclusively on the psychology of *fin' Amors*.

This composition appears to indicate that although the controversy over *trobar clus* and *trobar leu* had subsided some time previously,[1] the *trobar clus* is by no means extinct or decadent. Arnaut probably composed in it out of his admiration for earlier troubadours: Marcabru, Raimbaut, and perhaps Jaufré Rudel, and out of a preference for intellectual complexity.

4. 'Trobar prim'

The term *prim* is only mentioned by Arnaut once, in the song 'Chansson *do.ill* mot son plan e prim' (II). This song has smooth but mainly unusual rhymes (*im, or, uoilla, aill*), including the thin sound *im*, with short lines and a light and delicate style:

> Chansson do.ill mot son plan e prim
> farai puois que botono.ill vim
> e l'aussor cim
> son de color
> de mainta flor
> e verdeia la fuoilla,
> e.il chan e.il braill
> son a l'ombraill
> dels auzels per la bruoilla.   (1–9)

I shall compose a *chanso* where the words are smooth and delicate, since the osiers are budding and the highest tree-tops are coloured with many a bloom and the leaf grows green, and the songs and cries of the birds are shaded in the foliage.

nemo est qui reliquit domum aut parentes aut fratres, aut uxorem aut filios propter regnum Dei, et non recipiat multo plura in hoc tempore, et in saeculo venturo vitam aeternam.' (Cf. Arnaut's vv. 34–6.)

[1] The *tenso* between Giraut and Linhaure took place in about 1170 (Pattison, *Raimbaut d'Orange*, p. 23, n. 36); Arnaut's career appears to have begun in about 1180 (Toja, pp. 7–11).

A similar light, delicate texture is found in the song 'Quan chai la fuelha' (III):

> Quan chai la fuelha
> dels aussors entresims,
> e.l freg s'erguelha
> don seca.l vais e.l vims
> dels dous refrims
> au sordezir la bruelha,
> mas ieu soi prims
> d'amor, qui que s'en tuelha.   (1–8)

When the leaf falls from the topmost forked twigs, and the cold grows arrogant, withering hazel and osier, I hear the thicket muted in sweet refrains, but I am first in love, whoever else abandons it.

This texture follows the similar light, delicate, polished style of the *trobar prim* of Giraut and Raimbaut.[1] These are the only songs of Arnaut where this texture is maintained throughout, though like Raimbaut, Arnaut combines *prim* sounds with others elsewhere: with smooth sounds but fuller vowels in 'Lancan son passat li giure' (IV) (*iure, omba, embla, oma, il, oigna*).

5. *The richness of Arnaut's style*

Although the troubadours do not seem to have looked on *trobar ric* as a particular style in the same way as *trobar leu*, and although Arnaut is not the first to use a rich, elaborate style,[2] in his poetry *ric* or *car trobar* reaches its culmination.

One of the finest examples is the song 'L'aur' amara' (IX), which Dante quoted as one of the best songs on the theme of love.[3] Arnaut seeks the most concentrated effect of formal refinement and of the tight binding together of style and *razo* to produce a strong individual impression. Nearly a third of the syllables are governed by rhyme;[4] many of the rhymes are rare: *ara, uoills, ecs, encs, ortz, aut, oma*.[5] Striking sounds are closely packed together by the use of monosyllables: *aur', bruoills, dous', fuoills, letz, becs, ten balps e mutz, pars e non pars, de far e dir, a mains, per liei, bas d'aut* (stanza I). Rough and clenched sounds: *utz, etz, ecs, encs, ortz, aut*, are mixed with smoother ones: *ir, ars, ers, ei*, which set them in relief, and the stanza is rounded off as a compact unit by

---

[1] See pp. 138–9, 182–3.   [2] See pp. 86–7.
[3] *DVE* II. ii. 9.   [4] 17 out of 58 in the stanza.   [5] See pp. 213–20.

the single feminine, smoothly polished rhymes *ara*, *oma*, in the first and last lines. Alliteration and assonance bind the sounds more tightly together: 'L'aur'amara', 'bruoills brancutz', 'dous' espeis' ab fuoills', 'letz becs dels auzels ramencs', 'bruoills . . . fuoills', 'm'a virat bas d'aut'. Language is chosen for rarity and sound: *ramencs*, 'living among the branches', *balps* 'stuttering', *pars e non pars*, 'mated and unmated', *coma*, 'hair' for 'head', *goma*, 'balsam', *decs de totz mos fadencs*, 'boundary of all my follies', *brutz pars*, 'rough companions', *ufaut*, 'vainglory', for the more usual *ufana*. The effect of extreme compactness is reinforced by concise antitheses: 'L'aur' amara / fa.ls bruoills brancutz / clarzir / qe.l dous' espeis' ab fuoills' (1–4), 'car Pretz, / secs / sai, lai es doblencs' (90–2); and by images of the poet's feelings locked and crowded within him: 'ma.l cors ferms fortz / mi fai cobrir / mains vers' (45–7), 'dels qetz / precs / c'ai dedinz a rencs' (56–8). Several words suggest constriction, limitation, or suppression: 'balps e mutz', 'qe.t trencs', 'qetz / precs', 'qe.m brei', 'decs'. All aspects of the style and theme emphasize compactness, intensity, concentration.[1]

If this song is obscure it is for that reason, and not because it belongs to the *trobar clus*.[2] The theme is fundamentally straight-forward: the lover serves his lady though discouraged (stanza I), faithfully (stanza II), with silent hopes of reward (stanza III) and anticipation of being allowed to express his desires more openly (stanza IV); he addresses his love directly to the lady (stanza V) and sends his song to the king of Aragon (stanza VI), concluding with a reminder of his devotion in love (stanza VII). There is no conflict or development of thoughts such as were present in the *sestina*.

The richness of Arnaut's technique and the reasons why Dante must have admired him as a great craftsman have been amply discussed by Toja in his edition. Dante admired in particular the song 'Sols sui' (XV) as an example of 'gradus constructionis sapidus et venustus etiam et excelsus qui est dictatorum illustrium',[3] Arnaut's use of the stanza 'sub una oda continua',[4] and of the

---

[1] The rhyme scheme is a highly refined form of Arnaut's favourite scheme consisting of 7 *rimas dissolutas* (see pp. 227–8), here broken up by ten internal rhymes.

[2] Arnaut's *Vida* attributes the difficulty of his style to his use of *caras rimas* (Boutière and Schutz, p. 59: 'e pres una maniera de trobar en caras rimas, per que soas cansons no son leus ad entendre ni ad aprendre').

[3] *DVE* II. vi. 5–6; Toja, p. 66.   [4] *DVE* II. x. 2; Toja, p. 67.

'stantia sine rithimo'.[1] Arnaut's use of *rimas dissolutas*, more extensive than that of earlier troubadours,[2] arises from the correspondingly greater rarity of his rhymes.[3] He varies his rhythm by variety in short and long lines,[4] and the sound by the diversity and balance of vowel sounds: sometimes with thin and full vowels contrasted, sometimes with sounds linked in unrhymed assonance, sometimes with the vowels varied as much as possible.[5] In this he varies and refines techniques practised by earlier troubadours. A special innovation is Arnaut's extensive use of rare rhymes which are accented on the penultimate syllable, either smooth or slightly abrasive, such as *agre* (XI), *ampa* (XII), *arga* (XVII), *aura* (X), *ebres* (XVI), *embla* (IV), *emble* (III), *endi* (XII), *eri* (X), *erna* (X, XVI), *iula* (XI), *iure* (IV), *obra* (XII), *oigna* (IV, XVI), *ola* (VIII), *oli* (X), *oma* (IV, IX), *omba* (IV, XVII), *orda* (VIII), *orna* (V, VII), *outas* (XII).[6] These rhymes all have a certain weight or roundness, from the way they are accented, their full vowels or double consonants, and they give the style a stately elegance. Often they are combined with the decasyllabic line, which Dante praised for this same quality.[7] Bowra[8] pointed out that Dante probably admired Arnaut's use of *vocabula pexa et yrsuta*:[9] his combination of rough and smooth, 'shaggy and smooth-combed' words. Arnaut is the first troubadour to make such wide use of harsh sounds in love poetry. Although Peire d'Alvernhe was beginning to do this in 'Deiosta.ls breus iorns',[10] and Raimbaut d'Aurenga experiments with harsh rhymes in love poetry though often in a humorous way',[11] Arnaut takes this much further; he not only takes over the harsh sounds of

---

[1] *DVE* ii. xiii. 2; Toja, p. 67.

[2] Toja, p. 41. Toja equates *rima dissoluta* with *rima estrampa*, meaning a rhyme without correpondence within the stanza, as defined in the *Leys d'Amors*, ed. J. Anglade, ii. 105. Arnaut himself seems to have understood *rima estrampa* differently, since in the song 'Doutz brais e critz' (XII) composed of *rimas dissolutas*, he says he wants to avoid 'mot fals ni rim' estrampa' (8). Arnaut must have meant by *rim'* *estrampa* what the *Leys* meant by *rims espars* (p. 105), a completely unrhymed line.

[3] Toja, pp. 42 ff.　　　　　　[4] Toja, pp. 36–7.　　　　　　[5] Toja, pp. 46 ff.

[6] See pp. 213–30.

[7] V, XII, XIII, XVI, XVII, XVIII. See *DVE* ii. v. 3. On p. 37 Toja calls the lines of XV, XVII, XVIII *endecasillabi*, though on p. 36 and in the table on p. 37 he calls them decasyllables. Dante preferred to call the ten-syllable line the hendecasyllable, counting the final unstressed syllable of a line ending with a feminine rhyme, or an extra, silent syllable at the end of a masculine line.

[8] *S* xxvii (1952), 468–9.　　　　　　[9] *DVE* ii. vii. 1. See Toja, p. 70.

[10] See pp. 87 ff.　　　　　　[11] See pp. 86–7.

moralizing poetry but also some of its vocabulary, with its emphasis on physical detail: 'si m'art dinz la meola' (VIII. 21), 'pustell' ai en sa gauta' (VIII. 26), 'q'en la lenga.is morda' (VIII. 36), 'c'Amors l'afrena la gauta' (VIII. 56), 'et eu sentim n'ams los flancs' (XI. 18), 'traga.m ams los huoills crancs' (XI. 42), 'o.m peris el peleagre' (XI. 48), 'e no.m frezis freitz ni gels ni buerna, / ni.m fai dolor mals ni gota ni febres' (XVI. 41–2), 'Fals lausengier, fuocs las lengas vos arga, / e que perdatz ams los huoills de mal cranc' (XVII. 41–2).[1] In two songs especially this harsh, moralizing language is absorbed into the love theme in a special way: in 'Autet e bas' (VIII) it expresses Arnaut's way of being 'brus / ed estrus / ad autras' (50–2), in 'En breu brisara.l temps braus' (XI) it is part of a conceit from which the whole song is composed: a way to 'afrancar cor agre' (8).

Arnaut absorbs all the styles of the troubadours, from Marcabru onwards, into the love lyric. It is probably irrelevant to question his 'sincerity' or 'originality' in the actual content of his poems; he takes over the commonplaces of a century-old tradition as the basic material for his art, in which ideas are probably intended to be expressed not in personal but in universal terms.[2] It is true that the state of mind professed by Arnaut, and the ideas of a particular song, are often closely bound up with the style: in the *prim* songs, lightness of subject, harmonious joy correspond with the light, smooth, lulling style;[3] in 'L'aur' amara' the style corresponds to the poet's constricted feelings;[4] in the *sestina* intensely physical and disturbing images are bound up with the theme of intense conflict between physical desire and *fin' Amors*;[5] in 'Sols sui qui sai lo sobrafan qe.m sortz' (XV) the gravity and stateliness of the style reflect the mood of solitude, suffering, and the single-minded pursuit of love. But it may not be justifiable to look in this for Arnaut's 'absolute sincerity and intimate confession of his own secrecy',[6] his 'most intimate spiritual moments,[7] or 'individual feeling',[8] at least in terms of the ideas

---

[1] Giraut de Bornelh also used such images, e.g. XVIII. 43: 'Pustelh' en son olh e cranc'; see p. 141.

[2] Toja observes that Arnaut is entirely lacking in originality from the point of view of content, which simply repeats troubadour *topoi* (p. 127, following Viscardi, *Storia*, p. 178).

[3] See especially II. 19–24, 28–33; III. 9–12, 41–4.   [4] See p. 203.

[5] See pp. 193–201.   [6] Battaglia, *Le rime 'petrose'*, p. 63.

[7] Ibid., p. 35.   [8] Del Monte, *Studi*, p. 89.

expressed. The unity of individual form and ideas shows above all Arnaut's 'sincerity' in seeking the total harmony of his work: of language, ideas, sounds, and music. It is in this sense, in the context of troubadour *eloquentia*, that his love and art are inseparable: 'Obre e lim / motz de valor / ab art d'amor.'

CONCLUSION

THE troubadours examined cover a period of approximately seventy years, of the most creative time for Occitan civilization. Each of these poets makes his own individual impact on its literature.

Marcabru's attitude to eloquence is dualistic: he blames the false use of words through vague and illusory thinking or deliberate perversion; he also has detailed knowledge of Rhetorical techniques, especially those of law and debate. This emerges particularly in his methods of defining, clarifying, and arguing about *paraul' escura*,[1] and in the *gap*,[2] where he boasts of his skills in the art of verbal dispute. His own composition he calls *trobar naturau*, which means the art of composing according to an understanding of the moral order of things in nature, and which appears in his work especially in his use of nature imagery: of plants, animals, and birds as metaphors or symbols revealing some moral truth.[3] Although Marcabru makes no mention of the *trobar clus*, he is a model for later *clus* poets: in his awareness of a division in the audience between wise and foolish; in his technique of gradually unfolding meaning through symbols or the complex interweaving of thoughts, to reveal difficult truths and to arrive at clear thinking; and in his use of *colors*, in word-play,[4] in ambiguous meanings interwoven and finally bound up,[5] and in the double layer of meaning, deliberately misleading, in the *gap*.[2] Marcabru is also the model for later poets of the *trobar braus*, in his rough, anti-lyrical style which expresses his rejection of facility in both moral attitudes and style.[6]

While Marcabru mistrusts the power of eloquence, Peire d'Alvernhe considers it an essential courtly attribute.[7] He boasts of being the first to compose *vers entiers*; by this he primarily means songs in the highest stylistic level which are not 'broken' or disfigured by the vices, castigated by Rhetorical works, of obscurity or turgidness, resulting from excessive ambition on the part of lesser poets.[8] He claims that eloquence is closely bound up

[1] pp. 16 ff.   [2] pp. 19 ff.   [3] pp. 28 ff.   [4] pp. 50 ff.
[5] pp. 43 ff.   [6] pp. 52 ff.   [7] pp. 35 ff.   [8] pp. 58 ff.

with the inspiration of love and joy, and the control of wisdom.[1]
Bernart Marti attacks him for boasting that only he could compose
vers entiers, on the grounds that his vainglory demonstrates his
lack of moral integrity, essential in truly 'whole' poetry. Peire composes a song in the *trobar clus,* using ambiguity to suggest a sense of
personal mystery and significance,[2] and a *vers non-clus,* which suggests that popular opinion is already demanding a lighter style,
but that the *trobar leu,* so called, has not yet emerged. The *trobar
braus* he develops, not as a means of expressing moral conviction
but as a way of displaying his rhetorical virtuosity, his command
of a richly embellished, not over-polished style, in a set genre.[3] He
combines rough and smooth sounds in a rich style which anticipates the art of Arnaut Daniel, and which may be the reason for
Dante's description of him as one of the 'antiquiores doctores'.[4]

   Giraut de Bornelh theorizes in detail about the *trobar clus* and
trobar leu, and is probably the first troubadour to formulate the
trobar leu as a definite style from a theoretical standpoint. He sees
the *trobar clus* as a high level of style in which words are closely
locked together and bound up, a style enriched with 'colour':
meaning or formal embellishment, veiled and having unfamiliar
senses, and revealing its theme gradually and indirectly. This style
avoids obscurity, excessive ornamentation, and meagreness.[5]
Parallels can be drawn between Giraut's theory of the *trobar clus*
and Rhetorical theories of implying rather than stating meaning
in amplification and abbreviation, in particular those of Geoffrey
of Vinsauf.[6] In practice Giraut's *trobar clus* consists in the rich
rhetorical embellishment of straightforward material, and not the
working out of complex thoughts or states of mind through
interwoven meanings,[7] although a certain intentional ambiguity
may be present in 'Si.m sentis'.[8] Giraut defines the *trobar leu*
theoretically and may have 'invented' it, in the sense of having defined and named a light style opposed to the *trobar clus.* It may be
wondered how far the troubadours would ever have thought in
terms of separate, distinct styles, had it not been for Giraut and
his love of classification. He sees the *trobar leu* as easy to sing and
understand, light and entertaining, apparently carefree, smooth
and polished with obscurity planed away; and while he describes
it in deliberately pejorative terms to forestall criticism, he still

---

[1] pp. 69 ff.   [2] pp. 77 ff.   [3] pp. 74 ff.   [4] pp. 86 ff.
[5] pp. 90 ff.   [6] pp. 98 ff.   [7] pp. 117 ff.   [8] pp. 125 ff.

regards it as a high level of style.[1] To justify his change from *clus* to *leu* he draws on Rhetorical arguments: the level should be suited to the audience, and gravity of thought and craft should be combined with clarity, apparent ease, and lightness of touch.[2] Songs of the *trobar leu* he terms *chanso* rather then *vers*.[3] In practice, his *leu* style covers a wide range of styles from the starkly simple to the metaphorically elaborate, and it seems as if he modifies the simplicity of his early *leu* songs in response to the derision of his rivals.[4] He also composed in the *trobar prim*: a style with smooth sounds, light and polished, with a finely chiselled texture.[5] Giraut commands a wide diversity of techniques and interests, and seeks above all to make a new and strong impression with each song, through rhymes, versification, or the repetition of individual stylistic devices. His knowledge of literary theory, his importance in the formulation of the *trobar leu*, his didactic themes, learning, and range of interests and skills must have helped him to earn his title of 'master of the troubadours' and his prominence in Dante's *De Vulgari Eloquentia*.[6]

Raimbaut is the most individualistic of all these troubadours, repeatedly making fun of conventional ideas and expressions and refusing to accept Giraut's version of a light style. He rejects the *trobar leu* as easy, banal, and commonplace, and associates it with conventional attitudes to love.[7] He parodies it and turns it upside-down, especially through the twisting of conventional stylistic devices and clichés.[8] Although he defends the *trobar clus* in the *tenso* with Giraut only one of his works seems to be an entirely serious *clus* composition. In this, 'Cars douz', the interweaving of ideas and gradual unfolding of the *razo* reflect a personal struggle to maintain *joi* in the face of contaminating influences.[9] In 'Ar vei' he uses a *clus* framework for the comic purpose of speaking uncourtly words, and elsewhere elements of the *trobar clus* are used as a humorous background for jokes.[10] He experiments with many new rhymes and complex verse forms, especially looking for new sound effects with combinations of *prim* sounds: tight, minutely chiselled, with full, rough, or smooth ones. He is full of new departures and always looks for an original twist.[11]

Arnaut Daniel absorbs all the styles of earlier troubadours and

---

[1] pp. 101 ff.   [2] pp. 112 ff.   [3] pp. 115 ff.   [4] pp. 132 ff.
[5] pp. 136 ff.   [6] pp. 139 ff.   [7] pp. 169 ff.   [8] pp. 174 ff.
[9] pp. 147 ff.   [10] pp. 156 ff.   [11] pp. 178 ff.

harmonizes them in the love lyric. Without ever mentioning *trobar clus* or *trobar leu*, he refers to the *trobar clus* indirectly in evocative images describing his love and relationship with the lady.[1] He also appears to develop his own form of *trobar clus* in the *sestina*, binding up the double theme of physical love and *fin' Amors*, possibly even passing beyond this to a mystical love, and unfolding the thought through the refrain words, which change their figurative implications as the song develops.[2] He refines the light, delicate, finely-worked *prim* style and reaches a supreme concentration of effect in a rich style, exploiting rare vocabulary and new sounds—full, rounded, and smooth—or harsh sounds usually found in moralizing diction.[3] He seeks the complete harmony of craftsmanship, ideas, inspiration, sounds, and tone, in works which aspire to a unique expression in each, but at the same time aims to express ideas in universal rather than personal or individual terms.[4] In this Arnaut differs from Bernart de Ventadorn, who gives the appearance of relying on his own personal feelings of *jois* and fluctuations of mood, and Raimbaut d'Aurenga, who continually emphasizes the individuality of his feelings through his sense of humour. In the harmony of his work, the exploitation of techniques drawn from the complete troubadour tradition and applied to the love lyric alone, Arnaut marks the culmination of troubadour eloquence.

Just as each troubadour has his own idea of eloquence, so his methods vary within the general styles of *clus*, *leu*, or *braus*. The common qualities of the *clus* poems of Marcabru, Peire, Giraut, Raimbaut, and Arnaut appear to be the use of 'colours' or figurative meanings, and the gradual unfolding of the theme. But in Marcabru these elements appear in different ways in different songs: in 'Al departir' meaning is gradually revealed through nature symbols, and concerns society rather than the poet himself; in 'Contra l'ivern' Marcabru interweaves two strands of thought to express a moral conflict within his own mind, between awareness of illusion and desire; in the *gap* he binds up two entirely separate themes, the erotic boast and debating skill, and instead of resolving mystery and reaching clarity of thought he maintains a deliberate deviousness throughout. Peire's 'Be m'es plazen' concerns, as far as we can tell, only the theme of love and is expressed in blurred, and perhaps

[1] pp. 191 ff.   [2] pp. 193 ff.   [3] pp. 202 ff.   [4] pp. 205 ff.

mystical terms; there is no sense that he clarifies thought, he rather reaches into mystery for an esoteric meaning. Giraut's *trobar clus* expresses little conflict, ambivalence, or the working out of a mysterious idea: it is simply a form of embellishment of a basically plain theme. Raimbaut returns to the Marcabrunian technique of interweaving meanings and clarifying thought to express a personal struggle, but the struggle concerns the preservation of *jois* from corruption, not as in Marcabru a moral conflict of instinct and reason. Arnaut's *trobar clus* treats the conflict between physical desire and *fin'Amors*, perhaps introducing religious elements, and is influenced by Jaufré Rudel.

Similarly, the *trobar leu* of Giraut, learned and theoretical, is entirely different from the lyrical artlessness of Bernart de Ventadorn and the lighter style of Raimbaut d'Aurenga, who refuses to call any serious work in a light style by the name of *leu* or *plan*; and while the *trobar braus* was for Marcabru an expression of moral abrasiveness, in Peire d'Alvernhe it becomes a pretext for the display of rhetorical dexterity, and becomes absorbed, partly in Peire himself, more in Arnaut Daniel, into a rich style of the love lyric.

If the influence of medieval Rhetoric has been seen in these troubadours this influence has been by no means uniform: as indeed there is no reason why it should be, since medieval Rhetoric covers so many aspects of language and style and is treated by so many different authors. Marcabru's interest in Rhetoric lies in the techniques of definition and debate, and the idea of 'colours' or meanings: at the same time it follows a Christian tradition of Rhetoric which emphasizes the importance of truth before eloquence; Peire sees eloquence in terms of stylistic levels and their virtues and faults, from an aesthetic point of view; Giraut finds in Rhetoric a framework for his theories about *trobar clus* and *trobar leu*, and arguments on how to reconcile a high level of style with clarity. Raimbaut uses Rhetorical techniques to make fun of their over-learned use, while Arnaut, though supreme in eloquence, leaves this to appear in the finished work without pointing out his methods in detail.

The concept of a poetry of clichés, uniform by accident or design, impersonal, and lacking in individuality, is foreign to the aims and methods of any of these poets. Each one has his own intentions, of arguing, persuading, entertaining, instructing, expressing his own feelings, or creating a new and perfect work of art. Each is an 'inventor':

E son *inventores*
Dig tug li trobador.[1]

APPENDIX I. RHYMES[1]

	Marcabru	Peire	Raimbaut	Giraut	Arnaut	Bernart
a	7, 24	6, 15		25	7	
aba			13			
ac		12, 18				
aca			10			
ach	16, 24	15, 18	7	24		8
ada	5, 25, 28, 30		27	19		30
agra				66		
agre					11	
ai	6, 16, 20b, 25, 29, 31, 32	1, 18	16, 17, 19, 22, 36	2, 17, 22, 23, 24, 31, 35, 36, 38, 43, 49, 50, 73, 74, 7[6]		7, 10, 16, 17, 18, 25, 27, 33, 36, 37, 43
aiga			4			
aira			1			
aire	5, 9, 17, 24, 30, 32	1, 3, 10	1, 11, 25, 27	8, 13, 25, 31, 37, 45, 49, 54, 62		4, 12, 29, 30, 37, 44
aires		15				
ais	7	2, 4, 6, 8, 9, 13, 18	14, 15, 28	6, 14, 17, 20, 21, 22, 29, 35, 39, 45, 46, 52, 55, 68, 7[2], 73	1	
aisse			13	3		
aja	32		9			7
al	4, 20b, 22		25, 31, 36	2, 51, 58		28, 41
ala	11					
alba				54		
alh	4, 14, 16, 20b, 22	8, 11		11, 17, 32, 42, 47	2	
alha	14, 42			44		35
als		18	12	10, 27		15
am	6	3, 18		32	12	
ama	11			39	7	3, 12
ambra					18	
ampa					12	
ams			10	33		
an	2, 4, 7, 22, 24, 41, 44	18	1, 7, 16, 17, 22, 31, 34	9, 11, 22, 23, 25, 26, 27, 28, 30, 36, 41, 42, 43, 47, 51, 55, 58, 60, 61, 69, 7[2], 77	13, 14	4, 14, 28, 29, 31, 36, 37, 39, 45
ana	21, 30, 36		30, 34	20		22, 37

[1] I include Bernart de Ventadorn as an entirely *non-clus* poet for comparative purposes. Numbers refer to poems in the editions used.

	Marcabru	Peire	Raimbaut	Giraut	Arnaut	Bernart
anc		18	15	18	17	
ancas			34			
anchas					16	
ancs					11	
anda				57	7, 16	26
andres					13	
anh	4			16, 47		
anha				16, 28		19, 25
anhs				52		
ans	14, 25, 34	19	1, 14	5, 7, 10, 18, 19, 22, 29, 33, 35, 41, 42, 44, 46, 47, 48, 51, 65, 68, 70, 72,		15, 21, 26, 30, 33
ansa	13, 14, 18, 37	13, 14	12	11, 37, 69, 77		1, 25, 44, 45
anta	11		14		8	
ap			21			
api			39			
apis			39			
ar	1, 8, 15, 19, 20b, 23, 29, 32, 34, 40	8, 9, 17	17, 20, 22, 24, 26, 32, 35	2, 4, 12, 14, 17, 35, 41, 48, 51, 52, 53, 63, 65, 68, 71, 72, 77	3, 4, 15	4, 19, 39, 40
ara					9	3
arc					17	
arga					17	
arma					18	
ars		8, 12	7, 9, 20	3, 5, 14, 30, 46, 51, 64, 66, 74, 77	9	
art	16				13	
artz	24	12		12		
as	22, 25, 35	8, 19		3, 28, 74		
âs	20b	8, 11, 18	16, 19	26, 68		30
ast				56		
at	4, 25, 40	8, 19	37	1, 13		6, 30
ata	11, 18		37			
atge	28, 30	1		1, 34, 40, 54, 64, 72		19, 20, 23, 25, 42
atges				42		
atz	1, 6, 16, 18, 24, 25	1, 5, 9, 19	18, 30, 31	2, 8, 9, 10, 11, 13, 15, 16, 24, 26, 32, 33, 34, 36, 39, 40, 41, 42, 43, 44, 45, 46, 47, 52, 54, 55, 57, 58, 60, 63, 64, 70, 72, 73, 76, 77		16, 22, 24, 35

	Marcabru	Peire	Raimbaut	Giraut	Arnaut	Bernart
au	8, 19, 33, 38, 40	6				13, 21
auch			5, 21			
aucs		15				
auja			4			
aura					10	
aus	16, 35		20	62	11, 13	
aut			21		9	
auta					8	
autz		12				
auza	11					4
ava			14			
avi	18					
e	8	8, 11	26, 29, 36	2, 10, 15, 23, 24, 26, 27, 34, 38, 44, 50, 53, 63, 64	3	2, 3, 4, 16, 17, 25, 36, 41, 43
ebres					16	
ec		15	38	30		
èc	20b					
ech			17, 36	16		
echa	18, 24, 42					
echs				42		
ecs					9, 12, 14	
eda			4			
ega	18					
egra						3
egre			4			
ei	1, 7, 16, 23, 24, 25		33	24, 44, 45, 47, 60, 70, 73		5, 7, 21, 24
èi					9	
eira				56		
eire			4			
eis	20b, 22	7	16, 38	59, 72		
èis					14	
eja	37, 38	6				7, 29, 42
el	32					5
èl		18, 19	10, 34	54, 55		
ela			3			
èla					3	25
elh	1, 24, 42	11, 12	17, 19, 31	55, 58		7
elha		15				7
èlha	32					
els		6				
èls	16					
em		18			12	
embla					4	
emble					3	
emps		8				
ems	4		33	32, 74	8, 14	

H

	Marcabru	Peire	Raimbaut	Giraut	Arnaut	Bernart
en	11, 24, 44	8, 12, 14, 19	11, 27, 35, 36	1, 2, 17, 23, 24, 26, 31, 35, 36, 37, 38, 41, 43, 47, 49, 50, 59, 61, 77	7	2, 3, 6, 10, 13, 15, 16, 17, 20, 27, 30, 31
ena			5, 25	74		2
enc			18		8	
enca			39			
encs					9	
enda				75		9, 26
endi					12	
endre			3	45, 69		4
endres				3		
enga			13, 38			
enh	8, 40, 44		8	3, 23		
enha	18, 24	1, 3		47		3, 18
enhs			1			
enque			39			
ens	16, 23, 40, 44	5, 6, 8, 11, 18	6, 9, 12, 17	2, 4, 5, 7, 8, 12, 45, 51, 61, 63, 64, 71	17	1, 5, 39
ensa	26, 32	3, 6	5	15, 28		30
enta			15		3	37
eps		18				
er	23, 38	1, 10	12, 17, 22, 36	11, 29, 31, 35, 51, 59, 72		2, 4, 10, 15, 21, 25, 42, 43, 45
èr			22			
era	18					
èra			3, 26	7, 41, 43, 57		
erc			1	66	14	
erga			1, 4		18	
eri					10	
erma		6	4			
erna					10, 16	
ers		7		5, 6, 22, 51	9	
èrs	23		7	30	14	
èrsa			39			
èrse			39			
ert		18				
èrt			3		10	
ertre			39			
ertres			39			
èrtz			28	2	11	
es	6, 7, 15, 16, 25, 32, 35, 39, 40	12, 18, 19	24	2, 7, 11, 20, 23, 25, 33, 36, 41, 47, 50, 52, 66, 71, 75	6	2, 5, 10, 12, 14, 22, 31
ès		4	6, 33	9, 14, 20, 25, 26, 50		20
esc	14		1, 21			

	Marcabru	Peire	Raimbaut	Giraut	Arnaut	Bernart
esca	9, 14		1, 5			
èst			14	56		
esta			15		17	
èt	26	12				
etz	23	15	33	30, 49		
ètz	20b		26	32	9	
eu			18			
èu	24					
èus				12, 46		
eza		6	32			
i	4, 12b, 17, 26, 35, 44	18		48, 69		
ia	24, 25, 30, 32, 42, 44		29	5, 16, 18, 31, 34, 37, 38, 41, 49, 54, 69	3	17, 21, 25, 30, 45
ibres			10			
ic	20b, 22, 26, 32	8, 11	17, 38			24
icha				30		
ics	1	7	4	27		
ida	26, 36, 42			7, 31	3, 5, 7	23, 10
ier	1, 3, 19, 24, 40	4, 6, 11, 17	8, 25, 28	4, 51, 55, 59, 69		23
iers	41	6, 8, 11, 12, 15	37	12, 68, 75, 76	15	33
ieu	16, 26					
iga	24					
il			2, 4	16, 48	4	
ila			2			
ilh	33, 38	15	1, 2, 7, 33	19	1	
ilha	11, 21		2			
ils				19, 22		
im	13		2, 18		2	
ima			2, 3		10	
ims					3	
ina	31, 36, 37					18
inh			2			
inha	18		2			
ins		12				
int					13	
intra					18	
ir	7, 16, 20b, 22, 23, 34, 39, 41, 42	2, 16, 17, 19	3, 6, 16, 30	2, 7, 17, 18, 20, 21, 23, 36, 37, 38, 40, 48, 49, 77	3, 9	1, 2, 9, 13, 14, 25
ira			26	24, 25, 43		9, 18
ire				27, 37, 45	15	4, 9, 12, 25, 27, 30, 35, 44
irs			9	6, 66		

	Marcabru	Peire	Raimbaut	Giraut	Arnaut	Bernart
is	40	1, 2, 7, 12, 13, 16	29	1, 2, 7, 13, 33, 38, 66, 69	3	1, 20, 37
iscle			39			
iscles			39			
issa	30					
ist			4, 18	19, 56		
istz		18				
it	8					27
itz	4, 6, 19, 40, 44	9, 10, 11, 12, 18, 19	8, 33	18, 52, 55, 56, 60, 64, 65, 70, 71	12	33, 40
iu	8, 22, 24, 29					
iula					11	
iura			1			
iure			1, 4		4	
ius		18				
iva			5, 9, 19			
iza	11, 18, 28	4	3			44
o	4, 9, 16, 22, 31, 35					
obra					12	
oc	2, 31			17		
ocs					13	
oi			18, 39			
oire			1			
ois			39		15	
oja			13		3	44
òl	16	13	14, 18	19, 35, 44	6, 7	27
ol		18				
ola	38				8	
òla					16	
olh	6, 16, 23	8	33	15, 22, 29, 42	2	9, 25, 41
olha		6		15	2, 3, 11, 16	9, 25, 26, 27, 42
olhs					8, 9	
oli					10	
ols	20b		4			
òls			14			
olt			21			
olvre			4			
om			4, 13		17	
oma					4, 9	
omba					4, 17	
on	1, 2, 4, 6, 24			38	6	5, 43
ona		3		26, 39, 67		9, 23
onc					11	
oncas		15				
oncle					18	
onda	12b			57		26, 44

	Marcabru	Peire	Raimbaut	Giraut	Arnaut	Bernart
onge				17		
ongla					18	
onh		8	5, 18	3		
onha		2	28		4, 16	
onja	11					
op		16				
ops		18				
or	2, 6, 13, 20b, 24, 32, 35, 36, 40	17, 19	27, 36	1, 2, 6, 13, 21, 27, 29, 35, 36, 40, 50, 59, 62, 69	2, 3	2, 6, 13, 19, 25, 28, 31, 36, 39, 44
òr		8	17	2		41
ora		15		39		3
orda			34		8	
ordre			4			
orn		12		54		2, 12
orna					5, 7	
ors	1	12	20	9, 12, 14, 15, 19, 22, 32, 36, 44, 46, 47, 68, 73	5, 7, 13, 15	22
òrs		15	33			
ort	22, 34, 35	8	12, 21	2, 71, 72, 74, 46, 71	1, 6	25
ortz		19			9, 15	
os	4, 7, 29	4, 5, 18	19	2, 9, 14, 15, 17, 29, 38, 44, 47, 54, 61, 63, 66, 68, 70, 71, 73	3	8, 22, 28
osca	18					
ost				56		
ot	24					
ota		15				
otz		12, 16			15	
ou			10, 18		10, 14	
out		16				
outas					12	
outz		18				
oza						3
uch	8, 16			2	5, 11	
ucha				18		
ucs	3		36		14	
uda	5			23, 28, 41, 54, 57		8, 30
ufa	42					
ui	16, 26			10, 42, 44, 73		29
uja	18					
una	18					
ur	13, 16		1	11		
ura	9, 28, 30, 37	1, 13	11	61, 64, 72		8, 13, 16, 24, 30, 44
urs		5, 18	10	28		

	Marcabru	Peire	Raimbaut	Giraut	Arnaut	Bernart
us	4, 12b, 16, 20b, 25, 40	8, 18, 19	7		8	
usca	11					
ut	24		13	21, 24, 25		
utz	4, 26, 39	5, 14, 19	6	2, 8, 62	1, 9	12, 19
uza	42					

APPENDIX II. VERSIFICATION[1]

MARCABRU

VII	5,18	a a a a a a a a	7 7 7 7 7 7 7 7	
XLIV	40,2	a a a a b c b c	8 8 8 8 6′4 6′4	
VI	44,9	a a a b	8 8 8 8	
XXIII	44,8	a a a b	8 8 8 8	
XXX	51,5	a a a b a a b	7′ 7′ 7′ 7′ 7′ 7′ 7′	
I	54,1	a a a b a a c	8 8 8 8 8 8	U
XVIII	55,9	a a a b a b	7′ 7′ 7′ 3 7′ 7	[2]
XXIX	55,2	a a a b a b	8 8 8 8 8 8	[3]
XXV	84,1	a a a b c c c c c c b	7′ 7′ 7′ 7′ 3 3 3 3 3 3 7′	U[4]
XXVI	84,2	a a a b c c c c c c b	7′ 7′ 7′ 7′ 3 3 3 3 3 3 7′	
XV	91,8	a a b a a b	8 8 8 8 8 8	
XXII	91,9	a a b a a b	8 8 8 8 8 8	
VIII	117,3	a a b a b	8 8 8 8 8	
XVII	118,1	a a b a b a	7 7 7′ 7 7′ 7	U
V	157,1	a a b b c a	7′ 7′ 7′ 7′ 7′ 7′	U
XL	167,1	a a b b c c d	8 8 8 8 8 8 8	[5]
IX	190,1	a a b c b c	10′ 10′ 4 6′ 4 6′	[6]
XLI	193,3	a a b c c b	8 8 8 8 8 8	
XVI	193,7	a a b c c b	4 4 8 4 4 8	
XXb	193,8	a a b c c b	4 4 8 4 4 8	
XXIV	196,2	a a b c c b d d b	3 4 4 3 4 4 4 3 7 (3′ 3′ 3 3′ 3′ 3 3′ 7)	[7]
XIX	204,1	a a b c d d c c b	8 8 8 8 4 4 8 8 8	U[8]
IV	211,1	a b a a c b	8 8 4 8 8 8	U
XXI	223,5	a b a b a b	7′ 5′ 7′ 5′ 7′ 5′	
XXXIII	223,4	a b a b a b	8 8 8 4 8 4	
XXXII	266,1	a b a b a b b a c	4′ 6 4′ 6 4′ 6 4 6′ 4	U[9]
XL	359,1	a b a b c c a	8 8 8 8 8 8	[5]
XXXI	371,1	a b a b c c c d a	7′ 7 7′ 7 1 7 7 1 7′	U[10]

---

[1] Numbers in the first column refer to the songs in the editions used: in the second, to Frank's *Répertoire métrique*. U means the rhyme scheme is unique according to Frank.

[2] v. 4 *vilana*. [3] v. 4 refrain. [4] Probably: I–II, III, IV–V.

[5] After stanza II the rhyme scheme changes: compare 167,1 (stanzas III–VII) and 359,1 (I–II). This seems to have been intentional, as the order of lines in the stanzas cannot readily be changed.

[6] = 130, note: a a b b 10′ 10′ 10′ 10′, with internal rhyme.

[7] = 1, note: a a a 11 11 14, with internal rhyme.

[8] = 202b: a a b c d c c b 8 8 8 8 8 8 8, with internal rhyme (also U). v. 5 *cuidar*.

[9] = 82a: a a a b c 10 10 10 10 4, with internal rhyme (also U).

[10] vv. 5, 8 refrain.

XXVIII	376,16	a b a b c c d	7′ 7′ 7′ 7′ 7′ 7′ 7′	
XLII	376,13	a b a b c c d	7′ 7 7′ 7 7 7 7′	
XXXVI	403,5	a b a b c d	7′ 7 7′ 7 7′ 7′	1
XXXIV	405,5	a b a b c d c	8 8 8 8 8 8 8	
XXXIX	405,6	a b a b c d c	8 8 8 8 8 8 8	
XIII	407,16	a b a b c d c d	8 8 8 8 8 7′ 8 7′	
XXXVIII	430,6	a b a b c d e	7′ 7 7′ 7 7 7 7′	2
XXXV	456,1	a b a c d c d e f	8 8 4 8 8 8 8 8 8	U3
III	476,3	a b b a a b b a	8 8 8 8 8 8 8 8	4
XIIb	538,3	a b b a c	7′ 7 8 7′ 7	
XI	649,1	a b b a c d e d	7′ 7′ 7′ 7′ 7′ 7′ 7 7′	U
XXXVII	669,1	a b b c a d	7′ 7′ 7′ 7′ 7′ 7′	U
II	733,1	a b b c d	8 8 8 8 8	U?5
XIV	864,6	a b c d e f	7′ 7 7 7′ 7 7′	6

PEIRE D'ALVERNHE

IX	27,4	a a a a b b	7 7 7 7 7 7	
XII	91,11	a a b a a b	8 8 8 8 8 8	
XVIII	124,4	a a b a b b c	7 7 7 7 7 7 8	
II	178,3	a a b b c d c d	7 7 7 7 3 7′ 7 7′	7
XIV	193,4	a a b c c b	7 7 7′ 7 7 7′	
VIII	193,9	a a b c c b	4 4 8 4 4 8	
XIX	199,1	a a b c c c b	7 7 7 7 7 7 7	U8
VI	253,1	a b a b a b a b c c d d	7 5′ 7 5′ 7 5′ 7 5′ 8 8 8 8	U
I	378,1	a b a b c c d c c d	7′ 7 7′ 7 3 3 5′ 3 3 5′	
VII	405,1	a b a b c d c	8 8 8 8 10 10 10	
XV	421,32	a b a b c d d c	8 7′ 8 7′ 7′ 8 8 7′	
III	445,1	a b a c c d b e	7′ 7′ 7′ 7′ 7′ 7′ 7′ 7	U
XVI	457,1	a b a c d c e	8 8 8 8 8 8	U
X	557,2	a b b a c c b	7 7′ 7′ 7 7 7 7′	
XVII	612,7	a b b a c d c d	8 8 8 8 8 8 8 8	
IV	759,2	a b b c d e e	8 8 8 7′ 8 8 8	
V	775,1	a b c a b c d e d e	8 4 6 8 4 6 4 6 4 6	U9
XIII	793,1	a b c b d c e	8 7′ 7′ 7′ 7 7′ 7	U
XI	843,1	a b c d c e c e c d	8 8 4 6 4 6 4 6 4 6	U10

---

1 a: ida. b: or. c: ina × ana. d: ana × ina.

2 a: ola. b: er × au. c: au × er. d: ilh. e: eja.

3 a: i, i, es, es. b: o. c: or. d: aus. e: as, ort, as, ort. f: ort, as, ort, as.
v. 6 *lavador*.

4 v. 6 *saïcs*.

5 Variation in rhyme pattern, but the text is corrupt.

6 a: ansa × alh. b: alh × ansa. c: ans × alha. d: alha × ans. e: esc × esca.
f: esca × esc. Derivative rhymes 1/3, 2/4, 5/6.

7 v. 6 *conha*.

8 a: el, atz, ir, en, eis, ortz, as, o, o. b: atz, ir, en, eis, ortz, as, o, o, o. c: itz,
or, ans, uts, at, es, us, us, us. *Coblas capcaudadas.*

9 But cf. 358, note, a b a b c c 8 10 8 10 10 10 (not U).

10 = 844a: a b c d d c 8 8 10 10 10 10.

GIRAUT DE BORNELH

LXXIV	14,1	a a a a a a a b	7 7 7 7 7 7 7 7′	U¹
LVII	19,2	a a a a a b a b	10′ 10′ 10′ 10′ 10′4 10′ 6	
XXXVI	38,1	a a a a b b c c c c d d e	6 6 6 6 6 6 4 6 6 1 2 6 6	U
		e f f f g g g g h h h h h	6 6 6 6 4 6 6 6 6 6 6 6	
XXIII	39,1	a a a a b b c c d d e e f	1 2 4 5 2′ 3′ 2 4 5 2 3 5 5	U
		f e g g a a a h h c c h	3 2 5 5 2 4 5 3 5 5 5 5	
V	51,6	a a a b a a b	7 7 7 5′ 7 7 5′	
LXXVI	72,2	a a a b b b c c	8 4 8 8 4 8 8 8	
XXVI	78,1	a a a b b c c c d d c e e	5 5 5 5 5 5 5 5 5′ 5′ 5 3 5	U
		f f	7 7	
XXV	82,1	a a a b b c d d d e e f f	8 4 8 4 8 3 5 4 4 2′ 2′ 2 3	U¹
		f g g g f f	1 5′ 5′ 5′ 2 8	
LIV	156,2	a a b b c	10 10 10 10 6′	2
LIII	161,5	a a b b c c	8 8 8 8 8 8	
X	171,2	a a b b c c d d e e	5 5 5 5 5 5 5 5 10 10	
II	172,1	a a b b c c d d e e f f	8 4 4 8 8 8 2 8 4 8 8 8	
XIII	176,2	a a b b c c d e e d	4 6 6 6 6 6 10′ 10 10 10′	
VII	201,1	a a b c c d d e e b b f f	6 6 6 5′ 5′ 6 6 6 6 6 6 4 7	U
		d d g g	4 7 10′ 10′	
LXI	212,1	a b a a c c a a d d e e	7 7′ 7 5 7 5 7 7 3 7 7 7	U
XLIII	213,1	a b a a c c d e e e f f	5 5′ 5 5 5 5 5′ 5 5 5 5 5	U
LXVII	302,7	a b a b b a b a	7′ 7 7′ 7 8 7′ 7 6′	
XXXIV	382,38	a b a b c c d d	10 10′ 10 10′ 10 10 10 10′ 10′	
I	400,1	a b a b c c d e e	10 10 10 10 10 10 10 10′ 10 10	U
XL	424,6	a b a b c d d c d d	8 8 8 8 6′ 8 8 6′ 8 8	
XLV	446,1	a b a c c d c e e e f f a	7 7′ 7 5 5 7′ 5 5 5 5 5′ 5′ 4	
		g g	5 8	
XV	452,1	a b a c c d e e e f g	2 5 4 4 4 7′ 3 4 3 4′ 3	U³
LXV	480,1	a b b a a b b a c c	6 6 6 6 6 6 6 10 10	U
LXXV	482,1	a b b a a b b c c	8 8 8 8 8 8 10′ 10′	U
LX	484,1	a b b a a b b c d d	8 8 8 8 8 4 4 6 10	U
IX	490,1	a b b a a b c c d d e e	8 8 8 8 8 8 4 4 8 8 8	U
XII	511,1	a b b a a c c d d e e f f	8 8 8 4 8 8 8 8 4 8 8 8	U
LXIX	549,1	a b b a c c a a	10′ 10 10 10′ 10 10 10′ 10′	
LXIII	562,1	a b b a c c b d d e e b b	6 6 6 6 6 6 6 6 6 6 6 6	
VIII	566,2	a b b a c c c c c d	8 8 8 8 4 4 4 4 4 3′	4
LXII	571,13	a b b a c c d	7 7 7 7′ 7′ 7 7	
VI	577,212	a b b a c c d d	8 8 8 8 8 8 8 8	
XXI	577,290	a b b a c c d d	7 7 7 7 7 7 5 7	
LXIV	642,1	a b b a c d d c e f f g	7 7 7 7 7′ 7 7 7′ 7 7 7 7′	U
XXVII	647,1	a b b a c d d e e f f	7 7 7 7 5′ 2 3 4 7 7 7	
XVIII	653,1	a b b a c d e f	7′ 7 7 7′ 7 7 7 7′	U
LXX	679,1	a b b c c a a d d b b e	8 8 8 8 4 8 4 8 4 8 8 8	U
		b e	8 8	
XLVIII	693,1	a b b c c b b d e d	6 6 6 6 6 6 6 6 4 6	

---

¹ vv. 5, 8 equivocal rhymes; v. 8 *dol* . . . *pena.*
² v. 5 refrain. Frank: v. 5 masculine, but: *alba.*
³ Derivative rhymes 10/11.
⁴ = 571, note: a b b a c c d 8 8 8 8 8 8 7′, with internal rhyme.

L	696,1	a b b c c b d d e e f f	8 8 8 8 8 8 8 8 4 8 8	U
LXXIII	697,1	a b b c c b d d e e f f e	8 8 8 8 8 8 6 6 6 6 6 6	U
		e g g	6 6 6	
LVIII	705,9	a b b c c d d	8 8 8 4 4 8 8	1
LXVIII	709,1	a b b c c d d b b e f g g	6 6 6 6 6 6 6 6 6 6 6 10	U
XXXIII	712,1	a b b c c d d c c e e	8 8 8 8 4 8 4 8 4 10 10	U
LVI	713,1	a b b c c d c d c	8 8 8 7′ 7′ 7 7 7′ 7 7′	U
LIX	714,2	a b b c c d d e	8 8 8 8 8 8 8 8	
XLVI	720,2	a b b c c d d e e f f g g	6 6 6 6 6 4 6 6 6 6 10 10	
XXIX	722,1	a b b c c d d e f	8 8 8 8 4 8 4 8 8	
XXXI	723,1	a b b c c d d e f f f e	8 8 8 6′ 6′ 5′ 5′ 5′ 4 4 8 5′	U
XLVII	724,1	a b b c c d d e f f g g h h	3 3 6 4 4 5 4 6′ 4 4 6 6 6 6	U
		i i j k j	6 6 6 4 6	
XLIX	728,2	a b b c c d e d f	7 5 5 7 7 7′ 5 7′ 5′	
IV	734,1	a b b c d a a	7 7 7 7 7 7 7	U
LXXI	752,1	a b b c d d e e f f g g	8 8 8 8 4 8 8 4 8 8 8	U
XXX	754,2	a b b c d d e f f	4 6 10 7′ 7 7 7 7 7	
XXXVII	760,1	a b b c d e e c f	7′ 7 7 7′ 7′ 7 7 7′ 7′	U
XXVIII	763,1	a b b c d e e f g g	7 4 7 4 5′ 7 7 5′ 7′ 7′	U
LII	766,1	a b c a a d d e e f f	4 4 8 8 8 8 4 8 8 8	U
XXXIX	792,1	a b c b d b e e e	7′ 7 7′ 7 7 7 7 3 7 7	U
LV	795,2	a b c b d d a e e f f e e	6 6 6 6 6 6 6 6 6 6 6 6	
		f f	6 6	
XXIV	800,1	a b c b d e f f g h h	7 4 5 3 4 5′ 7 3 4 7 7	U2
LXVI	810,1	a b c b d e f g g	2′ 5 8 8 8 8 8 8	U3
LXXII	820,1	a b c c d c c e e f f g g	3 3 6 6 6 6 6 6′ 6′ 6 6 6 6	U4
		h h i i j j	6 6 6 6 6′ 6′	
XX	822,1	a b c c d d e	7′ 7 7 7 7 5 4	U
XI	824,1	a b c c d d e c c f f g g	3 5 8 8 8 4 6′ 8 4 8 4 8 8	U5
XIV	826,1	a b c c d d e e f a f	4 4 8 8 8 8 8 8 8 8 8	U6
XXXV	827,1	a b c c d d e e f f g g h	4 4 8 8 8 8 4 8 4 8 4 8 8	U7
		g h	8 8	
XLII	828,1	a b c c d d e e f f g g h h	3 3 6 6 6 6 6 4 6′ 6′ 6 6 6 6	
		h h h	6 6 6	
XLI	829,1	a b c c d d e e f f g g h	3 5 8 8 6′ 6′ 2 4 6′ 6′ 4 8 6′	U
		h i i	6′ 8 8	
LXXVII	830,1	a b c c d d e f d g f	4 4 8 8 8 8 4 6′ 8 8 6′	U
LI	844,1	a b c d c e e f f g g h h	4 6 4 6 6 6 6 6 6 4 6 6 6	U
		i i	6 6	
XLIV	848,1	a b c d d d e e f f g g h	4 4 2 6 6 6 6 6 6 6 6 6 6′	
		h i i	6′ 6 6	
XXXVIII	851,1	a b c d d e e f g g d c c	3 4 3 4 4 4 3 5′ 5 5 4 3 4	U8
		h h	5 5	

---

1 = 740, note: a b b c d d　8 8 8 8 8 8, with internal rhyme.
2 v. 3 *forfach.*
3 = 464, note: a b a c d e f f 8 8 8 8 8 8 8, with internal rhyme.
4 = 692a, note: a b b c b b d d e e f f g g h h i i　6 6 6 6 6 6′ 6′ 6 6 6 6 6 6 6
6′ 6′. vv. 19–20 refrain words alternated in pairs of stanzas.
5 Frank: a b c c d d e b b . . .
6 = 722a, note: a b b c c d d e f e　8 8 8 8 8 8 8 8 8 8. vv. 1–2 derivative rhymes
and word refrains alternated in pairs of stanzas.
7 vv. 13 and 15 alternatively, *senhor.*　　　　　8 Frank: v. 8 masculine, but: *ia.*

XVI	858,1	a b c d e e f e f f e e	7 7 7 7' 5 7 7' 5 5' 7' 7 7	U
XIX	860,1	a b c d e e f g	7 7 7 7 7 7 7 7'	U
XXXII	865,1	a b c d e f c c	8 8 8 8 8 8 8 8	U
III	866,1	a b c d e f d d	7' 7' 7 7 7 7 7 7	U
XVII	873,1	a b c d e f f g g h g h i	4 4 8 8 6' 4 8 4 8 8 8 8 4	U
		g h	4 8	
XXII	880,1	a b c d e f g h h	3 5 8 8 8 8 8 8 8	U¹

BERNART DE VENTADORN

XXVIII	5,20	a a a a a a a a	6 6 6 6 6 6 6 6	
XII	215,1	a b a b a a b	10 10' 10 10' 10 10 10'	
XXV	230,3	a b a b a b a b a b	5' 6 5' 6 5' 6 5' 6 5' 6 5' 6	
XXXVI	235,4	a b a b a b a b b	6 6 6 6 6 6 6 6	2
XXXVII	236,1	a b a b a b a b b a	6' 6 6' 6 6' 6 6' 6 6 6'	
XLIV	243,1	a b a b a b a b c c c b	7' 5' 7' 5' 7' 5' 7' 5' 6 6 7 5'	3
IV	263,1	a b a b a b b a	7' 7 7' 7 7' 7 7 7'	
IX	295,11	a b a b b a a b	7' 7 7' 7 7' 7' 7' 7	4
XIX	295,9	a b a b b a a b	8 7' 8 7' 7' 8 8 7'	
XXXV	321,1	a b a b b c	10' 10 10' 10 10 10'	
XXX	376,15	a b a b c c d	7' 7 7' 7 7' 7' 7	
VI	382,102	a b a b c c d d	7 7 7 7 7 7 7 7	
XXIX	382,97	a b a b c c d d	7' 7 7' 7 8 8 7' 7'	
XLI	382,75	a b a b c c d d	8 8 8 8 8 10 10	5
XXXIX	382,72	a b a b c c d d	8 8 8 8 10 10 10 10	
XLIII	407,9	a b a b c d c d	8 8 8 8 8 8 8 8	
X	408,1	a b a b c d c d c	8 8 8 8 4 6 4 6 10	6
XVII	421,28	a b a b c d d c	8 8 8 8 8 7' 7' 8	
XV	447,3	a b a c c d d	8 8 8 8 8 8 8	
XXI	448,2	a b a c c d d e	8 8 8 8 8 7' 7' 8	
XXIII	460,1	a b a c d d c b	7' 7' 7' 7 7 7' 7' 7 7'	U
XXVI	461,1	a b a c d d e	7' 7' 7' 7' 8 8 7'	
XL	476,2	a b b a a b b a	8 8 8 8 8 8 8 8	
XIV	547,15	a b b a c c	8 8 8 8 8 8	
V	571,6	a b b a c c d	8 8 8 8 8 8 8	
XLII	571,5	a b b a c c d	10' 10' 10' 10' 10 10 10'	7
I	577,239	a b b a c c d d	8 8 8 8 7' 7' 10 10	
XIII	589,6	a b b a c c d d e	8 8 8 8 8' 8' 10 10 10	8
XVI	620,1	a b b a c d c e	7 7 7 7 7 7 7 7'	U
II	621,7	a b b a c d d	8 8 8 8 7' 8 8	
VIII	624,86	a b b a c d d c	7 7 7 7 7' 7' 7' 7' 7'	

---

¹ = 878, note: a b c d e f g g 8 8 8 8 8 8 8 8 (not U).

² *Coblas capcaudadas.*

³ a: oja, ura, iza, ansa, onda, aire.   b: ura, iza, ansa, onda, aire, aire.   c: or. *Coblas capcaudadas*; v. 9 *amor.*

⁴ *Coblas capfinidas*; derivative rhymes 1/2, 3/4, 5/6, 7/8.

⁵ v. 6 *cor.*

⁶ = 376: a b a b c c d   8 8 8 8 10 10 10, with internal rhyme.

⁷ a: olha, eja, atge.   b: atge, olha, eja.   c: er.   d: eja, atge, olha. Stanzas I–IV–VII; II–V; III–VI. *Coblas capcaudadas.*

⁸ v. 8 *amor.*

XXXI	624,51	a b b a c d d c	8 8 8 8 8 8 8 8	[1]
XX	635,19	a b b a c d d c e e	7 7 7 7 7′ 7 3 4′ 7 7	[2]
XVIII	676,1	a b b c b b d	7′ 7 7 7′ 5 7 6′	U
XLV	705,13	a b b c c d d	7 7 7 7′ 7′ 7′ 7′	
XXVII	728,1	a b b c c d e d f	8 8 8 7′ 7′ 7 7′ 7 8	
XXXIII	743,10	a b b c d d c	8 8 8 8 8 8 8	
VII	753,1	a b b c d d e f	8 8 8 7′ 7′ 7′ 8 7′	U[3]
XXIV	779,1	a b c a c d d b	8 7′ 7 8 7 8 8 7′	U
XXII	796,1	a b c b d d e e	8 8 8 8′ 8′ 10 10	U
III	862,1	a b c d e e f g h g g	7′ 7′ 7′ 7′ 7 7 7′ 7 7′ 7 7	U

RAIMBAUT D'AURENGA

XXXIII	17,4	a a a a a b	6 10 6 6 6 6	[4]
XXXV	51,1	a a a b a a b	8 8 8 8 8 8 8	[5]
IV	121,1	a a b a b b	7′ 7′ 7 7′ 7 7	
VIII	143,1	a a b b a c	4 8 8 4 8 4	U[6]
XXXVII	160,3	a a b b c b c	8 8 8 7′ 8 7′	
XVII	182,1	a a b b c d d c e e c	4 4 4 4 8 4 4 8 4 4 8	U[7]
XVIII	197,1	a a b c c b d d b e b e	3 4 4 3 4 4 3 4 4 3 6 8	U[8]
XXX	200,2	a a b c c d d	7 7 7′ 7 7 7 7	
XX	209,1	a b a a b c d d	8 8 8 8 8 8 8 8	U
XXIV	223,2	a b a b a b	8 8 8 8 8 8	[9]
XXXVIII	377,2	a b a b c c d c	8 8 8 8 7′ 7′ 8 7′	[10]
XXVII	407,18	a b a b c d c d	8 7′ 8 7′ 8 7′ 8 7′	
XXV	447,4	a b a c c d d	7 7′ 7 7′ 7′ 8 8	
XXVI	451,1	a b a c c d e e	8 7′ 7 7 7 7′ 7 7	U
XVI	454,1	a b a c d b d e	4 4 8 4 4 8 8 8	U[11]
XXIX	455,1	a b a c d c d	7 7 7 7′ 7 7′ 7	U
XXI	475,1	a b b a a b b	7 5 7 7 7 7 7	U[12]
XI	565,1	a b b a c c c c a	7′ 7′ 7′ 7′ 3 3 3 7 7′	U
VI	571,11	a b b a c c d	8 8 8 8 8 8 8	

[1] a: an×en.   b: or.   c: en×an.   d: es. *Coblas capcaudadas.*

[2] = 620a, note: a b b a c d c e e   7 7 7 7 7′ 7 7′ 7 7.

[3] Derivative rhymes 1/4, 2/5, 3/6, 7/8.

[4] *Coblas capcaudadas.*

[5] *Coblas capfinidas.*

[6] v. 3 *denh* (or derivatives).

[7] Complex alternation of word-refrains in a, b, d, e:

     st. I a^1a^2 b^1b^2 d^1d^2 e^1e^2

     st. II a^3a^1 b^2b^3 d^3d^1 e^2e^3

     st. III a^2a^3 b^3b^1 d^2d^3 e^3e^1, in each group of 3 stanzas.

[8] Complex alternation of word-refrains in a, c, d, e:

     odd stanzas: a^1a^2 c^1c^2 d^1d^2 e^1e^2

     even stanzas: a^2a^1 c^2c^1 d^2d^1 e^2e^1

[9] Prose after each stanza.

[10] v. 5 *lenga.*

[11] = 777a, note: a b c a c d 8 8 8 8 8 8.

[12] Cf. 192*bis* 1: Frank gives the versification of a fragment of another song attributed to Raimbaut, with similar syllabic arrangements and rhymes, as 794,1 (XXVIII).

XXXII	656,1	a b b b b	10' 10 10 10 10	U[1]
XXXVI	657,1	a b b b b b	8 8 8 8 8 8	U[2]
XIX	701,1	a b b c c d a	7 7 7 7 7 7' 7	U
XXXI	705,9	a b b c c d d	8 8 8 4 4 8 8	
XXXIV	756,1	a b b c d e b b	7' 7 7 7' 7' 7 7 7	U[3]
XIV	764,2	a b b c d e f f g f	7' 3 5 7 7' 3 3 5 5 3	
III	765,1	a b b c d e f g	7' 7 7 7' 7' 7' 7' 7'	
XXVIII	794,1	a b c b d d	7 7 7' 7 7 7	U[4]
IX	816,1	a b c c b d e	4 3' 7 7 7' 7 7'	U[5]
XV	821,2	a b c c d d d	7 7' 7' 7' 8 8 8	6
V	834,1	a b c c d e f	7' 7' 7' 7' 8 7' 8	U[7]
XXII	847,1	a b c d d d e e	8 8 8 3 3 3 8 8	U
VII	852,1	a b c d d e f	8 8 8 8 8 8 8	U
XII	853,1	a b c d e a	8 8 8 7' 8 8	U
XXXIX	859,1	a b c d e e f f	7' 7' 7' 7' 7' 7' 8 8	U[8]
X	868,1	a b c d e f e d f	8 8 7' 8 7' 8 7' 8 8	U
XIII	869,2	a b c d e f e e	7' 8 7' 8 7' 8 8	
II	879,12	a b c d e f g h	7' 7 7 7' 7 7 7' 7	9
I	884,1	a b c d e f g h i j k	4 4 4 4 4 3' 4 3' 4 3' 7'	U[10]
		l m n	7' 7' 7'	

ARNAUT DANIEL

I	6,1	a a a a a a a a a	7 7 8 8 8 8 8 8 8	
III	302,14	a b a b b a b a	4' 6 4' 6 4 6' 4 6'	11
V	430,1	a b a b c d e	8 8 8 8 10 10' 10'	
VI	648,1	a b b a c d e	8 8 8 10 10 10	
II	664,1	a b b b c c d e e d	3 5 8 4 4 4 6' 4 4 6'	U[12]
VIII	861,1	a b c d e e f g h	8 8 7' 7' 3 3 7 7' 7'	U
XVIII	864,3	a b c d e f	7' 10' 10' 10' 10' 10'	13
IV	871,2	a b c d e f f e	7' 7' 7' 7' 8 7' 7' 8	
VII	874,1	a b c d e f f g g h h	8 8 8 7' 7' 4' 6' 4 2 4' 5'	U

---

[1] v. 3 *joglar*.

[2] v. 1 *malastrucs*.

[3] = 740, note: a b b c d d 8 8 8 8 8 8, with internal rhyme.

[4] See p. 226, n. 12.

[5] a: ars. b: iva×aja. c: irs×ens. d: ens×irs. e: aja×iva. v. 1 *clars*, vv. 5/7 *viva/gaja*.

   = 609, note: a b b a c d 7' 7 7 7' 7 7', with internal rhyme.

[6] v. 4 *genta*.

[7] v. 5 *gaug*.

[8] a: ersa×erse. b: ertres×ertre. c apis×api. d: enca×enque. e: iscles×iscle. f: ois×oi. 8 word-refrains alternated, with derivative rhymes; stanzas I, III, V 1–8 = II, IV, VI 1–8.

[9] Derivative rhymes 1/2, 3/5, 4/6, 7/8.

[10] = 881, note: a b c d e f g h i 8 8 7' 7' 7' 7' 7' 7' 7'. Derivative rhymes 2/14, 4/13, 8/12, 10/11.

[11] = 130, note: a a b b 10 10 10' 10'.

[12] = 202a, note: a a b c d c 8 8 8 10' 8 6', with internal rhyme. a: olh. b: im, or, alh. c: or, alh, im. d: olha. e alh, im, or. *Coblas capfinidas*.

[13] *Sestina*: word-refrains *intra, ongla, arma, verga, oncle, cambra*.

XV	875,1	a b c d e f g	10 10 10 10 10 10 10′	
XIII	875,3	a b c d e f g	8 8 8 8 10 10 10′	
XVI	875,5	a b c d e f g	7′ 7′ 7′ 7′ 10′ 10′ 10′	
X	875,7	a b c d e f g	7′ 7′ 7 7 7′ 7 7 7′	
IX	876,1	a b c d e f g b h h i c j k l c m	3′ 4 2 6 2 1 5 4 1 3 4 4 2 4 6 4 6′	U[1]
XVII	879,1	a b c d e f g h	10′ 10 10 10′ 10 10 10 10′	
XIV	879,9	a b c d e f g h	8 8 8 8 8 8 8 10	
XI	879,11	a b c d e f g h	7 7 7 7′ 7′ 8 8 7′	
XII	879,14	a b c d e f g h	4 6′ 10 10 10 10′ 10′ 10′	2

[1] = 875, note: a b c d e f g   8 8 8 8 10 10 10′, with internal rhyme.
[2] = 875, note: a b c d e f g   10′ 10 10 10 10′ 10′ 10′, with internal rhyme.

APPENDIX III. VOCABULARY

Tables A and B are intended to indicate the comparative richness of vocabulary of Marcabru, Peire d'Alvernhe, Giraut de Bornelh, Bernart de Ventadorn, Raimbaut d'Aurenga, and Arnaut Daniel. They were derived from word-frequency lists produced by computer at the Chilton Atlas Laboratory, from the texts of these troubadours as they appear in the editions used in this work.

Table A is based on all of their songs, and shows the total number of words used by each poet, the size of his vocabulary, and the number of words he uses only once, the last being a guide to his use of rare words. Table B, for clearer comparison, is based on samples of approximately equal size from the works of each poet. Words of under three letters have been ignored. The figures are approximate and generally higher than the actual number of words used since they do not take spelling variations into account, or the fact that certain editors partially unified the spelling; neither has any attempt been made to unify inflected forms.

TABLE A

	Marcabru	*Peire*	*Giraut*	*Bernart*	*Raimbaut*	*Arnaut*
Total no. of words	11,761	7,140	31,758	15,081	14,557	6,199
Size of vocabulary	3,392	2,240	4,374	2,365	3,168	1,781
No. of words used once	2,324	1,612	2,396	1,293	2,023	1,203

TABLE B

	Marcabru	*Peire*	*Giraut*	*Bernart*	*Raimbaut*	*Arnaut*
No. of words in sample	6,136	6,143	6,137	6,142	6,140	6,135
Size of vocabulary	2,113	1,957	1,575	1,398	1,799	1,773
No. of words used once	1,527	1,407	996	842	1,218	1,196

From these it appears that Marcabru has the richest vocabulary, and is followed by Peire, Raimbaut, Arnaut, Giraut, and Bernart in that order.

BIBLIOGRAPHY AND ABBREVIATIONS

The Bibliography includes only works referred to more than once in
the text and footnotes

DICTIONARIES

Du Cange   C. Du Cange, *Glossarium manuale ad scriptores mediae et
infimae latinitatis*, Halle, 1772–84.

Godefroy   F. Godefroy, *Dictionnaire de l'ancienne langue française et de
tous ses dialectes du IXe au XVe siècle*, Paris, 1880–1902.

Godefroy, *Lex.*   *Lexique de l'ancien français*, Paris and Leipzig, 1901.

L & S   C. T. Lewis and C. Short, *A Latin Dictionary*, Oxford,
1869; rep. 1962.

Meyer-Lübke   *Romanisches etymologisches Wörterbuch*, Heidelberg, 1935.

Mistral   F. Mistral, *Lou Tresor dou felibrige, ou Dictionnaire provençal-
français embrassant les divers dialectes de la langue d'oc moderne.
Éd. du centenaire sous la direction de V. Tuby*, Paris, 1932.

PD   E. Levy, *Petit Dictionnaire provençal-français*, Heidelberg,
1961.

Rayn.   M. Raynouard, *Lexique roman*, Paris, 1836–44.

SWB   E. Levy, *Provenzalisches Supplement-Wörterbuch*, Leipzig,
1894–1924.

TL   A. Tobler and E. Lommatzsch, *Altfranzösisches Wörterbuch*, Berlin, 1925–.

CHURCH FATHERS

PL   J. P. Migne, *Patrologiae cursus completus. Series latina*. Paris,
1844–64.

PERIODICALS

Actes ... Ier congrès: *Les Actes et mémoires du Ier Congrès International de
Langue et de Littérature du Midi*, Avignon, 1957.

Actes ... IIe congrès: *Actes et Mémoires du IIe Congrès International de Langue
et de Littérature du Midi de la France*, Avignon, 1958.

AdM   *Annales du Midi.*

Arch.   *Archiv für das Studium der neueren Sprachen und Literatur.*

Arch. Rom.   *Archivum Romanicum.*

CAIEF   *Cahiers de l'Association internationale des Études françaises.*

CCM   *Cahiers de civilisation médiévale.*

CN   *Cultura Neolatina.*

DDJ   *Deutsches Dante-Jahrbuch.*

FR   *Filologia romanza.*

GRM   *Germanisch-romanische Monatsschrift.*

MA   *Medium Aevum.*

MIL   *Memorie dell'Istituto Lombardo.*

MLN   *Modern Language Notes.*

N   *Neophilologus.*

NMi   *Neuphilologische Mitteilungen.*

ÖAW   *Österreichische Akademie der Wissenschaften.*

R   *Romania.*

RC   *Revue critique.*

RF   *Romanische Forschungen.*

RLR   *Revue des langues romanes.*

RN   *Romance Notes.*

RP   *Romance Philology.*

RSH   *Revue des sciences humaines.*

S   *Speculum.*

SFR   *Studi di filologia romanza.*

SM   *Studi medievali.*

SP   *Studies in Philology.*

WIJ   *Warburg Institute Journal.*

ZFSL   *Zeitschrift für französische Sprache und Literatur.*

ZRP   *Zeitschrift für romanische Philologie.*

J. Anglade, *Grammaire de l'ancien provençal*, Paris, 1921 (*Grammaire*).

—— *Histoire sommaire de la littérature méridionale*, Paris, 1921 (*Hist. somm.*).

—— *Les Troubadours*, Paris, 1908 (*Les Troubadours*).

—— *Peire Vidal — poésies*, Paris, 1966 (2ᵉ édition revue).

C. Appel, *Bernart von Ventadorn*, Halle, 1926 (*Bernart*).

—— *Die Singweisen Bernarts von Ventadorn*, Halle, 1934 (*ZRP*, Beiheft lxxxi).

—— *Provenzalische Chrestomathie, mit Abriss der Formenlehre und Glossar*, Leipzig, Reisland, 1895 (*Chrest.*).

—— *Provenzalische Inedita aus Pariser Handschriften*, Wiesbaden, 1967 (reprint of edition of 1892) (*Prov. Inedita*).

—— *Raimbaut von Orange*, Berlin, 1928 (*Abhandlungen der Gesellschaft der Wissenschaften zu Göttingen*, Philol.-hist. Klasse, N.F. vol. xxi, no. 2) (*Raimbaut von Orange*).

—— 'Zu Marcabru', *ZRP* xliii (1923), 403–69 ('Zu Marcabru').

S. C. Aston, *Peirol, Troubadour of Auvergne*, Cambridge, 1953.

A. S. Avalle, *Peire Vidal, Poesie*, Milano and Napoli, 1960.

K. Bartsch, *Provenzalisches Lesebuch*, Eberfeld, 1855.

—— *Chrestomathie provençale*, Berlin, 1892 (5th edition) (*Chrest.*).

S. Battaglia, *Le rime 'petrose' e la sestina*, Napoli, 1964 (*Le rime 'petrose'*). This essentially repeats his *Poesia e tecnica*, Napoli, 1949.

G. Bertoni, 'Due note provenzali, I. Marcabruno', *SM* iii (1911), 638–57 ('Due note').

—— Review of Lewent, 'Beiträge', *RLR* lxi (1913), 496 ('Lewent').

P. Boissonnade, 'Les personnages et les événements de l'histoire d'Allemagne, de France et d'Espagne dans l'œuvre de Marcabru', *R* xlviii (1922), 207–42.

J. Boutière and A. Schutz, *Biographies des troubadours*, Paris, 1964.

M. Bowra, 'Dante and Arnaut Daniel', *S* xxvii (1952), 459–74.

F. Branciforti, *Il canzoniere di Lanfranco Cigala*, Firenze, 1954.

E. de Bruyne, *Études d'esthétique médiévale*, Bruges, 1946.

U. A. Canello, *La vita e le opere del trovatore Arnaldo Daniello*, Halle, 1883 (Canello).

A. Cavaliere, *Le poesie di Peire Raimon de Tolosa*, Firenze, 1935 (Biblioteca dell'*Archivum Romanicum*, ser. i, vol. xxii).

P. Chabaille, *Li Livres dou tresor*, Paris, 1863.

J. Chailley, 'Les premiers troubadours et les versus de l'école d'Aquitaine', *R* lxxvi (1955), 212–39.

H. J. Chaytor, *From Script to Print*, Cambridge, 1945 (*From Script to Print*).

Cicero, *De Inventione*, ed. Loeb Classical Library, London and Cambridge, Mass., 1949 (*De Inv.*).

E. Cnyrim, *Sprichwörter, sprichwörtliche Redensarten und Sentenzen bei den provenzalischen Lyrikern*, Marburg, 1888 (*Sprichwörter*).

J. Coulet, 'Spécimen d'une édition des poésies de Peire d'Alvernhe', *Mélanges Chabaneau*, Erlangen, 1907, 777–89.

E. R. Curtius, *European Literature and the Latin Middle Ages*, New York, 1953 (originally Bern, 1948).

J.-M.-L. Dejeanne, 'Alegret, jongleur gascon du xiie siècle', *AdM* xix (1907), 221–31.

—— 'À propos d'une chanson de Peire d'Alvernhe', *AdM* xvi (1904), 341–7.

—— *Poésies complètes du troubadour Marcabru*, Toulouse, 1909 (Dejeanne).

M. Delbouille, 'Les senhals littéraires désignant Raimbaut d'Orange et la chronologie de ces témoignages', *CN* xvii (1957), 49–73.

A. Del Monte, *Peire d'Alvernha: liriche*, Torino, 1955 (*Peire*).

——*Studi sulla poesia ermetica medievale*, Napoli, 1953 (*Studi*).

F. Diez, *Leben und Werke der Troubadours*, Leipzig, 1882.

R. Dragonetti, *La Technique poétique des trouvères dans la chanson courtoise. Contribution à l'étude de la rhétorique médiévale*, Bruges, 1960. This is based on his thesis of 1943. Cf. P. Zumthor's review in *R* lxxxii (1961), 418–22.

G. Errante, *Marcabru e le fonti sacre dell'antica lirica romanza*, Firenze, 1948.

E. Faral, *Les Arts poétiques aux XIIe et XIIIe siècles*, Paris, 1958.

I. Frank, *Répertoire métrique de la poésie des troubadours*, Paris, 1953–7.

M. Gatien-Arnoult, *Las Flors del Gay Saber*, Paris and Toulouse, 1841.

F. Ghisalberti, 'Medieval Biographies of Ovid', *WIJ* ix (1946), 10–59 ('Biographies').

—— 'Arnolfo d'Orléans. Un cultore di Ovidio nel sec. XII'. *MIL*, Classe di Lettere, vol. xxiv, fasc. IV ('Arnolfo d'Orléans').

R. Guiette, 'D'une poésie formelle en France au moyen-âge', *RSH* liv (1949), 61–8.

W. Hensel, 'Die Vögel in der provenzalischen und nordfranzösischen Lyrik des Mittelalters', *RF* xxvi (1909), 584–670. ('Vögel').

E. Hoepffner, *Les Poésies de Bernart Marti*, Paris, 1929.

Horace, *Ars Poetica*.

A. Jeanroy, *Jongleurs et Troubadours gascons des XIIᵉ et XIIIᵉ siècles*, Paris, 1957 (*Jongleurs*).

—— *La Poésie lyrique des troubadours*, Toulouse and Paris, 1934 (*Poésie lyrique*).

—— *Les Chansons de Guillaume IX, duc d'Aquitaine*, Paris, 1964.

—— *Les Chansons de Jaufré Rudel*, Paris, 1924.

—— *Les Poésies de Cercamon*, Paris, 1922.

—— and J.-J. Salverda de Grave, *Poésies de Uc de Saint-Circ*, Toulouse, 1913.

E. Köhler, *Trobadorlyrik und höfischer Roman*, Berlin, 1962.

A. Kolsen, 'Dante und der Trobador Arnaut Daniel', *DDJ* viii (1924), 47–59.

—— *Guiraut von Bornelh, der Meister der Trobadors*, Berlin, 1894.

—— *Sämtliche Lieder des Trobadors Giraut de Bornelh*, Halle, 1910 (*Giraut de Bornelh*).

Cf. the corrections of:

A. Jeanroy, *AdM* xix (1907), 389–90;

—— *AdM* xxi (1909), 363–8;

—— *RC* (1908), no. i, pp. 148–50;

—— *RC* (1909), no. i, pp. 511–12;

G. Bertoni, *RLR* liii (1910), 516–22;

A. Stimming, *Lit. Zentralblatt*, 1910, col. 1090.

See also Lewent, *Zum Text*; Salverda de Grave, *Observations*.

A. Kressner, 'Über die Tierbücher des Mittelalters nebst einem Bruchstücke aus einer provenzalischen Handschrift', *Arch.* lv (1876), 241–96.

H. Lausberg, *Handbuch der literarischen Rhetorik*, München, 1960.

R. Lavaud, 'Les poésies d'Arnaut Daniel', *AdM* xxii (1910), 17–55, 162–79, 300–39, 446–66; *AdM* xxiii (1911), 5–31.

M. Lazar, *Bernard de Ventadour, troubadour du XIIᵉ siècle: chansons d'amour*, Paris, 1966.

R. Lejeune, 'Rôle littéraire d'Aliénor d'Aquitaine et de sa famille', *CN* xiv (1954), 5–57.

—— 'Thèmes communs de troubadours et vie de société', *Actes . . . IIᵉ Congrès* (1958), 74–88. ['Thèmes'].

K. Lewent, 'Beiträge zum Verständnis der Lieder Marcabrus', *ZRP* xxxvii (1913), 313–37, 427–51 ('Beiträge'). (Cf. Bertoni, 'Lewent' and Spitzer, 'Lewent'.)

—— *Zum Text der Lieder des Giraut de Bornelh*, Firenze, 1938 (Biblioteca dell'*Archivum Romanicum*, ser. i, vol. xxvi) (*Zum Text*).

J. Linskill, *The Poems of the Troubadour Raimbaut de Vaqueiras*, The Hague, 1964.

C. de Lollis, *Vita e poesie di Sordello di Goito*, Halle, 1896.

G. Mari, 'Ritmo latino e terminologia ritmica medievale' *SFR* viii (1901), 35–88.

A. Marigo, *Dante: De Vulgari Eloquentia*, ridotto a miglior lezione, commentato e tradotto da A. Marigo, Firenze, 1957 (*DVE*).

J. H. Marshall, 'On the text and interpretation of a poem by Raimbaut d'Orange (*Cars douz*; ed. Pattison, I)', *MA*, vol. xxxvii, no. 1 (1968), 12–36.

F. Maus, *Peire Cardenals Strophenbau in seinem Verhältnis zu dem anderer Trobadors*, Marburg, 1882.

U. Mölk, *Trobar clus — trobar leu*, München, 1968.

J. Morawski, *Proverbes français antérieurs au XVe siècle*, Paris, 1925 (*Proverbes*).

J. Mouzat, 'Les poèmes perdus d'Eble II, vicomte de Ventadorn. Recherches et suggestions", *Actes* . . . *IIe congrès* (1958), 89–103.

E. Müller, *Die altprovenzalische Versnovelle*, Halle, 1930.

M. F. Nims, *Poetria Nova of Geoffrey of Vinsauf* (translation), Toronto, 1967.

Ovid, *Ars amatoria*, Loeb Classical Library, London and Cambridge, Mass., 1962.

—— *Metamorphoses*, Loeb Classical Library, London and Cambridge, Mass., 1960.

B. Panvini, *Giraldo di Bornelh, trovatore del secolo XII*, Catania, 1949.

W. Pattison, *The Life and Works of the Troubadour Raimbaut d'Orange*, Minneapolis, 1952.

A. Pillet, *Beiträge zur Kritik der ältesten Troubadours*, Breslau, 1911 (Sonderabdruck aus dem 89. Jahresbericht der Schlesischen Gesellschaft für vaterl. Kultur.

—— and H. Carstens, *Bibliographie der Troubadours*, Halle, 1933 (P–C).

F. Pirot, 'Bibliographie commentée du troubadour Marcabru', *Moyen Age* lxxiii (1967), 87–126.

L. Pollmann, '*Trobar clus*', *Bibelexegese und hispano-arabische Literatur*, Münster, Westfalen, 1965 ('*Trobar clus*'). Reviewed by S. Jauernick, *GRM* xvi (1966), 427–9.

F. Quadlbauer, 'Die antike Theorie der Genera dicendi im lateinischen Mittelalter', *Österreichische Akademie der Wissenschaften*, Philos.-hist. Klasse, Sitzungsberichte Band 241, Abhandlung 2, Wien 1962 (Quadlbauer).

Quintilian, *Institutio oratoria*, Loeb Classical Library, Cambridge, Mass., 1958–60.

F. J. E. Raby, *The Oxford Book of Medieval Latin Verse*, Oxford, 1959.

Rhetorica ad Herennium, Loeb Classical Library, Cambridge, Mass., and London, 1964 (*Rhet. ad Her.*).

M. de Riquer, *La lírica de los trovadores* (tomo I: *Poetas del siglo XII*), Barcelona, 1948 (*Lírica*).

D. W. Robertson, 'Five poems by Marcabru', *SP* li (1954), 539–60 ('Five poems').

—— 'Some medieval terminology, with special reference to Chrétien de Troyes', *SP* xlviii (2) (1951), 669–92.

—— 'The doctrine of charity in medieval literary gardens', *S* xxvi (1951), 24–49 ('Gardens').

A. Roncaglia, 'Carestia', *CN* xviii (1958), 121–37.

—— 'Per un'edizione e per l'interpretazione dei testi del trovatore Marcabruno', *Actes* . . . *Ier Congrès*, 47–55 ('Per un'edizione').

—— 'I due sirventesi di Marcabruno ad Alfonso VII', *CN* x (1950), 153–83 [Dejeanne, XXII and XXIII].

—— 'Il *gap* di Marcabruno', *SM* xvii (1951), 46–70 [Dejeanne, XVI; 'Il *gap*'].

—— 'Lo vers comens quan vei del fau', *CN* xi (1951), 25–48 [Dejeanne, XXXIII; 'Lo vers comens'].

—— 'Al departir del brau tempier', *CN* xiii (1953), 5–33 [Dejeanne, III; 'Al departir'].

—— 'Aujatz de chan', *CN* xvii (1957), 20–48 [Dejeanne, IX].

—— 'Cortesamen voill comensar', *Rivista di cultura classica e medioevale*, vii (1965), 948–61 [Dejeanne, XV].

—— ' "Trobar clus": discussione aperta' *CN* xxix (1969), 5–55.

Dr. Sachs, *Le Trésor de Pierre de Corbiac en vers provençaux*, Brandenbourg, 1859.

J.-J. Salverda de Grave, *Observations sur l'art lyrique de Giraut de Borneil*, Amsterdam, 1928 (*Mededeelingen der koninklijke nederlandsche Akademie van Wetenschappen, afd. letterkunde*, Nieuwe reeks, deel 1, no. 1) (*Observations*).

J.-J. Salverda de Grave, 'Giraut de Bornelh et la poésie obscure', *Mélanges de linguistique et de philologie offerts à Jacq. van Ginneken*, Paris, 1937, pp. 297–306.

F. Saxl, 'A spiritual encyclopaedia of the later Middle Ages', *WIJ* v (1942), 82–134.

F. Schalk, 'Zur Interpretationsmethode in der romanischen Philologie', *Studium Generale*, vii (1954), 410–16.

D. Scheludko, 'Anlässlich des Liedes von Raimbaut d'Aurenga *Cars douz*', *Arch. Rom.* xxi (1937), 285–97.

—— 'Beiträge zur Entstehungsgeschichte der altprovenzalischen Lyrik', *Arch. Rom.* xi (1927), 273–312; xii (1928), 30–127; xv (1931), 137–206 ('Beiträge').

—— 'Religiöse Elemente im weltlichen Liebeslied der Trobadors', *ZFSL* lx (1935–7), 18–35.

—— 'Über die religiöse Lyrik der Troubadours', *NMi* xxxviii (1937), 224–50.

—— 'Zur Geschichte des Natureingangs bei den Trobadors', *ZFSL* lx (1935–7), 257–334 ('Natureingang').

W. P. Shepard and F. M. Chambers, *The Songs of Aimeric de Peguilhan*, Evanston, Ill., 1950.

H. Spanke, 'Untersuchungen über die Ursprungen des altprovenzalischen Minnesangs, II. Marcabrustudien', Göttingen, 1940, *Abhandlungen der Gesellschaft der Wissenschaften zu Göttingen*, Philol.-hist. Klasse, 3. F., no. 24 ('Marcabrustudien').

L. Spitzer, 'Trouver', *R* lxvi (1940–1), 1–11.

—— 'Zu K. Lewents Beiträgen', *ZRP* xxxix (1917–19), 221–3 ('Lewent').

H. Springer, *Das altprovenzalische Klagelied mit Berücksichtigung der verwandten Literaturen*, Berlin, 1895 (*Klagelied*).

E. Stengel, *Die beiden ältesten provenzalischen Grammatiken, 'Lo Donatz proensals' und 'Las rasos de trobar'*, Marburg, 1878.

A. Stimming, *Bertran de Born, sein Leben und seine Werke*, Halle, 1879.

J. Storost, *Ursprung und Entwicklung des altprovenzalischen Sirventes bis auf Bertran de Born*, Halle, 1931.

S. Stroński, *Le Troubadour Folquet de Marseille*, Cracovie, 1910.

A. Thomas, *La Chanson de Sainte Foi d'Agen*, Paris, 1925.

A. Tobler, *Li Proverbe au vilan*, Leipzig, 1895. (*Proverbe*).

G. Toja, *Arnaut Daniel, Canzoni*, Firenze, 1960. Cf. editions by Canello and Lavaud (cited in Bibliography).

L. Topsfield, 'The burlesque poetry of Guilhem IX of Aquitaine', *NMi*, vol. lxix, no. 2 (1968), 280–302.

—— *Les Poésies du troubadour Raimon de Miraval*, Paris, 1971.

E. Vinaver, 'A la recherche d'une poétique médiévale', *CCM* ii (1959), 1–16.

A Viscardi, *Storia delle letterature d'oc e d'oïl*, Milano, 1952 (*Storia*).

K. Vossler, 'Der Trobador Marcabru und die Anfänge des gekünstelten Stiles', *Sitzungberichte der Königlichen Bayerischen Akademie der Wissenschaften*, Philos.-philol. und hist. Klasse, Jahrg. 1913, Abhandlung xi, pp. 1–65 ('Der Trobador Marcabru'). Reviewed by W. Küchler, *Die neueren Sprachen*, xxvi (1918-19), 279–80.

—— *Die göttliche Komödie*, Heidelberg, 1925.

H. Walther, *Proverbia sententiaeque Latinitatis Medii Aevi. Lateinische Sprichwörter und Sentenzen des Mittelalters in alphabetischer Anordnung*. Göttingen, 1963–7.

R. Zenker, *Die Lieder Peires von Auvergne*, Erlangen, 1900 (*Peire*).

—— *Die provenzalische Tenzone*, Leipzig, 1888 (*Tenzone*).

P. Zumthor, *Langue et techniques poétiques à l'époque romane*, Paris, 1963 (*Langue et techniques*).

—— 'Recherches sur les topiques dans la poésie lyrique des xiie et xiiie siècles', *CCM* ii (1959), 409–27 ('Recherches').

GENERAL INDEX

INDEX OF PROVENÇAL LITERARY TERMINOLOGY AND RELATED VOCABULARY

entresejn, 124

escas, 96, 101, 155n

esciens, 71

esclaire, 109, motz esclairatz, 92

esclarzir, 104, 107

escrimir, 28

escubel, 63n

escur, 71, 72, 73, 84, 95, 98, 137, 156, 160n, 162, 187n; escur saber, 138

escurzir, 104, 107, 119

eslaissatz, 98, 100

esmerar un chan, 10

espars, 204n

esproar, 14n

esprovaire, 11

essejn, 97, 124

estacar, 160n, 162

estoc breto, 22n, 23, 25, 160n

estoriar, 96n

estranhs sens naturals, 97, 101, 131

estribot, 68

fabreich, 137

fatz, 16n, 107, 110, 170, 171, 174

fenhz, 150n, 151n

fermar, 170

flor (del trobar), 76, cf. 187

fol sobreparlar, 8

fols mentirs, vanars, 67, 68

forbir un chan, 109

frag, frait, 8, 10, 58, 59, 67, 68, 139

fraichura, 10n, 16

gap, 11, 19

gaujar, 65n

gejn, genh, 120n, 124

   giens ginhos, 25, 70, 71

gignos, 19, 24, 25, 26, 28, 97

greu, 104, 118, 170

intrar en plait, 22n, 23

inventores, 212n

joglar, 27, 40, 80, 212

jonher, 94

jutgar razo, 28

lais, 121n

laner, 163

lassar, 11, 170

lengatge, 92

lengua-plana, 74

lengua traversana, 9n

leu, 88, 90, 91, 101, 102, 103, 104, 106, 110, 116, 117, 133, 136, 167, 171; see *trobar leu* in General Index

leuger, leugier, 104, 105, 106, 110, 116, 117, 133, 139, 167, 172, 179

levatz, 111n, 112

levet, 103, 105, 106n, 107, 110, 116, 163, 191

liar, 95

lima, 137

limar, 137, 153, 187, 189n

maestria, 107, 108, 110, 137

menut, 95, 182

menut trobador, 28, 37

mostraire, 14, 15

mostrar, 13

mot(z) apostitz, 54

   borrel, 63n, 65, 66, 67

   cobertz, 92, 100

   en fre, 98, 101n

   entrebeschar, 91

   escurs, 160n

   fals, 54, 76, 188

   leugiers, 167, 168, 172, 179

   peceiatz, 104, 139; cf. peceiar sos digz, 137

   politz, 54, 189n

   romputz, 71, 84

   serratz, 80, 93, 95

   vila, 54

natural (naturau, 29), 97, 98, 125, 131

nier(s), 63n, 67

non-clus, 84, 85, 101

nosens, 98, 100

obra, 137, 188; obra polia, 95

obrar, 187

obrier, 137

oc e no, 9n

onher, 122n

ort serrat e fort, 80

pairon, 62n, 63n

pan, 20, 62n

paraula follesca, 43, sana, 174

paraulas, 27

paraul'escura, 16

parauletas, 23

parladura, 57

parlier, 27, 60; li mielhs parlan, 167

partimen, 13